Relation of Alvar Nuñez Cabeça de Vaca : translated from the Spanish.

Núñez Cabeza de Vaca, Alvar

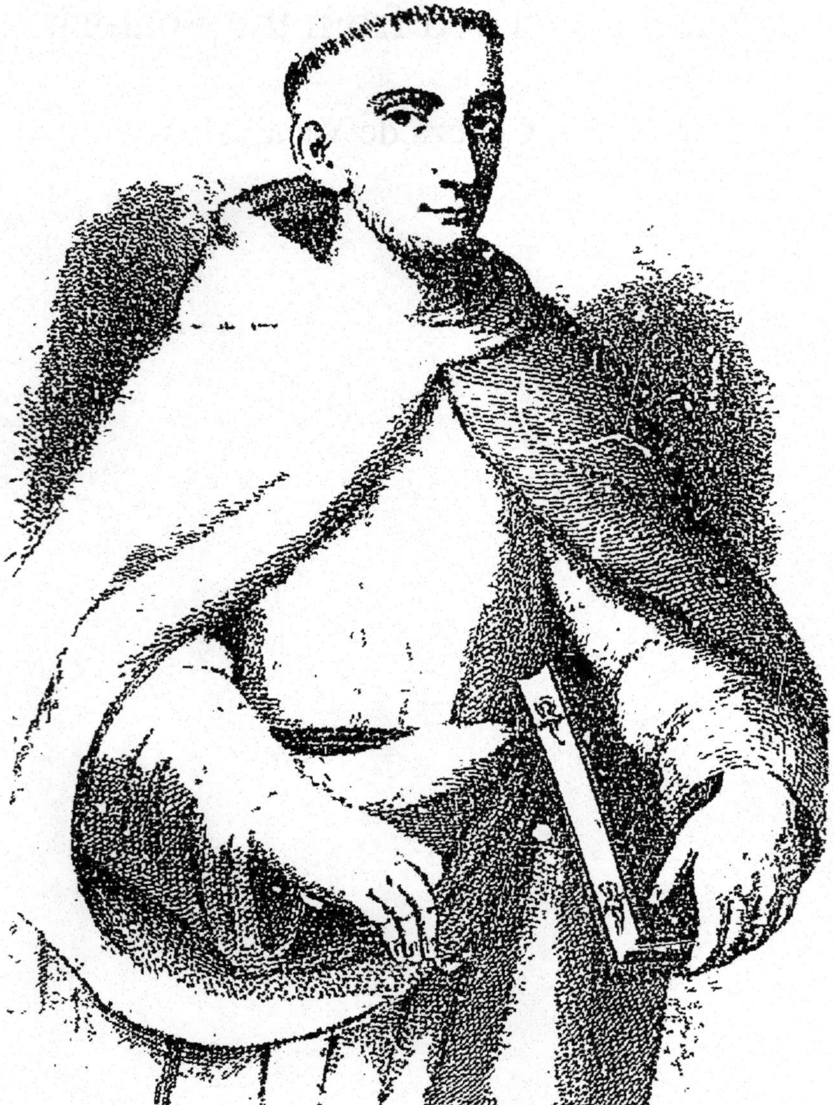

RELATION

OF

ALVAR NUÑEZ CABEÇA DE VACA

Translated from the Spanish

BY

BUCKINGHAM SMITH

NEW YORK
1871

Entered according to Act of Congress in the year 1871,
By the Estate of BUCKINGHAM SMITH,
In the office of the Librarian of Congress at Washington.

EDITION, 100 COPIES ONLY.

TO THE READER.

The sudden death of the author of this volume, while its first sheets were passing through the press, devolved upon his friends the duty of completing its publication. He had carefully revised the entire translation and notes, but had not prepared as he had intended, two maps showing the route of Alvar Nuñez, somewhat differently from what he had conceived in the former edition, and the work appears accordingly without them. These differences related principally, it is believed, to the place on the Gulf of Mexico where the adventurer spent the long interval during which his narrative is silent, and the inland point from whence he afterwards started on his western route. While it is to be regretted that we are thus deprived of the conclusions upon this interesting inquiry of one who had made the subject a study of years, the question is one after all, perhaps, upon which readers will prefer to decide for themselves. The translator in a note on page 44 promised to furnish in the Appendix a paper respecting the hieroglyph of Don Pedro to be found in that note. No such paper has been discovered. It was his intention, also to have given a sketch of the life of Alvar Nuñez, but some documents only for that purpose were found among his papers. These were placed in the hands of Thomas W. Field, Esq., who has drawn up the very interesting account inserted in the Appendix. The reading of the proof sheets was committed by Mr. Smith in his life time to Miss Maria J. B. Browne, of New York, who has faithfully performed the task.

This volume, signalized as it is, by the sad occurrence which calls forth this prefatory note, required some memorial of the translator, for the narrative not only occupied his thoughts in an extraordinary degree, as presenting one of the earliest explorations by Europeans of the land of his birth, and an original picture of the savage tribes of the southern and western territories of the United States, when first discovered by the white man, but has received much elucidation by his valuable annotations. The lovers of our early history for whose especial gratification this edition sees the light, will be pleased for this reason to have the memoir written by his distinguished friend, Dr. J. Gilmary Shea, which is appended to the work.

BROOKLYN, *May* 1871.

INTRODUCTION.

To no one more appropriately than to George W Riggs of Washington, could these remarks be addressed. The occasion is agreeably recalled, when near twenty years ago a first translation into English, of this tract, with maps and notes that attempted to trace the route of the army of Narváez, was greeted in the library of Peter Force Although the narrative had appeared in other languages, the points of march were at no time indicated, nor was it thought possible to ascertain them, and, finally, the story itself, though perused with delight in the beginning, went not unchallenged, and at the close of three centuries, amidst the most solemn protestations of sincerity, came to be condemned by no mean authority, as deformed by bold exaggerations and the wildest fiction Opinion under the array of facts is yielding to the force of truth Things that the author speaks of as "very new and most difficult of belief," instruct and find credence in the last third of the nineteenth century

While filling an official position in Mexico, due to the influence of Jackson Morton, Senator from Florida, the translator found a field for historical investigation ; and, later, to William Pitt Fessenden of Maine, he is indebted for a like position near the court at Madrid, that presented a still more extensive area. These admissions of obligation can have no significancy in the future, no word of salutation from the past. It is but an acknowledgment made to generous spirits in the account of years

The first imprint of the *Relacion*, a book extremely rare, was made in the year 1542 It comprises sixty-seven leaves octavo, with the following title page and colophon ·

¶ La relacion que dio Aluar nu- ‖ ñez cabeça de vaca de lo acaescido en las Indias ‖ en la armada donde yua por gouernador Pá ‖ philo de narbáez, desde el año de veynte ‖ y siete hasta el año de treynta y seys ‖ que boluio a Seuilla con tres ‖ de su compañia.. ‖

¶ Fue impresso el presente tra- ‖ tado en la magnifica, noble, y antiquissima ciudad ‖ de Zamora por los honrrados varones Augu || stin de paz y Juan Picardo compañeros im || pressores de libros vezinos de la dicha çiu || dad. A costa y espensas del virtuoso va || ron Juan pedro musetti mercader || de libros vezino de Medina del || campo Acabose en seys dias || del mes de Octubre Año || del nasçimiento de nro Sal || uador Jesu Cristo de || mil y quinientos y || quarenta y dos || Años

The next edition, in nearly the same form and black letter, printed in the year 1550, is connected with a work from another hand. The title page gives the subjects of both volumes.

The text of the latter edition differs from the earlier one in the spelling of the names of several Indian nations, the omission of one name, and in the failure to mention that of an island. These may be only changes made by the author. The matter is likewise differently divided. The chapters have headings, and the pages a running title. There is also a table of the contents of chapters, and a numbering of leaves to lvj which closes with the line, Deo Gracias. The enumeration continues through the *Comentarios*, written by Pero Fernandez to leaf cxliuj.

¶ La relacion y comentarios del gouernador Aluar nuñez cabeça de vaca, de lo acaescido en las dos jornadas que hizo a las Indias. Con priuilegio

Esta tassada por los señores del consejo en Ochēta y cinco mrs.

The third and last issue in Spanish was imprinted in the year 1799, folio, among the *Historiadores Primitivos de las Indias Occidentales* of Bárcia. It is a copy of the second edition, with an index to the contents, the proem and table being omitted. The text continues without paragraphing. The title is

Navfragios || De Alvar Nuñez || Cabeza De Vaca; || y || Relacion De La Jornada, || que hizo á la Florida con el Adelantado || Pánfilo de Narváez

In the *Historical Collection* of Ramusio, a translation was published in Italian at Venice, made from the first edition. The single edition in French is of H. Ternaux Compans, Paris, 1837.

The only version in English, intended to be literal, was printed in the year 1851, in one hundred copies, for a gentleman conversant with the history of American discovery, who desired to place in the hands of students and a few acquaintances, one of the earliest authentic relations. In the unavoidable absence of the translator, a friend obligingly gave it his editorial supervision.

When the survivors of those who under Narvaez had designed the conquest of Florida, arrived in Mexico, they wrote to the *Audiencia* of Española an account of the fate of the armament, their own toil, suffering and servitude, the countries whither they had wandered and the character of their discoveries. From this letter, which is not supposed to exist, was taken the relation given in the *Historia de las Indias*. Although Oviedo assures us of his care in trimming away redundancies, to touch nothing of value, he has certainly been at fault. His remarks and reflections in running commentary with the narration, while not without fitness and even wit, we would willingly spare for what might be the uncouth proportions of the original, with the unmistakable features of genuineness. The facts in the chronicle, not to be found in the *Relacion*, or not in exact accord with it, have been carefully culled and placed in the margins of the translated pages or are carried in sections to the Addenda.

In Mexico before the survivors of the enterprise separated, Mendoza required of them a map of the territories over which they had traveled. They accordingly made one and placed it in the hands of the viceroy.[1] It is believed not to exist

On the arrival of Alvar Nuñez at Sevilla, he was summoned to declare before the counsel of Indias what he saw and knew of Florida He answered that he was on the eve of departure to report in person to the emperor.[2] A royal order had already required his presence, and at once he responded to it. Hastening to Valladolid he appeared before Charles V The hide of the bison, a few emeralds, a handful of turquoise, with the relation of an impracticable fortune, were the only evidences of diligence and good conduct he could lay at the feet of his imperial master.

---

[1] *Crónica de Mechoacan* by the *R Pe Fray* PABLO BEAUMONT, MS
[2] Letter of ZARATE and CAVALLEROS to the King, 8th Nov 1537, MS in the Lonja

RELATION

THAT

ALVAR NUÑEZ CABEÇA DE VACA

GAVE OF

What befel the Armament in Indias

WHITHER

PÁNFILO DE NARVÁEZ WENT FOR GOVERNOR

FROM

THE YEAR 1527 TO THE YEAR 1537

WHEN WITH THREE COMRADES HE RETURNED AND
CAME TO SEVILLA

PROEM.

Sacred Cesarian Catholic Majesty:[1]

Among the many who have held sway, I think no prince can be found whose service has been attended with the ardor and emulation shown for that of your Highness at this time. The inducement is evident and powerful: men do not pursue together the same career without motive, and strangers are observed to strive with those who are equally impelled by religion and loyalty.

Although ambition and love of action are common to all, as to the advantages that each may gain, there are great inequalities of fortune, the result not of conduct, but only accident, nor caused by the fault of any one but coming in the providence of God and solely by His will. Hence to one arises deeds more signal than he thought to achieve; to another the opposite in every way occurs, so that he can show no higher proof of purpose than his effort, and at times even this is so concealed that it cannot of itself appear.

As for me, I can say in undertaking the march I made on the main by the royal authority, I firmly trusted that my conduct and services would be as evident and distinguished as were those of my ancestors, and that I should not have to speak in order to be reckoned among those who for diligence and fidelity in affairs your Majesty honors. Yet as neither my counsel nor my constancy availed to gain aught for which we set out agreeably to your interests, for our sins, no one of the many armaments that have gone into those parts has been permitted to find itself in straits great like ours, or come to an end alike forlorn and fatal. To me one only duty remains, to present a relation of what was seen and heard in the ten years I wandered lost

---

[1] Addressed to Charles V., Emperor of Germany, being Charles I, King of Spain of the Sicilies, etc., etc.

and in privation through many and remote lands.[1] Not merely a statement of positions and distances, animals and vegetation, but of the diverse customs of the many and very barbarous people with whom I talked and dwelt, as well as all other matters I could hear of and discern, that in some way I may avail your Highness. My hope of going out from among those nations was always small, still my care and diligence were none the less to keep in particular remembrance everything, that if at any time God our Lord should will to bring me where I now am, it might testify to my exertion in the royal behalf.

As the narrative is in my opinion of no trivial value to those who in your name go to subdue those countries and bring them to a knowledge of the true faith and true Lord, and under the imperial dominion, I have written this with much exactness; and although in it may be read things very novel and for some persons difficult to believe, nevertheless they may without hesitation credit me as strictly faithful. Better than to exaggerate, I have lessened in all things, and it is sufficient to say the relation is offered to your Majesty for truth. I beg it may be received in the name of homage, since it is the most that one could bring who returned thence naked.

[1] The fleet arrived at the Island of Santo Domingo from Spain about the month of September 1527, and Cabeça de Vaca left Cuba, returning, on the 2d day of June 1537, so that he was absent nearly ten years. From the time he landed in Florida the 14th of April 1528, until he arrived at the Spanish settlements on the Gulf of California in 1536, there was an interval of eight years; and one year more elapsed before he went from Veracruz to Spain.

RELATION

OF

ALVAR NUÑEZ CABEÇA DE VACA.

CHAPTER I.

IN WHICH IS TOLD WHEN THE ARMADA SAILED, AND OF THE OFFICERS AND PERSONS WHO WENT IN IT.

On the seventeenth day of June,* in the year fifteen-hundred and twenty-seven, the Governor Pámphilo de Narváez left the port of San Lúcar de Barrameda, authorized and commanded by your Majesty to conquer and govern the provinces of the main, extending from the river Palmas to the cape of Florida.¹ The fleet he took was five ships, in which went six hundred men, a few more or less, the officers (for we shall have to speak of them), were these, with their rank: Cabeça de Vaca, Treasurer and High-sheriff; Alonzo Enriquez, Comptroller; Alonzo de Solis, Distributor to your Majesty and Assessor; Juan Xuarez, a friar of Saint Francis, Commissary, and four more friars of the same order.

We arrived at the island of Santo Domingo, where we tarried near forty-five days, engaged in procuring for ourselves some necessary material, particularly horses. Here we lost from our fleet more than one

* June 17.

hundred and forty men, who wished to remain, seduced by the *partidos*, and advantages held out to them by the people of that country.

We sailed from the island and arrived at Santiago, a port of Cuba, where, during some days that we remained, the Governor supplied himself further with men, also with arms and horses. It happened there that a gentleman, Vasco Porcallo of Trinidad,³ which is also on the island, offered to give the Governor some provisions which he had in the town, a hundred leagues from the port of Santiago.⁴ Accordingly the Governor set out with all the fleet for Trinidad, but coming to a port half way, called Cabo de Santa Cruz, he thought it well to wait there, and send a vessel to bring the stores. To this end he ordered that a Captain Pantoja should go for them with his ship, and for greater security, that I should accompany him with another. The Governor remained with four ships, having bought one at the island of Santo Domingo.

We having arrived with the two vessels at the port of Trinidad, Captain Pantoja went with Vasco Porcalle to the town, a league off, to receive the provisions, while I remained at sea with the pilots, who said we ought to go thence with the greatest dispatch possible, for it was a very bad port in which many vessels were lost. As what there occurred to us was very remarkable, it appears to me not foreign to the purpose with which I write this, to relate it here.

The next morning began to give signs of bad weather. Rain commenced falling, and the sea ran so high, that, although I gave the men permission to go on shore, many of them returned to the ship to avoid exposure to the wet and cold, and because the town was a league away. In this time a canoe came off, bringing me a letter from a resident of the place, asking me to come for the needed provisions that were there, from which request I excused myself, saying that I could not leave the ships. At noon the canoe returned with another letter, in which I was solicited again with much urging, and a horse was brought for me to ride. I gave the same answer as before, that I could not leave the ships; but the pilots and the people entreated me to go, so that I might hasten the provisions as fast as possible, and we might join the fleet where it lay, for they had great fear lest remaining long in this port, the ships should be lost. For these reasons, I determined to go to the town; but first I left orders with the pilots, that if the south wind which often wrecks vessels there, came on to blow, and they should find themselves in much danger, to put the ships on shore at some place where the men and horses could be saved. I wished to take some of the men with me for company; but they said the weather was too rainy and cold, and the town too far off; that to-morrow, which was Sunday, they would come, with God's help, and hear mass.

An hour after I left, the sea began to rise very high and the north wind was so violent that neither the boats dared come to land, nor could the vessels be let drive on shore, because of the head wind, so that the people remained severely laboring against the adverse weather, and under a heavy fall of water all that day and Sunday until dark. At this time, the rain and the tempest had increased to such a degree, there was no less agitation in the town than on the sea; for all the houses and churches fell, and it was necessary in order to move upright, that we should go seven or eight holding on to each other that the wind might not blow us away; and walking in the groves, we had no less fear of the trees than of the houses, as they too were falling and might kill us under them. In this tempest and danger we wandered all night, without finding place or spot where we could remain a half hour in safety. During the time, particularly from midnight toward, we heard much tumult and great clamor of voices, the sound of timbrels, flutes and tamborines, as well as other instruments, which lasted until the morning, when the tempest ceased. Nothing so terrible as this storm, had been seen in those parts before. I drew up an authenticated account of it, and sent the testimony to your Majesty."

On Monday morning we went down to the harbor, but did not find the ships. The buoys belonging to them were floating on the water, whence we knew the ships were lost, and we walked along the shore to see if any thing could be found of them. As nothing was discovered, we struck into the woods, and, having traveled about a quarter of a league in water, we found the little boat of a ship lodged upon some trees. Ten leagues thence along the coast, two bodies were found, belonging to my ship, and some lids of boxes, but the persons were so disfigured by beating against the rocks that they could not be recognized. A cloak too was seen, also a coverlet rent in pieces, and nothing more. Sixty persons were lost in the ships, and twenty horses. Those who had gone on shore the day of our arrival, who may have been as many as thirty were all the survivors of both ships. During some days we were struggling with much hardship and hunger; for the provisions and subsistence were destroyed, and some herds. The country was left in a condition piteous to behold; the trees prostrate, the woods parched, there being neither grass nor leaf.

Thus we lived until the fifth day of November,* when the Governor arrived with four ships, which had lived through the great storm, having run into a place of safety in good time. The people who came in them, as well as those on shore, were so intimidated by what had passed, that they feared to go on board in the winter, and they besought the Governor to spend it there. Seeing their desire, and that it was also the wish of the townspeople, he staid through the season. He gave the ships and people into my charge, that I might go with them to pass the winter at the port of Xagua, twelve leagues thence, where I remained until the twentieth day of February.†

* November 5, 1527. † February 20, 1528.

‡ Rio de las Palmas on the western shore of the gulf of Mexico, on modern charts in latitude 23° 48′ north. Oviedo says, on the authority of CHAVES, that near Rio de las Palmas crosses Tropic of

Cancer, thence to Rio Pánuco are more than thirty leagues and thence to Veracruz, seventy leagues.

[2] " ... and for Aldermen of the first town that they should erect, went Miguél de Lambreras, Geronimo Lopez, Andrés Dorantes, Diego de Cueto, and for those of the second, Juan de Mayorga, Bartholomé Hernandez Franco, Juan de Guijón, Alonzo de Herrera."—HERRERA.

In the *Archivo de Indias*, is the original commission issued by the King and Doña Joana, his mother, to Juan Velazquez de Salazar, of the royal household, to be Mayor of the first and principal town of Christians in Florida.

[3] Vasco Porcallo de Figueroa went afterwards with Soto from Cuba to Florida as his Lieutenant general; but, having some misunderstanding with him, returned to the Island soon after the first skirmish with the natives.—OVIEDO. GARCILASSO.

[4] Seventeen and a half leagues, according to the usage of the Spanish and Portuguese navigators of the time, measured one degree, which gives three and a half geographical miles to the league. A mile will be found about the distance accounted "league" in the narrative. A personal experience has shown the day's journey, *jornada*, to be about twenty two miles.

[5] From Xagua, the 15th day of Feb., 1528, he wrote an account to the Emperor of all that had befallen the armament to that time.—OVIEDO.

Official accounts are extant of a very destructive hurricane that visited the Antillas in the same month of October, the year before, which should have a record. The excerpta are in the handwriting of Muñoz in the LXXVIIIth volume of his Collection in the Academy of History at Madrid. The *Audiencia* wrote from Española 20th of May, 1526. "The population is in very necessitous condition. The pestilence of small pox has finished the Indians. The war with France, and his Majesty having taken as borrowed the gold sent to Spain for supplies, have carried up the prices of Spanish goods. The inhabitants notwithstanding have exerted themselves to build sugar mills and other structures for permanency; for the storm or uracan in last October threw down many of the sugar-works and destroyed most of the plantations, although so much has been set up since that the labor is expected to be over with in a short time."
To the Emperor from Portorico, 27th March, 1526.

(San Juan.) "On the night of the 4th of October last there came on such a storm of wind and water, called here uracan, that in twenty four hours it demolished the greater part of this city including the church, doing so great damage to the plantations in the country, because of the freshes in the river, that the like is not remembered on this Island." Many rich have been made poor.

CHAPTER II.

THE COMING OF THE GOVERNOR TO THE PORT OF XAGUA AND WITH A PILOT

At this time, the Governor arrived with a brigantine bought in Trinidad, and brought with him a pilot named Miruelo, who was employed because he said he knew the position of the river Palmas, and had been there, and was a thorough pilot for all the coast of the North.[1] The Governor had also purchased and left on the shore of Havana another vessel, of which Alvaro de la Cerda remained in charge, with forty infantry and twelve cavalry.

The second day after arrival the Governor set sail with four hundred men and eighty horses, in four ships and a brigantine.* The Pilot being again on board, put the vessels among the shoals they call Canarreo, and on the day following we struck; thus we were situated fifteen days, the keels of our vessels frequently touching bottom. At the end of this time,† a tempest from the south threw so much water upon the shoals that we could get off, although not without danger. We left this place and arrived at Guaniguanico, where another storm overtook us, in which we

* Feb. 20   † March 1   1528

were at one time near being lost. At cape Corrientes we had still another, which detained us three days. These places being passed, we doubled Cape Sant Anton, and sailed with head winds until we were within twelve leagues of Havana. Standing in the next day to enter the harbor, a wind came from the south which drove us from the land towards the coast of Florida. We came in sight on Tuesday, the twelfth day of April,* and sailed along the coast. On Holy Thursday † we anchored near the shore in the mouth of a bay at the head of which we saw some houses or habitations of Indians.

* April 12 † April 14 1528

¹ This was Diego the younger Miruelo, nephew, according to BARCIA, of the one of the name who died in the armament of Ayllón. The elder had sailed with Pineda for Garay in a voyage from Española to the northern shore of the Gulf of Mexico, so that, upon a comparison of authorities in the year 1519, he had seen all the shore from the cape of Florida to the river Pánuco in going and again in returning.— NAVARRETE. *Viages Menores. Ensayo Cro.*

CHAPTER III

OUR ARRIVAL IN FLORIDA.

On the same day the Comptroller, Alonzo Enriquez, landed on an island in the bay. He called to the Indians, who came and remained with him some time, and in barter gave him fish and several pieces of venison. The day following, which was Good Friday,* the governor debarked with as many of the people as the boats he brought could contain. When we came to the buhios,¹ or houses that we had seen, we found them vacant and abandoned, the inhabitants having fled at night in their canoes. One of the buhios was very large: it could hold more than three hundred persons. The others were smaller. We found a tinklet of gold among some fish nets.

The next day the Governor raised ensigns for your Majesty,† and took possession of the country in your royal name. He made known his authority, and was obeyed as governor, as your Majesty had commanded. At the same time we laid our commissions before him, and he acknowledged them according to their tenor. Then he ordered that the rest of the people and the horses should land. Of the beasts there were only

* April 15   † April 16   1528

forty-two; by reason of the great storms and the length of time passed at sea, the rest were dead. These few remaining, were so lean and fatigued, that for the time, we could have little service from them. The following day * the Indians of the town came and spoke to us, but as we had no interpreter we could not understand what they meant. They made many signs and menaces, and appeared to say we must go away from the country. With this they left us and went off, offering no interruption.

* April 17   1528

[1] OVIEDO speaks of the *buhio* as distinguished from other forms of Indian habitations, in being "fechas a dos aguas," made with two sheds. The Yucayo word was early taken up by the Spaniards into their speech, and carried from the Antillas to the main, where it is in use. The subject of Indian dwellings is treated of both for the islands and tierra firme, in a full chapter with plates for illustration, in the *Historia General y Natural de las Indias* 1ª P, Lo VI, Cap 1

CHAPTER IV

OUR ENTRANCE INTO THE COUNTRY.

The day following,* the Governor resolved to make an incursion to explore the land, and see what it might contain. With him went the Commissary, the Assessor, and myself with forty men, among them six cavalry, of which we could make little use. We took our way towards the north,† until the hour of vespers, when we arrived at a very large bay that appeared to stretch far inland. We remained there that night, and the next day we returned to the place where were our ships and people.‡ The Governor ordered that the brigantine should sail along the coast of Florida and search for the harbor that Miruelo, the pilot, said he knew, (though as yet he had failed to find it, and could not tell in what place we were, or where was the port), and that if it were not found, she should steer for Havana and seek the ship of which Alvaro de la Cerda was in command, § and, taking provisions, together, they should come to look for us.

---

* April 18.   ‡ April 19.   1528

† Northeast. *Letter* written by Alvar Nuñez and Andres Dorantes in Oviedo.

§ In which were coming forty men and twelve horses.—*Letter.*

After the brigantine left, the same party, with some persons more, returned to enter the land. We kept along the shores of the bay we had found, and, having gone four leagues,* we captured four Indians. We showed them maize, to see if they had knowledge of it, for up to that time we had seen no indication of any. They said they could take us where there was some, so they brought us to their town near by, at the head of the bay, and showed us a little corn not yet fit for gathering.

There we saw many cases, such as are used to contain the merchandise of Castilla, in each of them a dead man, and the bodies were covered with painted deer skins. This appeared to the Commissary to be a kind of idolatry, and he burned the cases with the bodies. We also found pieces of linen and of woolen cloth, and bunches of feathers which appeared like those of New Spain.[1] There were likewise traces of gold. Having by signs asked the Indians whence these things came, they motioned to us that very far from there, was a province called Apalachen, where was much gold, and so the same abundance in Palachen[2] of every thing that we at all cared for.

Taking these Indians for guides, we departed, and traveling ten or twelve leagues we came to a town of fifteen houses. Here a large piece of ground was cultivated in maize then ripe, and we likewise found some already dry. After staying there two days, we returned to where the Comptroller tarried with the

---

* From whence we started.—*Letter*.

men and ships, and related to him and the pilots what we had seen, and the information the natives had given.

The next day, the first of May,* the Governor called aside the Commissary, the Comptroller, the Assessor, myself, a sailor named Bartolomé Fernandez and a Notary, Hieronymo Alaniz. Being together he said that he desired to penetrate the interior, and that the ships ought to go along the coast until they should come to the port which the pilots believed was very near on the way to the river Palmas. He asked us for our views.

I said it appeared to me that under no circumstances ought we to leave the vessels until they were in a secure and peopled harbor; that he should observe the pilots were not confident, and did not agree in any particular, neither did they know where we were; that, more than this, the horses were in no condition to serve us in such exigencies as might occur. Above all, that we were going without being able to communicate with the Indians by use of speech, and without an interpreter, and we could but poorly understand ourselves with them, or learn what we desired to know of the land, that we were about entering a country of which we had no account, and had no knowledge of its character, of what there was in it, or by what people inhabited, neither did we know in what part of it we were, and beside all this, we had not food to sustain us in wandering we knew not whither; that with regard to the stores in the ships, rations could

* May 1.

not be given to each man for such a journey, more than a pound of biscuit and another of bacon: that my opinion was, we should embark and seek a harbor and a soil better than this to occupy, since what we had seen of it was desert and poor, such as had never before been discovered in those parts.

To the Commissary every thing appeared otherwise. He thought we ought not to embark; but, that always keeping the coast, we should go in search of the harbor, which the pilots stated was only ten or fifteen leagues from there, on the way to Pánuco, and that it was not possible, marching ever by the shore, we should fail to come upon it, because they said it stretched up into the land a dozen leagues, that whichever might first find it should wait for the other, that to embark would be to brave the Almighty after so many adversities encountered since leaving Spain, so many storms, and so great losses of men and ships sustained before reaching there: that for these reasons we should march along the coast until we reached the harbor, and those in the ships should take a like direction until they arrived at the same place.

This plan seemed the best to adopt, to the rest who were present, except the Notary, who said that when the ships should be abandoned they ought to be in a known, safe haven, a place with inhabitants, that this done the Governor might advance inland and do what might seem to him proper.

The Governor followed his own judgment and the council of others. Seeing his determination, I required him in behalf of your Majesty, not to quit the ships before putting them in port and making them secure, and accordingly I asked a certificate of this under the hand of the Notary. The Governor responded that he did but abide by the judgment of the Commissary, and of the majority of the officers, and that I had no right to make these requirements of him. He then asked the Notary to give him a certificate, that inasmuch as there was no subsistence in that country for the maintenance of a colony, nor haven for the ships, he brake up the settlement he had placed there, taking its inhabitants in quest of a port and land that should be better. He then ordered the people who were to go with him to be mustered, that they might be victualed with what was needed for the journey. After they had been provided for, he said to me, in the hearing of those present, that since I so much discouraged and feared entering the land, I should sail in charge of the ships and people in them, and form a settlement, should I arrive at the port before him; but from this proposal I excused myself.

After we had separated, the same evening, having said that it did not appear to him that he could entrust the command to any one else, he sent to me to say that he begged I would take it; but finding, notwithstanding he so greatly importuned me, that I still refused, he asked me the cause of my reluctance. I answered that I rejected the responsibility, as I felt certain and knew that he was never more to find the ships, nor the ships him, which might be foreseen in the slender outfit we had for entering the country; that I desired rather to expose myself to the danger which he and the others adventured, and to pass with them what he and they might go through, than to take charge of the ships and give occasion for it to be said I had opposed the invasion and remained behind from timidity, and thus my courage be called in question. I chose rather to risk my life than put my honor in such position. Seeing that what he said to me availed nothing, he begged many persons to reason with me on the subject and entreat me. I answered them in the same way I had him, so he appointed for his lieutenant of the ships an Alcalde he had brought with him, whose name was Caravallo.

[1] To the Commissary and the friars it appeared to be idolatry, and the Governor ordered the bodies to be burned. Pieces of shoes, canvas, broadcloth and iron were likewise found. The Indians on being questioned, answered by signs that they had brought those things from a vessel which had been lost on the shore of that bay.—*Latter*

[2] Thus is the name differently spelled. In the second edition the n is omitted in every instance.

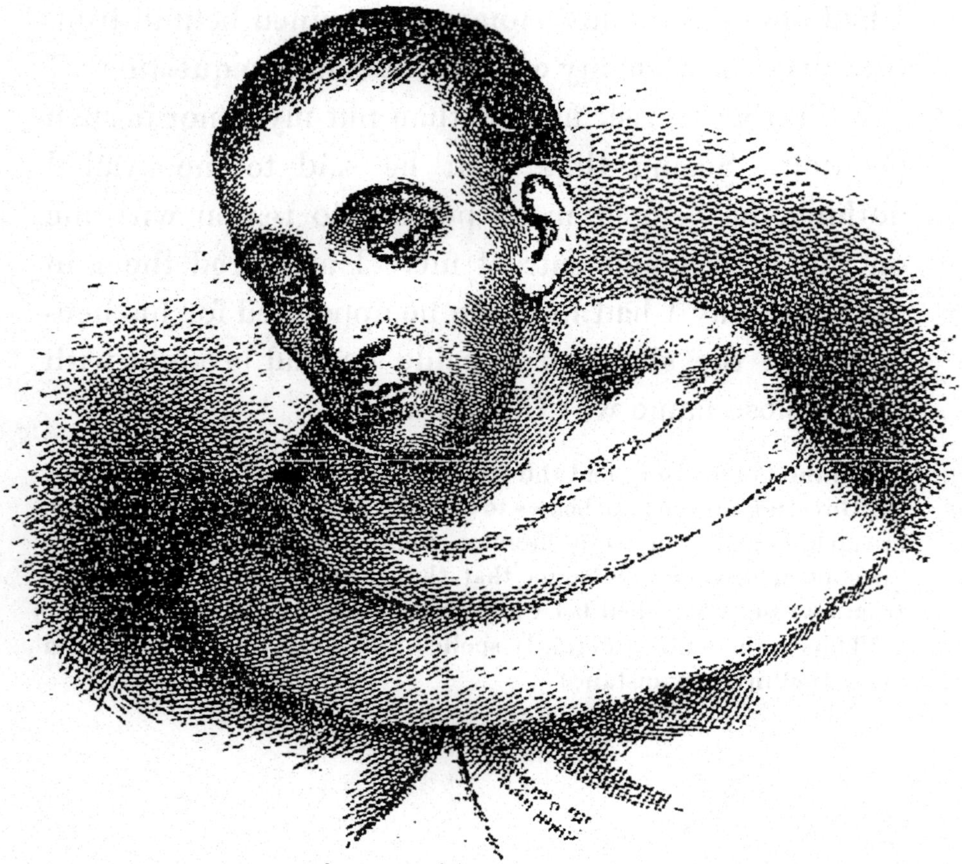

CHAPTER V

THE GOVERNOR LEAVES THE SHIPS

On Sunday, first of May,* the date of this occurrence, the Governor ordered to each man going with him, two pounds of biscuit and half a pound of bacon; and, thus victualed we took up our march into the country. The whole number of men was three hundred: among them went the Commissary, Friar Juan Xuarez, and another friar, Juan de Palos, three clergymen and the officers. We of the mounted men consisted of forty. We traveled on the allowance† we had received fifteen days,[1] without finding any other thing to eat than palmitos,[2] which are like those of Andalusia. In all that time we saw not an Indian, and found neither village nor house. Finally we came to a river, which we passed with great difficulty, by swimming and on rafts. It detained us a day to cross because of the very strong current.[3] Arrived on the other side,‡ there appeared as many as two hundred natives, more or less. The Governor met them, and conversing by signs they so insulted us with their gestures, that we were forced to break with them. We seized upon five or six, and they took us to their houses half a league off.[4] Near

* May 1   † May 15   ‡ May 16   1528

by we found a large quantity of maize in a fit state to be gathered. We gave infinite thanks to our Lord for having succored us in this great extremity, for we were yet young in trials, and besides the weariness in which we came, we were exhausted from hunger.

On the third day after our arrival,* the Comptroller, the Assessor, the Commissary and I met, and together besought the Governor to send to look for the sea, that if possible we might find a port, as the Indians stated there was one not a very great way off. He said that we should cease to speak of the sea, for it was remote, but as I chiefly importuned him, he told me to go and look for it, and seek for a harbor, to take forty men and to travel on foot.⁵ So the next day † I left with Captain Alonzo del Castillo and forty men of his company. We marched until noon, when we arrived at some sea sands that appeared to be a good ways inland. Along this sand we walked for a league and a half,⁶ with the water half way up the leg, treading on oysters, which cut our feet badly and made us much trouble, until we reached the river we had before crossed, emptying into this bay. As we could not cross it by reason of our slim outfit for such purpose, we returned to camp and reported what we had discovered. To find out if there was a port and examine the outlet well, it was necessary to repass the river at the place where we had first gone over, so the next day the Governor ordered a captain,‡ Valenzuela by

* May 17.   † May 18.   ‡ May 19.   1528

name, with sixty men and six cavalry,* to cross, and following the river down to the sea, ascertain if there was a harbor. He returned after an absence of two days,† and said he had explored the bay, that it was not deeper any where than to the knee, and that he found no harbor. He had seen five or six canoes of Indians passing from one shore to the other, wearing many plumes.

With this information, we left the next day † going ever in quest of Apalache, the country of which the Indians told us, having for our guides those we had taken. We traveled without seeing any natives who would venture to await our coming up with them until the seventeenth day of June ‡ when a chief approached, borne on the back of another Indian and covered with a painted deer-skin. A great many people attended him, some walking in advance, playing on flutes of reed. In this manner he came to where the Governor stood and spent an hour with him. By signs we gave him to understand that we were going to Apalachen, and it appeared to us by those he made that he was an enemy to the people of Apalachen, and would go to assist us against them. We gave him beads and hawk-bells with other articles of barter, and he having presented the Governor with the skin he wore, went back, when we followed in the road he took.

That night we came to a wide and deep river with a very rapid current. As we would not venture to

* May 20 † May 21 ‡ June 17 1528

cross on rafts, we made a canoe for the purpose, and spent a day in getting over.* Had the Indians desired to oppose us, they could well have disputed our passage, for even with their help we had great difficulty in making it. One of the mounted men, Juan Velazquez by name, a native of Cuellar, impatient of detention, entered the river, when the violence of the current casting him from his horse, he grasped the reins of the bridle, and both were drowned. The people of that chief, whose name was Dulchanchellin, found the body of the beast, and having told us about where in the stream below, we should find the corpse, it was sought for. This death caused us much regret, for until now not a man had been lost. The horse afforded supper to many that night.

Leaving that spot, the next day we arrived at the town of the chief,† where he sent us maize. During the night one of our men was shot at in a place where we got water, but it pleased God that he should not be hit. The next day we departed,‡ not one of the natives making his appearance, as all had fled. While going on our way a number came in sight, prepared for battle, and though we called to them, they would not return nor await our arrival, but retired following us on the road. The Governor left some cavalry in ambush, which sallying as the natives were about to pass, seized three or four, who thenceforth served as guides. They conducted us through a country very

* June 18   † June 19   ‡ June 20   1528

difficult to travel and wonderful to look upon. In it are vast forests, the trees being astonishingly high. So many were fallen on the ground as to obstruct our way in such a manner that we could not advance without much going about and a considerable increase of toil. Many of the standing trees were riven from top to bottom by bolts of lightning which fall in that country of frequent storms and tempests.

We labored on through these impediments until the day after Saint John's,* when we came in view of Apalachen, without the inhabitants being aware of our approach. We gave many thanks to God at seeing ourselves so near, believing true what had been told us of the land, and that there would be an end to our great hardships, caused as much by the length and badness of the way as by our excessive hunger; for although we sometimes found maize, we oftener traveled seven and eight leagues without seeing any; and besides this and the great fatigue, many had galled shoulders from carrying armor on the back, and even more than these we endured. Yet, having come to the place desired, and where we had been informed were much food and gold, it appeared to us that we had already recovered in part from our sufferings and fatigue.

* June 25.   1528

¹ A daily ration of one pound of bread and half a pound of salted pork for fifteen days.—*Letter.*

² This is the dwarf fan palm, not the cabbage palm, to which we often inadvertently apply the diminutive termination *ito*, misspelled *etto*.

³ This river should be the Withlacooche (*Oiua Slakhi uche*, water long narrow) of the Seminole, called Cale by Oviedo, in the account given of the march of Soto on the authority of Ranjel.

⁴ This appears to be the first dissension that took place between the invaders and natives. When Soto came with his army to a town of Tampa bay, the Cacique there refused to entrust him with his person, giving as a reason that Narváez had caused his nose to be cut off and his mother to be torn in pieces by dogs. Such is the recital in Garcilasso where the Fidalgo of Elvas is silent. Nothing of this is to be found in Ranjel's account out of which Oviedo wrote, nor in the report of Biedma, not in the letter of Soto to the municipality of Santiago de Cuba, giving a circumstantial relation of what had occurred since leaving Havana to the 9th of July, within a short time of his march to the interior; neither does any thing appear in the text of Herrera drawn from other authorities. It an act so cruel had been perpetrated, it was little likely to fade from the retentive memory of the High sheriff, and quite as improbable that he would fail in his narrative to make it known. The character of Narváez does not appear open to the charge of cruelty, even from one who knew him well: the misfortunes he brought upon others with himself, arose out of an easy nature that was justly his reproach.

⁵ Because horses could not be taken.—*Letter*

⁶ A matter of two leagues.—*Letter*

⁷ Six cavalry and forty infantry.—*Letter*

⁸ In the same way, eleven years later, the people under Soto approaching this river, which can be no other than the Sawane, were met by the Indians 'playing upon flutes, a sign among them to others that they come in peace.'—*Relaçam* The name of the chief, found in this territory now just passed over, is spelled by the Fidalgo of Elvas *Uzachil*, in Oviedo *Ucachila*, in Garcilasso *Ochile*, by Biedma *Veachile*, in Herrera *Osachile*. The words may be one with that in the text: the name of the region, probably, as well as of the chief.

CHAPTER VI.

OUR ARRIVAL AT APALACHE.

When we came in view of Apalachen, the Governor ordered that I should take nine cavalry with fifty infantry and enter the town.* Accordingly the Assessor and I assailed it, and having got in, we found only women and boys there, the men being absent; however these returned to its support, after a little time while we were walking about, and began discharging arrows at us. They killed the horse of the Assessor, and at last taking to flight, they left us.

We found a large quantity of maize fit for plucking, and much dry that was housed; also many deer-skins, and among them some mantelets of thread, small and poor, with which the women partially cover their persons. There were numerous mortars for cracking maize. The town consisted of forty small houses, made low, and set up in sheltered places because of the frequent storms. The material was thatch. They were surrounded by very dense woods, large groves and many bodies of fresh water, in which so many and so large trees are fallen, that they form obstructions rendering travel difficult and dangerous.

*June 25.

CHAPTER VII.

THE CHARACTER OF THE COUNTRY.

The country where we came on shore to this town and region of Apalachen, is for the most part level, the ground of sand and stiff earth. Throughout are immense trees and open woods, in which are walnut, laurel and another tree called liquid-amber,[1] cedars, savins, evergreen oaks, pines, red-oaks and palmitos like those of Spain. There are many lakes, great and small, over every part of it; some troublesome of fording, on account of depth and the great number of trees lying throughout them. Their beds are sand. The lakes in the country of Apalachen are much larger than those we found before coming there.

In this Province are many maize fields; and the houses are scattered as are those of the Gelves. There are deer of three kinds,[2] rabbits, hares, bears, lions and other wild beasts. Among them we saw an animal with a pocket on its belly, in which it carries its young until they know how to seek food; and if it happen that they should be out feeding and any one come near, the mother will not run until she has gathered them in together. The country is very cold. It has fine pastures for herds. Birds are of various kinds. Geese in great numbers. Ducks, mallards,

royal-ducks, fly-catchers, night-herons and partridges
abound. We saw many falcons, gerfalcons, sparrow-
hawks, merlins, and numerous other fowl.

Two hours[3] after our arrival at Apalachen,[4] the
Indians who had fled from there came in peace to us,
asking for their women and children, whom we released, but the detention of a cacique by the Governor
produced great excitement, in consequence of which
they returned for battle early the next day,* and attacked us with such promptness and alacrity that they
succeeded in setting fire to the houses in which we
were. As we sallied they fled to the lakes near by,
because of which and the large maize fields, we could
do them no injury, save in the single instance of one
Indian, whom we killed. The day following,† others
came against us from a town on the opposite side of
the lake,[5] and attacked us as the first had done, escaping in the same way, except one who was also slain.

We were in the town twenty-five days,‡ in which
time we made three incursions, and found the country
very thinly peopled and difficult to travel for the bad
passages, the woods and lakes. We inquired of the
cacique we kept and the natives we brought with us,
who were the neighbors and enemies of these Indians,
as to the nature of the country, the character and condition of the inhabitants, of the food and all other
matters concerning it. Each answered apart from the
rest, that the largest town in all that region was Apa-

* June 26   † June 27   ‡ July 19   1528

lachen; the people beyond were less numerous and poorer, the land little occupied, and the inhabitants much scattered; that thenceforward were great lakes, dense forests, immense deserts and solitudes. We then asked touching the region towards the south, as to the towns and subsistence in it. They said that in keeping such a direction, journeying nine days, there was a town called Aute,⁶ the inhabitants whereof had much maize, beans and pumpkins, and being near the sea they had fish, and that those people were then friends.

In view of the poverty of the land, the unfavorable accounts of the population and of everything else we heard, the Indians making continual war upon us, wounding our people and horses at the places where they went to drink, shooting from the lakes with such safety to themselves that we could not retaliate, killing a lord of Tescuco,⁷ named Don Pedro, whom the Commissary brought with him, we determined to leave that place and go in quest of the sea, and the town of Aute of which we were told.

At the termination of the twenty-five days after our arrival we departed,* and on the first day got through those lakes and passages without seeing any one, and on the second day we came to a lake difficult of crossing, the water reaching to the paps, and in it were numerous logs. On reaching the middle of it we were attacked by many Indians from behind trees, who

* July 19, 20.
1528

thus covered themselves that we might not get sight of them, and others were on the fallen timbers. They drove their arrows with such effect that they wounded many men and horses, and before we got through the lake they took our guide. They now followed, endeavoring to contest the passage; but our coming out afforded no relief, nor gave us any better position; for when we wished to fight them they retired immediately into the lake, whence they continued to wound our men and beasts. The Governor, seeing this, commanded the cavalry to dismount and charge the Indians on foot. Accordingly the Comptroller alighting with the rest, attacked them, when they all turned and ran into the lake at hand, and thus the passage was gained.

Some of our men were wounded in this conflict, for whom the good armor they wore did not avail. There were those this day who swore that they had seen two red oaks, each the thickness of the lower part of the leg, pierced through from side to side by arrows; and this is not so much to be wondered at, considering the power and skill with which the Indians are able to project them. I myself saw an arrow that had entered the butt of an elm to the depth of a span.

The Indians we had so far seen in Florida are all archers. They go naked, are large of body, and appear at a distance like giants. They are of admirable proportions, very spare and of great activity and strength. The bows they use are as thick as the arm, of eleven or twelve palms in length, which they will discharge at two hundred paces with so great precision that they miss nothing.

Having got through this passage, at the end of a league we arrived at another of the same character, but worse, as it was longer, being half a league in extent. This we crossed freely, without interruption from the Indians, who, as they had spent on the former occasion their store of arrows, had nought with which they dared venture to engage us. Going through a similar passage the next day,* I discovered the trail of persons ahead, of which I gave notice to the Governor, who was in the rear guard, so that though the Indians came upon us, as we were prepared they did no harm. After emerging upon the plain they followed us, and we went back on them in two directions. Two we killed, and they wounded me and two or three others. Coming to woods we could do them no more injury, nor make them further trouble.

In this manner we traveled eight days.† After that occurrence we were not again beset until within a league of the place to which I have said we were going. There, while on our way, the Indians came about us without our suspicion, and fell upon the rear guard. A hidalgo, named Avellaneda, hearing the cries of his serving boy, went back to give assistance, when he was struck by an arrow near the edge of his cuirass, and so severe was the wound, the shaft having passed almost entirely through his neck, that

* July 21   † July 29   1528

he presently died. The corpse was carried to Aute, where we arrived at the end of nine days travel from Apalache.* We found all the inhabitants gone and the houses burned. Maize, beans and pumpkins, were in great plenty, all beginning to be fit for gathering. Having rested two days,† the Governor begged me to go and look for the sea, as the Indians said it was near, and we had before discovered it, while on the way, from a very large stream to which we had given the name of river of the Magdalena.

Accordingly, I set out the next day after,‡ in company with the Commissary, Captain Castillo Andrés Dorantes, seven more on horseback and fifty on foot. We traveled until the hour of vespers, when we arrived at a road or entrance of the sea. Oysters were abundant, over which the men rejoiced, and we gave thanks to God that he had brought us there. The following morning I sent twenty men to explore the coast and ascertain its direction.§ They returned the night after, reporting that those creeks and bays were large, and lay so far inland as made it difficult to examine them agreeably to our desires, and that the sea shore was very distant.

These tidings obtained, seeing our slender means, and condition for exploring the coast, I went back to the Governor. On our arrival we found him and many others sick. The Indians had assaulted them the night before, and because of the malady that

* July 28   † July 30   ‡ July 31   § August 1   1528

had come upon them, they had been pushed to extremity. One of the horses had been killed. I gave a report of what I had done, and of the embarrassing nature of the country. We remained there that day

¹ Sweet gum

² The varieties of the deer must have included those found farther west, by the *Sierra Madre* or the *Cordillera* of the Andes, then within the limits of the extensive region known as Florida, on the west defined by those mountains

Strange to say no mention is made anywhere in the narrative either of the turkey or alligator

³ The first edition and the *Letter* says two days

⁴ The name of the territory or town, probably in the language of the Timuqua Indians. It is once spelled Palache in the second edition, and also in the *Relaçam Verdadeira* of the march of Soto, and not probably by accident in either instance. The *á* to *á la*, to the are prefixes that native names appear to take upon them in some unaccountable way from the Spanish. Timuqua has oftentimes received the *a*, and so incorrectly have other names. Perhaps the Anagados of this narrative are the Nagadoch. A-la Tama Alatamaha, A la Chua, Alachua are instances of the double prefix, and Alapaha, Alafaya, ancient names, may be suspected of bearing it

⁵ From other towns another people —*Letter*

⁶ The name of this town is spelled Ochete in the *Relaçam* of the march of Soto by the Knight of Elvas

⁷ Spelled Tezuco in the first edition. Although this lord was by seniority and descent on the father's side heir to the throne of Tetzcoco, the selection was made by the nobles. Not being given to arms he was considered of a nature too pacific for the government of an extensive territory. On the other hand the election of either of his brothers Cohuanatco or Yxtlixochitl, was opposed for their want of years. In this dissension the influence of Moctezuma prevailed, and their half brother Cacama became elected. He was the son of Netzaxualpilli, the father of those princes, by a sister of the Emperor. Cohuanatco in the council approved of the selection. Yxtlixochitl protested and withdrew taking with him numerous adherents. Beyond the city he called together all those who would oppose Moctezuma of whom Cacama had asked support. Although permitted to possess the extensive mountainous portion of the domain, Yxtlixochitl maintained a position hostile to the Em-

peror, threatened the capital, challenged his forces and even engaged them with success.

At this juncture the Spaniards having arrived on the coast, Ixtlxochitl informed them of the condition of affairs and offered his assistance. The invasion followed; and Cortés, who without scruple or distinction of race or rank, seems to have taken off most of those standing in his way or entrusting him with their persons, despatched Cacama on the retreat from Mexico, after the death of Moctezuma, whose successor he had been declared.

On the second approach to the capital Cohuanateo who reigned in Tetzcoco, at once gave his support to the Emperor Guatimo, successor of Cuitlahuac the successor of Moctezuma, in a last struggle for the mastery. On the side of the Spaniards, with the forces of the allies were Ixtlxochitl as king of Tetzcoco appointed by Cortés, and the Prince *Ithlhuchuczpuizlt* his brother otherwise *Don Pedro* with an immense army, the one accompanying Cortés in the assault on the capital, the other aiding Olid and Alvarado. Their assistance probably decided the terrible contest.

The house of Netzahualcoyotl the father of Netzaxualpath suffered for their conduct. Cohuanateo with other princes were hanged while accompanying Cortés in the invasion of Ibueras. The descendant of Ixtlxochitl in the fifth generation after a lapse of eighty years states in his record of the conquest written near the close of life that his daughters were without a protector poor, retired with scarce a roof over their heads and even from that they were liable to be expelled.

Their great ancestor Netzaxualcoyotl esteemed for his wisdom his abilities as a lawgiver and warlike qualities is remembered as the composer of song. Of sixty canticles two remain and portions of two others are preserved by his descendant in the *Historia de los Chichimecas*. They are conceived in no spirit of prophecy, but are rather the melancholy forebodings that attend thoughts on the mutability of earthly things. They were chanted at the dedication of palaces and at royal festivals. One of them entitled Song of Spring commences:

'Listen to what the king Netzahualcoyotl says in his lamentations over the calamities and oppressions which his realms and principalities are to suffer. When you are gone from the present to the future O King Totontzin! (this other name he bore Don trim) the time will come when your vassals will be overpowered and dispersed, all things avoiding the darkness of oblivion. Then in truth power and command will not be in your hand but in that of God.

then will come the afflictions, the miseries that your children and grandchildren will undergo, who, weeping, will remember you have left them orphans, the servants of strangers, in Acolhuan their country. To this doom come away empires and lordships, which have no stability and last only a little time. The things of this life are lent; in a moment we are to leave the world as others have left it."

In the year 1467 the edifice dedicated to Huitzilipuztli, the largest in the city of Tezcoco was completed. At the opening the king sang:

"In some such year as this, when the temple which is now being consecrated shall be destroyed, who will be here? Shall it be my son or my grandson? The earth will continue lessening in her increase, and the rulers will be no more. The magueys small and untimely will be blasted, the dwarfed trees will yield no fruit, and the defective earth go on still becoming worse."—YXTLILXOCHITL *Cap XLVI* in IX vol of Kingsborough, p 259.

It was his grandchildren who, in the heat of rivalry, forgot their country, giving it over as a possession to the invader. Let us hope that not for safety was Don Pedro accompanying the friar of Huehotzinco.

I have been favored from Mexico with the figure denoting the name of Don Pedro together with an explanation of its meaning that will be placed in the addenda. My friend says, and I translate:

I too think that the Tezcucan in company with Alvar Nuñez was Don Pedro Tetlahuehuetzquititzin, own brother of Ixtlilxochitl. The true orthography of his name I believe is as I write it, according perfectly with his glyph which represents the name phonetically in this wise

It denotes symbolically and figuratively the mask of the jester or juggler who directs the Matachin dances of the ancient Mexicans, which you may have witnessed here. It may signify the epigrammatic and malignant man who makes jest of every thing besides one who jokes and is witty, though in some degree epigrammatic. By abbreviation he is now called by the populace *Huehue* old man, and that was likewise a part he represented.

With the Comptroller and the Inspector.—*Letter*

CHAPTER VIII

WE GO FROM AUTE

The next morning we left Aute,* and traveled all day before coming to the place I had visited. The journey was extremely arduous. There were not horses enough to carry the sick, who went on increasing in numbers day by day, and we knew of no cure. It was piteous and painful to witness our perplexity and distress. We saw on our arrival how small were the means for advancing farther. There was not anywhere to go; and if there had been, the people were unable to move forward, the greater part being ill, and those were few who could be on duty. I cease here to relate more of this, because any one may suppose what would occur in a country so remote and malign, so destitute of all resource whereby either to live in it or go out of it; but most certain assistance is in God, our Lord, on whom we never failed to place reliance. One thing occurred, more afflicting to us than all the rest, which was, that of the persons mounted, the greater part commenced secretly to plot, hoping to secure a better fate for themselves by abandoning the Governor and the sick, who were in a state of weak-

* August 1.

ness and prostration. But, as among them were many hidalgos and persons of gentle condition, they would not permit this to go on, without informing the Governor and the officers of your Majesty; and as we showed them the deformity of their purpose, and placed before them the moment when they should desert their captain, and those who were ill and feeble, and above all the disobedience to the orders of your Majesty, they determined to remain, and that whatever might happen to one should be the lot of all, without any forsaking the rest.

After the accomplishment of this, the Governor called them all to him, and of each apart he asked advice as to what he should do to get out of a country so miserable, and seek that assistance elsewhere which could not here be found, a third part of the people being very sick, and the number increasing every hour; for we regarded it as certain that we should all become so, and could pass out of it only through death, which from its coming in such a place was to us all the more terrible. These, with many other embarrassments being considered, and entertaining many plans, we coincided in one great project, extremely difficult to put in operation, and that was to build vessels in which we might go away. This appeared impossible to every one: we knew not how to construct, nor were there tools, nor iron, nor forge, nor tow, nor resin, nor rigging; finally, no one thing of so many that are necessary, nor any man who had a knowledge of their manufacture, and, above all, there was nothing to eat, while building, for those who should labor. Reflecting on all this, we agreed to think of the subject with more deliberation, and the conversation dropped from that day, each going his way, commending our course to God, our Lord, that he would direct it as should best serve Him.

The next day it was His will,* that one of the company should come saying, that he could make some pipes out of wood, which with deer-skins might be made into bellows; and, as we lived in a time when any thing that had the semblance of relief appeared well, we told him to set himself to work. We assented to the making of nails, saws, axes and other tools of which there was such need, from the stirrups, spurs, crossbows and the other things of iron there were; and we laid out for support, while the work was going on, that we would make four entries into Aute, with all the horses and men that were able to go; and that on every third day a horse should be killed to be divided among those who labored in the work of the boats and the sick. The incursions were made with the people and horses that were available, and in them were brought back as many as four hundred fanegas of maize;¹ but these were not got without quarrels and contentions with the Indians. We caused many palmitos to be collected for the woof or covering, twisting and preparing it for use in the place of tow for the boats.

* August 4.
1528

We commenced to build on the fourth,* with the only carpenter in the company, and we proceeded with so great diligence that on the twentieth day of September,† five boats were finished twenty-two cubits in length, each caulked with the fibre of the palmito. We pitched them with a certain resin, made from pine trees by a Greek, named Don Theodoro, from the same husk of the palmito, and from the tails and manes of the horses we made ropes and rigging, from our shirts, sails, and from the savins growing there, we made the oars that appeared to us requisite. Such was the country into which our sins had cast us, that only by very great search could we find stone for ballast and anchors, since in it all we had not seen one. We flayed the horses, taking the skin from their legs entire, and tanning them to make bottles wherein to carry water.

During this time some went gathering shell-fish in the coves and creeks of the sea, at which employment the Indians twice attacked them and killed ten men in sight of the camp, without our being able to afford succor. We found their corpses traversed from side to side with arrows, and for all some had on good armor, it did not give adequate protection or security against the nice and powerful archery of which I have spoken. According to the declaration of our pilots under oath, from the entrance to which we had given the name *Bahia de la Cruz* to this place, we had traveled two

---

* August 4.   † September 20.   1528

hundred and eighty leagues or thereabout.[2] Over all that region we had not seen a single mountain, and had no information of any whatsoever.

Before we embarked there died more than forty men of disease and hunger, without enumerating those destroyed by the Indians. By the twenty-second of the month of September,* the horses had been consumed, one only remaining, and on that day we embarked in the following order. In the boat of the Governor went forty-nine men; in another, which he gave to the Comptroller and the Commissary, went as many others; the third, he gave to Captain Alonzo del Castillo and Andrés Dorantes, with forty-eight men; and another he gave to two captains, Tellez and Peñalosa, with forty-seven men. The last was given to the Assessor and myself, with forty-nine men. After the provisions and clothes had been taken in, not over a span of the gunwales remained above water; and more than this, the boats were so crowded that we could not move; so much can necessity do, which drove us to hazard our lives in this manner, running into a turbulent sea, not a single one who went, having a knowledge of navigation.

* September 22.   1528

[1] Five fanegas measure nearly eight bushels, so that the quantity of maize got in Aute was about six hundred and forty bushels.—KERR's *Universal Cambist.*

[2] In fact, about this number of geographical miles.

REVIEW OF FORCE TO THIS TIME

Sailed from Spain,	.	600 men, more or less		
Left the fleet at Santo Domingo,	140	"	and over	
Lost in the ships at Trinidad de Cuba,	60	"	20 horses	
	—200	"		
Sailed from Xagua, in Cuba,		400	" 80 "	
Landed at *Bahía de la Cruz*,		"	" 42 "	
Left on board the vessels, near		100 persons*		
Set out to enter the country,		300 men 40 horses		
Drowned, or killed on the march,	3	"	3 "	
Killed in *Bahía de Caballos*,	. 10	"	—	
Died of disease and hunger, more than	40	"	37 "	
	—53	"		
	247			
Embarked in the five boats 49, 49, 48, 47, 49, —	.	242	" 40 "	killed for subsistence

If to those in the five boats be added the Governor and the four other officers appointed by the king, the account of persons will be complete

* Stated in the final chapter, of whom ten were women

CHAPTER IX.

WE LEAVE THE BAY OF HORSES

The haven we left bears the name *Bahía de Caballos*.[1] We passed waist deep in water through sounds without seeing any sign of the coast, and at the close of the seventh day,* we came to an island near the main. My boat went first, and from her we saw Indians approaching in five canoes, which they abandoned and left in our hands, finding that we were coming after them. The other boats passed ahead, and stopped at some houses on the island, where we found many dried mullet and roes, which were a great relief in our distress. After taking these we went on, and two leagues thence, we discovered a strait the island makes with the land, which we named Sant Miguel, for having passed through it on his day.† Coming out we went to the coast, where with the canoes I had taken, we somewhat improved the boats, making waist-boards and securing them, so that the sides rose two palms above the water. This done we returned to move along the coast in the direction of the river Palmas, our hunger and thirst continually increasing; for our scant subsistence was getting near the end, the water

---

* September 28.   † September 29.

was out, and the bottles made from the legs of the horses having soon rotted, were useless. Sometimes we entered coves and creeks that lay far in, and found them all shallow and dangerous. Thus we journeyed along them thirty days, finding occasionally Indian fishermen, a poor and miserable people.

At the end of this time, while the want of water was great,† going near the coast at night we heard the approach of a canoe, for which, so soon as it was in sight we paused, but it would not meet us, and, although we called, it would neither come nor wait for us. As the night was dark, we did not follow, and kept on our way. When the sun rose we saw a small island,† and went to it to find water; but our labor was vain, as it had none. Lying there at anchor, a heavy storm came on, that detained us six days,‡ we not daring to go to sea, and as it was now five days since we had drunk, our thirst was so excessive that it put us to the extremity of swallowing salt water, by which some of the men became so crazed that three or four suddenly died. I state this so briefly, because I do not believe there is any necessity for particularly relating the sufferings and toils amidst which we found ourselves, since, considering the place where we were, and the little hope we had of relief, every one may conceive much of what must have passed.

Although the storm had not ceased, as our thirst increased and the water killed us, we resolved to com-

* October 21.   † October 22.   ‡ October 27.   1528

mend ourselves to God our Lord, and adventure the peril of the sea rather than await the end which thirst made certain. Accordingly we went out by the way we had observed the canoe go the night we came.* On this day we were ourselves many times overwhelmed by the waves, and in such jeopardy that there was not one who did not suppose his death inevitable. Thanks be to Him, that in the greatest dangers, He was wont to show us his favor; for at sunset doubling a point made by the land, we found shelter with much calm.

Many canoes came off with Indians who spoke with us and returned, not being disposed to await our arrival. They were of large stature and well formed; they had no bows and arrows. We followed them to their houses near by, at the edge of the water, and jumped on shore. Before their dwellings were many clay pitchers with water, and a large quantity of cooked fish, which the chief of these territories offered to the Governor and then took him to his house. Their dwellings were made of mats, and so far as we observed, were not movable. On entering the house the cacique gave us fish, and we gave him of the maize we brought, which the people ate in our presence. They asked for more and received it and the Governor presented the cacique with many trinkets. While in the house with him, at the middle hour of night, the Indians fell suddenly upon us, and on those who were very sick, scattered along the shore. They

* October 27.

also beset the house in which the Governor was, and with a stone struck him in the face. Those of our comrades present seized the cacique; but his people being near liberated him, leaving in our hands a robe of civet-marten.

These skins are the best, I think, that can be found; they have a fragrance that can be equalled by amber and musk alone, and even at a distance is strongly perceptible. We saw there other skins, but none comparable to these.

Those of us around, finding the Governor wounded, put him into his boat; and we caused others of our people to betake themselves likewise to their boats, some fifty remaining to withstand the natives. They attacked us thrice that night, and with so great impetuosity, that on each occasion they made us retire more than a stone's cast. Not one among us escaped injury. I was wounded in the face. They had not many arrows, but had they been further provided, doubtless they would have done us much harm. In the last onset, the Captains Dorantes, Peñalosa, and Tellez put themselves in ambuscade with fifteen men, and fell upon the rear in such manner that the Indians desisted and fled.

The next morning I broke up more than thirty canoes,* which were serviceable for fuel in a north wind in which we were kept all day suffering severe cold, without daring to go to sea, because of the rough weather

* October 28

upon it. This having subsided, we again embarked, and navigated three days.* As we brought little water and the vessels were few, we were reduced to the last extremity. Following our course, we entered an estuary, and being there we saw Indians approaching in a canoe. We called to them and they came. The Governor, at whose boat they first arrived, asked for water, which they assented to give, asking for something in which they might bring it, when Dorotheo Theodoro, a Greek spoken of before, said that he wished to go with them. The Governor tried to dissuade him, and so did others, but were unable: he was determined to go whatever might betide. Accordingly he went, taking with him a negro, the natives leaving two of their number as hostages. At night the Indians returned with the vessels empty and without the Christians; and when those we held were spoken to by them, they tried to plunge into the sea. Being detained by the men, the Indians in the canoe thereupon fled, leaving us sorrowful and much dejected for our loss.

* October 29.   1528.

¹ The appearance that *Bahía de los Caballos* presented in the year 1539, when visited by Juan de Añasco with a squadron from the army of Soto, is thus stated by the INCA. CHARLEVOIX, who was at San Marcos de Apalache there wrote in the year 1722. Cette Baye est précisément ce que Garcilasso de la Vega appelle dans son Histoire de la Floride la Port d'Auté.—*Lettre XXXIV.*

"Guided by three Indians they arrived at a very wide and spacious bay, and keeping its shore they came to the place at which Pánphilo de Narvaez had stopped. They saw where had been a furnace in which were made the spikes for his boats, and much charcoal was lying about. They saw also some large hollowed logs, used as troughs for feeding horses.

"The Indians showed them the place where ten of the Spaniards were killed, as Cabeça de Vaca writes in his history. They took them step by step over all that Narváez had gone, pointing to the spots where such and such an event took place. Finally they left no memorable thing which had occurred to Pámphilo de Narváez in that bay untold, by signs and by words well or badly understood, some of them spoken in Castillian, which they had learned aforetime.

"Captain Añasco and his soldiers sought diligently in holes and under the bark of trees for letters, in the places where it was the custom of the discoverers to conceal them, that they might have account of what those who went before had seen and learned; but they discovered nothing which they desired to find. After this they followed the shore of the bay to the sea three leagues, and with the ebb tide ten or twelve swimmers went out in some old canoes they found abandoned, and sounded the depths of the bay in mid channel."

Among the collection of Ancient Charts in fac-simile published by Jomard, is a *mappemonde* from the hand of SEBASTIAN CABOT, upon which is inscribed at Apalache bay, *baya de miruelo*

aqui de san barco panflo de narnez

which were enough to convince, were other evidence wanting, that this map is little likely to have been engraved where the Spanish was spoken.

The chart refers in different places to the Tabvla Prima and Tabula Secvnda (both omitted to be published), the former on the originals to the left of the spectator, numbering ten sections, alternately Spanish and Latin, the latter on the right, twelve sections, in the same languages. They cover eight pages folio, on paper pasted as was the custom once on the margin outside of the map. The impression is ancient, unofficial, appears to have been taken from a cut on wood, and in the opinion of an excellent judge, Sr. d. P. de Gayangos, who attentively examined it for me, "was probably printed in Brussels or Amsterdam or some such place." In two corners of the map are ornaments with frivolous or rather senseless inscriptions. "It has been in the *Biblioteque Impériale* about twenty years," said M. Richard Cortambert, the distinguished *Membre des Comité d'archéologie américaine*, of France, in October, 1868. The chart is colored green, blue, red; a double eagle is outside of the field of the hemispheres, with columns of Hercules. It bears the title

"Sebastian Caboto Capitan, y piloto mayor de la S. c. e. m. del Imperador don Carlos quinto deste nombre, y Rey nuestro sennor hizo esta figura extensa en plano, anno del nascim⁰ de ñro salvador Iesu Christo de M D XLIIII, annos tirada por grados de latitud y longitud con sus mentos como carta de marcar, imitando en parte el Ptolomeo, y en parte a los modernos descobridores, assi Epannoles como Portugueses, y parte por su padre, y por el descubierto por donde podras nauegar como por carta de marcar."

"Sebastian Caboto captain and chief pilot of the Sacred Caesarean Catholic Majesty the Emperor Don Carlos fifth of the name and the King our master, made this extensive configuration in plano year of the birth of our Lord Jesus Christ 1544 years, drawn in degrees of latitude and longitude with points of compass like a marine chart, imitating that of Ptolomeus in part, and the modern discoverers Spaniards as well as Portuguese, partly by his father and by him discovered, wherewith you may navigate as by a sea card."

"§ 8 Terram hanc olim nobis clausam aperuit Ioannes Cabotus Venetus, necnō Sebastianus Cabotus eius filius, anno ab orbe redempto 1494 die uero 24 July, hora 5 sub diluculo qua terrā primū uisam appellarūt & Insulā quandā magnā ei oppositā, Insula diui Ioannes nominarunt, quippe quae solemni die festo diui Ioannis aperta fuit."

"Esta tierra fue descubierta por Juan Caboto Venetiano, y Sebastian Caboto su hijo, anno del nascimiento de nuestro Saluador Iesu Christo de MCCCCXCIIII a ueinte y quatro de Junio por la mañana, a la qual pusieron nōbre prima tierra uista, y a un isla grade que esta par de la dha tierra le pusieron nombre Sant Joan, por auer sido descubierta el mismo dia la gente della andan uestidos de pieles de orsos, planeos y cieruos muy grandes como cauallos, y otras muchas animales, y semeiantmēte ay pescado infinito, sollos salmōes, lenguados muy grandes de uara en largo y otras muchas diuersidades de pescados, y la mayor multitud dellos se dizen bacallaos, y asi mismo ay en la dha tierra Halcones prietos, como cueruos, Aguilas Perdices, Pardillas, y otras muchas aues de diuersas maneras."

"This land was discovered by Juan Caboto, Venetian, and Sebastian Caboto, his son, year of the birth of our Saviour Jesus Christ 1494, the 24th of June in the morning, to which they gave the name First Land seen and to a large island along said land they gave the name Sant Joan for having been discovered on the same day. The people of it go dressed in figured bear-skins and in those of very large stags like horses, and of many other animals. In like manner there is an infinity of fish, pikes, salmon sole very large, a yard in length, and many other sort of fish the greatest number called bacallaos and likewise in that country are falcons, black as crows, eagles, partridges, linnets, and many other birds of different kinds."

F. A. DE VARNHAGEN has stated with greater exactness the position of the Bay: "Tocobaga, more recently called Miruelo." *Le premier royage de Amerigo Vespucci*, Vienne, 1869, p. 30. The bay was the present Tampa and formerly Espiritu Santo, the entrance in latitude 27° 35' north, on the western coast of the Peninsula of Florida.

² Killing three men.—*Letter.*

CHAPTER X.

THE ASSAULT FROM THE INDIANS

The morning having come,* many natives arrived in canoes who asked us for the two that had remained in the boat. The Governor replied that he would give up the hostages when they should bring the Christians they had taken. With the Indians had come five or six chiefs, who appeared to us to be the most comely persons, and of more authority and condition than any we had hitherto seen, although not so large as some others of whom we have spoken. They wore the hair loose and very long, and were covered with robes of marten such as we had before taken. Some of the robes were made up after a strange fashion, with wrought ties of lion skin, making a brave show. They entreated us to go with them, and said they would give us the Christians, water, and many other things. They continued to collect about us in canoes, attempting in them to take possession of the mouth of that entrance; in consequence, and because it was hazardous to stay near the land, we went to sea, where they remained by us until about mid-day. As they would not deliver our people, we would not give up theirs, so they began

* October 31.

to hurl clubs at us and to throw stones with slings, making threats of shooting arrows, although we had not seen among them all more than three or four bows While thus engaged, the wind beginning to freshen, they left us and went back.

We sailed that day until the middle of the afternoon, when my boat, which was first, discovered a point made by the land, and against a cape opposite, passed a broad river I cast anchor near a little island forming the point, to await the arrival of the other boats. The Governor did not choose to come up, and entered a bay near by in which were a great many islets We came together there, and took fresh water from the sea, the stream entering it in freshet. To parch some of the maize we brought with us, since we had eaten it raw for two days, we went on an island, but finding no wood we agreed to go to the river beyond the point, one league off. By no effort could we get there, so violent was the current on the way, which drove us out, while we contended and strove to gain the land The north wind, which came from the shore, began to blow so strongly that it forced us to sea without our being able to overcome it We sounded half a league out, and found with thirty fathoms we could not get bottom; but we were unable to satisfy ourselves that the current was not the cause of failure.[1] Toiling in this manner to fetch the land, we navigated three days,* and at the end of this time, a little before

---

* November 2   1528

the sun rose, we saw smoke in several places along the shore. Attempting to reach them, we found ourselves in three fathoms of water, and in the darkness we dared not come to land; for as we had seen so many smokes, some surprise might lie in wait, and the obscurity leave us at a loss how to act. We determined therefore to stop until morning.

When day came, the boats had lost sight of each other. I found myself in thirty fathoms. Keeping my course until the hour of vespers, I observed two boats, and drawing near I found that the first I approached was that of the Governor. He asked me what I thought we should do. I told him we ought to join the boat which went in advance, and by no means to leave her, and, the three being together, we must keep on our way to where God should be pleased to lead. He answered saying that could not be done, because the boat was far to sea and he wished to reach the shore, that if I wished to follow him, I should order the persons of my boat to take the oars and work, as it was only by strength of arm that the land could be gained. He was advised to this course by a captain with him named Pantoja, who said that if he did not fetch land that day, in six days more they would not reach it, and in that time they must inevitably famish. Discovering his will I took my oar, and so did every one his, in my boat, to obey it. We rowed until near sunset, but the Governor having in his boat the healthiest of all the men, we could not by any means hold with or follow her. Seeing this, I asked him to give me a rope from his boat, that I might be enabled to keep up with him, but he answered me that he would do no little, if they, as they were, should be able to reach the land that night. I said to him, that since he saw the feeble strength we had to follow him, and do what he ordered, he must tell me how he would that I should act. He answered that it was no longer a time in which one should command another, but that each should do what he thought best to save his own life; that he so intended to act, and saying this, he departed with his boat.

As I could not follow him, I steered to the other boat at sea, which waited for me, and having come up, I found her to be the one commanded by the Captains Peñalosa and Tellez.

Thus we continued in company, eating a daily allowance of half a handful of raw maize, until the end of four days, when we lost sight of each other in a storm; and such was the weather, that only by God's favor, we did not all go down. Because of winter and its inclemency, the many days we had suffered hunger, and the heavy beating of the waves, the people began next day to despair in such a manner that when the sun sank, all who were in my boat were fallen one on another, so near to death that there were few among them in a state of sensibility. Of the whole number at this time not five men were on their feet; and when night came, only the master and myself were left, who

* November 4   1528

could work the boat. Two hours after dark, he said to me that I must take charge of her as he was in such condition he believed he should die that night. So I took the paddle, and going after midnight to see if the master was alive, he said to me he was rather better, and would take the charge until day. I declare in that hour I would more willingly have died than seen so many people before me in such condition. After the master took the direction of the boat, I lay down a little while; but without repose, for nothing at that time was farther from me than sleep.

Near the dawn of day,* it seemed to me I heard the tumbling of the sea; for as the coast was low, it roared loudly. Surprised at this, I called to the master, who answered me that he believed we were near the land. We sounded and found ourselves in seven fathoms. He advised that we should keep to sea until sunrise; accordingly I took an oar and pulled on the land side, until we were a league distant, when we gave her stern to the sea. Near the shore a wave took us, that knocked the boat out of water the distance of the throw of a crowbar,³ and from the violence with which she struck, nearly all the people who were in her like dead, were roused to consciousness. Finding themselves near the shore, they began to move on hands and feet, crawling to land into some ravines. There we made fire, parched some of the maize we brought, and found rain water. From the warmth of the fire

* November 5. 1528

the people recovered their faculties, and began somewhat to exert themselves. The day on which we arrived was the sixth of November *

* November 6   1528

¹ In the year 1540 the soldiers under Soto on their way to the town of Mavila, came to a large river which they believed to be the one entering the bay of Chuse. They heard that the boats of Narváez had been there below for water, that Don Theodoro and his companion had remained among the Indians, and were shown likewise a dirk that had been his.—BIEDMA

The bay of Achuse was afterwards called Panzacola by the Spaniards.—BÁRCIA *Ensayo Cro*

On the authority of that gentleman who had followed Soto to see the world, and who for recreation, kept a journal that he might know how his days passed away, OVIEDO states that at Piahi, a town built on the steep bluff of a river, the Spaniards heard of Theodoro and the negro, and that they had been killed. From these statements it would appear that the army of Soto, moving westwardly had not at that time reached the Coosa river

² "The boat, in which the Treasurer was, arrived at a point made by the coast, behind which was a river that flowed broad and swollen from freshet a little behind, the boat of the Governor with the others anchored among some islands near by, whither the Treasurer went and made known the discovery of that river. As they found no wood with which to parch the maize they had been eating raw for two days, they agreed to enter that river, of which they took up fresh water in the sea, but, on drawing near to it, the violence of the current at the entrance did not permit them to gain the land."—*Letter* This river is supposed to be the Mississippi. The date is about the 2d of November, 1528

³ *Juego de herradura.* The reference is to the distance the bar of iron may be thrown in the exercise of *juego de la barra*, practiced in Spain, particularly among the women of Navarra. The instrument, often a crowbar, is grasped in the middle and cast the distance possible, to fall erect

CHAPTER XI.

OF WHAT BEFEL LOPE DE OVIEDO WITH THE INDIANS.

After the people had eaten, I ordered Lope de Oviedo, who had more strength and was stouter than any of the rest, to go to some trees that were near by, and climbing into one of them to look about and try to gain knowledge of the country. He did as I bade, and made out that we were on an island. He saw that the land was pawed up in the manner that ground is wont to be where cattle range, whence it appeared to him that this should be a country of Christians, and thus he reported to us. I ordered him to return and examine much more particularly, and see if there were any roads that were worn, but without going far, because there might be danger.

He went, and coming to a path, took it for the distance of half a league, and found some huts, without tenants, they having gone into the woods. He took from these an earthen pot, a little dog, some few mullets, and returned. As it appeared to us he was gone a long time, we sent two men that they should look to see what might have happened. They met him near by, and saw that three Indians with bows and arrows followed and were calling to him, while he, in the same way, was beckoning them on. Thus he arrived where we were, the natives remaining a little way back, seated on the shore. Half an hour after, they were supported by one hundred other Indian bowmen,[2] who if they were not large, our fears made giants of them. They stopped near us with the first three. It were idle to think that any among us could make defence, for it would have been difficult to find six that could rise from the ground. The Assessor and I went out and called to them, and they came to us. We endeavored the best we could to encourage them and secure their favor. We gave them beads and hawk-bells, and each of them gave me an arrow, which is a pledge of friendship. They told us by signs that they would return in the morning and bring us something to eat, as at that time they had nothing.

[1] The word *perrillo*, meaning diminutive dog, is familiarly used by old writers for *perro mudo*, or dumb dog, inhabiting the Antillas, Tierra firme and New Spain. An additional word in the text, *pequeño*, little, seems to attach a particular meaning to the first. The natives of Española reared the perrillo in their dwellings for food and the hunting of small game, but it appears to have been a different animal from the *Procyon lotor* of the continent. In the account of the expedition of Soto, given in Oviedo, it is stated that while the army was in a certain region of country (now covered by the state of Georgia), it was plentifully supplied with *perrillos* by the Indians. We may suspect that the raccoon in this instance, was intended to be understood, and that *perrillo pequeño* marks the specific animal distinctively with its size.

[2] Two hundred archers with holes in their ears in which were joints of cane.—*Letter.*

CHAPTER XII.

THE INDIANS BRING US FOOD.

At sunrise the next day,* the time the Indians appointed, they came according to their promise, and brought us a large quantity of fish with certain roots, some a little larger than walnuts, others a trifle smaller, the greater part got from under the water and with much labor. In the evening they returned and brought us more fish and roots. They sent their women and children to look at us, who went back rich with the hawk-bells and beads given them, and they came afterwards on other days, returning as before. Finding that we had provision, fish, roots, water and other things we asked for, we determined to embark again and pursue our course. Having dug out our boat from the sand in which it was buried, it became necessary that we should strip, and go through great exertion to launch her, we being in such a state that things very much lighter sufficed to make us great labor.

Thus embarked, at the distance of two cross-bow shots in the sea we shipped a wave that entirely wet us. As we were naked, and the cold was very great, the oars loosened in our hands, and the next blow the

* November 7.

sea struck us, capsized the boat. The Assessor and two others held fast to her for preservation, but it happened to be far otherwise, the boat carried them over, and they were drowned under her. As the surf near the shore was very high, a single roll of the sea threw the rest into the waves and half drowned upon the shore of the island, without our losing any more than those the boat took down. The survivors escaped naked as they were born, with the loss of all they had, and although the whole was of little value, at that time it was worth much, as we were then in November, the cold was severe, and our bodies were so emaciated the bones might be counted with little difficulty, having become the perfect figures of death. For myself I can say that from the month of May passed, I had eaten no other thing than maize, and sometimes I found myself obliged to eat it unparched, for although the beasts were slaughtered while the boats were building, I could never eat their flesh, and I did not eat fish ten times. I state this to avoid giving excuses, and that every one may judge in what condition we were. Besides all these misfortunes, came a north wind upon us, from which we were nearer to death than life. Thanks be to our Lord that in looking among the brands we had used there, we found sparks from which we made great fires. And thus were we asking mercy of Him and pardon for our transgressions, shedding many tears, and each regretting not his own fate alone, but that of his comrades about him.

At sunset, the Indians thinking that we had not gone, came to seek us and bring us food; but when they saw us thus, in a plight so different from what it was before, and so extraordinary, they were alarmed and turned back. I went toward them and called, when they returned much frightened. I gave them to understand by signs that our boat had sunk and three of our number had been drowned. There, before them, they saw two of the departed, and we who remained were near joining them. The Indians, at sight of what had befallen us, and our state of suffering and melancholy destitution, sat down among us, and from the sorrow and pity they felt, they all began to lament so earnestly that they might have been heard at a distance, and continued so doing more than half an hour. It was strange to see these men, wild and untaught, howling like brutes over our misfortunes. It caused in me as in others, an increase of feeling and a livelier sense of our calamity.[1]

The cries having ceased, I talked with the Christians, and said that if it appeared well to them, I would beg these Indians to take us to their houses. Some who had been in New Spain, replied that we ought not to think of it; for if they should do so, they would sacrifice us to their idols. But seeing no better course, and that any other led to a nearer and more certain death, I disregarded what was said, and besought the Indians to take us to their dwellings. They signified that it would give them delight, and that we should tarry a little, that they might do what we asked. Presently thirty men loaded themselves with wood and started for their houses, which were far off, and we remained with the others until near night, when, holding us up, they carried us with all haste. Because of the extreme coldness of the weather, lest any one should die or fail by the way, they caused four or five very large fires to be placed at intervals, and at each they warmed us; and when they saw that we had regained some heat and strength, they took us to the next so swiftly that they hardly let us touch our feet to the ground. In this manner, we went as far as their habitations, where we found that they had made a house for us with many fires in it. An hour after our arrival, they began to dance and hold great rejoicing, which lasted all night, although for us there was no joy, festivity nor sleep, awaiting the hour they should make us victims. In the morning,* they again gave us fish and roots, showing us such hospitality that we were re-assured, and lost somewhat the fear of sacrifice.

* November 8   1528

[1] "The Indian and the white man having made each other presents, they thereby became friends, so as to make it the duty of each to weep for the affliction of the other. The dances that follow the wailing," says Peter P. Pitchlynn, an educated English half blood, chief of the 'hatas, who considers that he perfectly comprehends the conduct of these natives, "was to cheer and sooth the strangers that they might the less feel their loss. It is a duty, he says, among his people, to mourn with friends in their bereavement. Even persons long separated, when they meet, though it should be on a road and after a death has long occurred, sit down together and the friends lament the lost one, with tears and sorrowing hearts. Long journeys are made to show this act of respect for the one that is not; the name

of the deceased never being mentioned in the presence of a relative. It is etiquette to allow the persons bereaved first to speak of their loss, a delicate consideration for their feelings to be invariably observed."

Some missionaries to the Indians appear not to have known and to have been puzzled with this observance common among the natives, of not naming the dead. Two Jesuits in a report of their visit to the Kalo at the Capes of Florida, in the year 1743, write to Horcasitas, Captain General of Cuba: "To close their mouths we have had to take the method of proving to them the immortality of the soul by their own strange custom of offering to the dead, and the killing of children to serve the deceased chief; but on naming death or the dead they go away with fear or some other emotion we do not distinguish."—*MS*

CHAPTER XIII.

WE HEAR OF OTHER CHRISTIANS

This day I saw a native with an article of traffic I knew was not one we had bestowed; and asking whence it came, I was told by signs that it had been given by men like ourselves who were behind. Hearing this I sent two Indians, and with them two Christians to be shown those persons. They met near by, as the men were coming to look after us; for the Indians of the place where they were, gave them information concerning us. They were the Captains Andrés Dorantes and Alonzo del Castillo, with all the persons of their boat. Having come up they were surprised at seeing us in the condition we were, and very much pained at having nothing to give us, as they had brought no other clothes than what they had on.

Thus together again, they related that on the fifth day of that month,* their boat had capsized a league and a half from there, and they escaped without losing any thing. We all agreed to refit their boat,¹ that those of us might go in her who had vigor sufficient and disposition to do so, and the rest should remain until they became well enough to go, as they best

* November 5

might, along the coast until God our Lord should be pleased to conduct us alike to a land of Christians. Directly as we arranged this, we set ourselves to work. Before we threw the boat out into the water, Tavera, a gentleman of our company, died, and the boat, which we thought to use, came to its end, sinking from unfitness to float.

As we were in the condition I have mentioned, the greater number of us naked, and the weather boisterous for travel, and to cross rivers and bays by swimming, and we being entirely without provisions or the means of carrying any, we yielded obedience to what necessity required, to pass the winter in the place where we were. We also agreed that four men of the most robust should go on to Panuco, which we believed to be near, and if, by Divine favor, they should reach there, they could give information of our remaining on that island, and of our sorrows and destitution. These men were excellent swimmers. One of them was Alvaro Fernandez, a Portuguese sailor and carpenter, the second was named Mendez, the third Figueroa, who was a native of Toledo, and the fourth Astudillo, a native of Çafra. They took with them an Indian of the island of Auia.[2]

---

[1] The *Letter* says the boat of the Treasurer, and this evidently is correct.

[2] The last two words of the sentence are dropped in the second edition. HERRERA says, "an Indian of the island of Cuba." We infer the name to be the Indian one of Malhado, though there was another island situated back of it according to the *Letter*. ANTONIO GALVANO writes that the island was called Xamo, but he does not state the source of his information. As he was a wide traveler and may have been in Spain, very probably it was Nuñez himself.

CHAPTER XIV.

THE DEPARTURE OF FOUR CHRISTIANS

The four Christians being gone, after a few days such cold and tempestuous weather succeeded that the Indians could not pull up roots,[1] the cane weirs in which they took fish no longer yielded any thing, and the houses being very open, our people began to die. Five Christians, of a mess on the coast, came to such extremity that they ate their dead; the body of the last one only was found unconsumed. Their names were Sierra, Diego Lopez, Corral, Palacios and Gonçalo Ruiz. This produced great commotion among the Indians, giving rise to so much censure that had they known it in season to have done so, doubtless they would have destroyed any survivor, and we should have found ourselves in the utmost perplexity. Finally, of eighty men who arrived in the two instances, fifteen only remained alive.

After this, the natives were visited by a disease of the bowels, of which half their number died. They conceived that we had destroyed them, and believing it firmly, they concerted among themselves to dispatch those of us who survived. When they were about to execute their purpose, an Indian who had charge of me, told them not to believe we were the cause of those deaths, since if we had such power we should also have averted the fatality from so many of our people, whom they had seen die without our being able to minister relief, already very few of us remaining, and none doing hurt or wrong, and that it would be better to leave us unharmed. God our Lord willed that the others should heed this opinion and counsel, and be hindered in their design.

To this island we gave the name Malhado.[2] The people we found there are large and well formed: they have no other arms than bows and arrows, in the use of which they are very dexterous. The men have one of their nipples bored from side to side, and some have both, wearing a cane in each, the length of two palms and a half, and the thickness of two fingers. They have the under lip also bored, and wear in it a piece of cane the breadth of half a finger.[3] Their women are accustomed to great toil. The stay they make on the island is from October to the end of February. Their subsistence then is the root I have spoken of, got from under the water in November and December. They have weirs of cane and take fish only in this season; afterwards they live on the roots. At the end of February, they go into other parts to seek food, for then the root is beginning to grow and is not good.

Those people love their offspring the most of any in the world, and treat them with the greatest mildness. When it occurs that a son dies, the parents and kindred weep as does every body; the wailing continu-

¹ As illustrative of the neat and skilful manner in which the natives made weirs on the coasts, see the engravings in DE BRY'S Voyages and Discoveries, Part I, plate XIII, and Part II, plate III.

² Ill luck, or misfortune.

³ RIBAS, a missionary in Cinaloa about the opening of the second quarter of the seventeenth century, states that the Acaxee, an agricultural people living in the mountains of Topia, were eaters of human flesh. Their residences of adobe were usually on eminences of difficult ascent and in sheltered situations. They would seek an enemy as they would hunt a deer for his flesh. When one killed a fellow man for the first time, he was presented with the first dish of the food; and if he had not already a hole under his nether lip from boyhood, made by his mother, one would be opened in which a little bone of the person killed would be fitted, to distinguish him ever after as a brave among his nation. p. 473.

If to wear a trophy should be considered the probable original purpose of this incision, the Mexicans in advancing to a state of comparative civilization appear to have substituted a dirk of jade or other stone for ornament instead. Padre DURAN, who wrote in the sixteenth century, speaks of it, and once in this manner in giving account of the ceremonies attending the choice of a new incumbent for the throne of Mexico. A ball took place attended in court suit by the kings and nobles of the country.

When they were all engaged in the slow and solemn dance Auitzotl came forth wearing a crown of gold set with gems and having rich plumes and golden pendants. In his ears were green stones round and very bright in gold. A fine emerald was in his mouth, and another green stone highly transparent traversed the nose, in each end of which was a tuft of small blue feathers, the colors giving agreeable and changing shades. He wore bracelets.

In a note Sr. Don José F. Ramirez describes the fashion of the lip stones, found in the ancient tombs of the country, which the Spaniards call *bezote*, from *bezo* the ancient word for lip, and the Mexicans *tentetl*, from *tentli* lip and *tetl* stone. It is half an inch in diameter, and in shape a hat, the smaller end projecting, and that with the brim being on the inside of the mouth to keep it in place. *Historia de las Indias de Nueva España y Yslas de Tierra Firme*, pp. 154, 319.

⁴ ROMANS speaks of such a custom among the Chicasas:

—— the nearest relatives mourn over it ——the body—' with awful lamentations, the women are very vociferous in it, but the men do it in silence taking great care not to be seen any more than heard. At this business, the mourning continues about a year, which they know by counting the moons, every morning and evening, and at first throughout the day, they are at different times employed in the exercise of this last duty.—*A Concise Natural History of East and West Florida*, p. 71.

⁵ Pitchlynn says, that these and other passages contain a better account of what are the customs of the Indian than the white man can give now. Among the Chatas, after marriage the mother and son in-law speak not to each other, except in cases of urgent necessity, and then with their heads bowed and faces covered. This conduct is maintained through life, although their houses should be in the same yard, or they should live in adjoining rooms, as happens since it is usual that the daughter remains with the mother until she have her first offspring, and it is old enough to run about. Custom equally separates him from her aunts and grandmother. When they are in the way of meeting, one will stop until the other passes, or they will go round turning away the face. Still however, the son in law is the constant subject of conversation with the mother, and through every circumstance of life she is very solicitous for his welfare, and holds him in the highest respect. They are each to the other too sacred to be spoken to. It is the Indian idea that he is to increase her line and not his own.

⁶ "The natives eat oysters for three or four months in the year without any other thing; at a time they experience hunger, and continual exertion day and night to protect themselves from mosquitos which are in such numbers as to render the endurance of them scarcely supportable. Brackish water only is to be got, and no wood. In other four months of the year, they eat blackberries and the green things growing wild; for two other months, they suck certain roots and eat lizards, snakes, rats, and great spiders; and for the other two months they live on fish. They go after another root like the ground truffle, got in water. At times there are deer, which they kill from canoes. The people are very comely; the women undergo excessive hard labor."—*Letter*.

⁷ LORD HURTADO thus wrote to Charles V. from Santiago in Cuba on the 20th of the ensuing month of May 1529. "A caravel has arrived here from searching after Narvaez, and brings eight Indians from the coast. They state by signs that he is inland with his men, who do little else than eat, drink and sleep."—*MS*.

⁸ AREYTO, the Lucayo word for the mystic dancing and singing of Indians, which corresponds to the Mexican *mitote*.

CHAPTER XV.

WHAT BEFEL US AMONG THE PEOPLE OF MALHADO.

On an Island of which I have spoken, they wished to make us physicians without examination or inquiring for diplomas. They cure by blowing upon the sick, and with that breath and the imposing of hands they cast out infirmity. They ordered that we also should do this, and be of use to them in some way. We laughed at what they did, telling them it was folly, that we knew not how to heal. In consequence, they withheld food from us until we should practice what they required. Seeing our persistence, an Indian told me I knew not what I uttered, in saying that what he knew availed nothing, for stones and other matters growing about in the fields, have virtue, and that passing a pebble along the stomach would take away pain and restore health, and certainly then we who were extraordinary men must possess power and efficacy over all other things. At last, finding ourselves in great want we were constrained to obey, but without fear lest we should be blamed for any failure or success.

Their custom is, on finding themselves sick to send for a physician, and after he has applied the cure, they give him not only all they have, but seek among their relatives for more to give. The practitioner scarifies over the seat of pain, and then sucks about the wound. They make cauteries with fire, a remedy among them in high repute, which I have tried on myself and found benefit from it. They afterwards blow on the spot, and having finished, the patient considers that he is relieved.[1]

Our method was to bless the sick, breathing upon them, and recite a Pater-noster and an Ave-Maria, praying with all earnestness to God our Lord that he would give health and influence them to make us some good return. In his clemency he willed that all those for whom we supplicated, should tell the others that they were sound and in health, directly after we made the sign of the blessed cross over them. For this the Indians treated us kindly; they deprived themselves of food that they might give to us, and presented us with skins and some trifles.

So protracted was the hunger we there experienced, that many times I was three days without eating. The natives also endured as much; and it appeared to me a thing impossible that life could be so prolonged, although afterwards I found myself in greater hunger and necessity, which I shall speak of farther on.

The Indians who had Alonzo del Castillo, Andrés Dorantes and the others that remained alive, were of different tongue and ancestry from these, and went to the opposite shore of the main to eat oysters, where they staid until the first day of April, when they returned. The distance is two leagues in the widest part. The island is half a league in breadth and five leagues in length

The inhabitants of all this region go naked. The women alone have any part of their persons covered, and it is with a wool that grows on trees.[2] The damsels dress themselves in deerskin. The people are generous to each other of what they possess. They have no chief. All that are of a lineage keep together. They speak two languages, those of one are called Capoques, those of the other, Han. They have a custom when they meet, or from time to time when they visit, of remaining half an hour before they speak, weeping, and, this over, he that is visited first rises and gives the other all he has, which is received, and after a little while he carries it away, and often goes without saying a word. They have other strange customs; but I have told the principal of them, and the most remarkable, that I may pass on and further relate what befel us.

---

[1] No doubt the Indian juggler has had knowledge of animal magnetism and the force (if it be not the same) applied in social entertainments now a days to table tipping. Their practice of healing was early and carefully observed in the Jesuit Mission of Sonora. Ribas about a century after the passage of Cabeça de Vaca, with whose relation he was acquainted, gives account of the art in substance as follows

"The method of cure the possessed practitioners have, is sucking the part that aches if it be injured, blowing on it, which for the effort and force, may be heard many steps off. The process is so surrounded by superstition and fancy, we do not feel assured that it is entirely free from deceit and covenant with the Devil. They give the sick to understand that the causes of their illness are the sticks, thorns and pebbles in their bodies which they take out. This is false

They have the things in the mouth or held craftily in the hand and afterwards exhibit them as our tooth pullers do teeth, on a string, as evidences of their professional skill. Their manner of healing arrow wounds is by sucking them and instantly spitting out the poison, the sound tongue receiving no serious injury, nor is the poison mortal unless it become incorporated with the blood. The remedy is so good a one that generally in making use of it they are accustomed to work entirely outside of their pact with the evil one."

² The moss *Tillandsia usneoides*, was everywhere the covering of the matrons where it grew in the south. Landonnere and Hawkins found them dressed in it on the eastern coast of Florida soon after the middle of the sixteenth century, and Le Moyne so represented them in pictures of that age from his own observation. Escalante Fontaneda, a little later, during a long captivity among the fierce barbarians at the capes of Florida, found the female there removed only by the same rural dress, from a state of nature.

CHAPTER XVI.

THE CHRISTIANS LEAVE THE ISLAND OF MALHADO.

After Dorantes and Castillo returned to the Island, they brought together the Christians, who were somewhat separated, and found them in all to be fourteen. As I have said, I was opposite on the main, where my Indians had taken me, and where so great sickness had come upon me, that if anything before had given me hopes of life, this were enough to have entirely bereft me of them.

When the Christians heard of my condition, they gave an Indian the cloak of marten skins we had taken from the cacique, as before related, to pass them over to where I was that they might visit me. Twelve of them crossed, for two were so feeble that their comrades could not venture to bring them. The names of those who came were Alonzo del Castillo, Andrés Dorantes, Diego Dorantes, Valdevieso, Estrada, Tostado, Chaves, Gutierrez, Asturiano a clergyman, Diego de Huelva, Estevanico a black, and Benitez; and when they reached the main land, they found another, who was one of our company, named Francisco de Leon. The thirteen together followed along the coast. So soon as they had come over, my Indians informed me of it, and that Hieronymo de Alvaniz and Lope de Oviedo remained on the island. But sickness prevented me from going with my companions or even seeing them.

I was obliged to remain with the people belonging to the island more than a year, and because of the hard work they put upon me and the harsh treatment, I resolved to flee from them and go to those of Charruco, who inhabit the forests and country of the main, the life I led being insupportable. Besides much other labor, I had to get out roots from below the water, and from among the cane where they grew in the ground. From this employment I had my fingers so worn that did a straw but touch them they would bleed. Many of the canes are broken, so they often tore my flesh, and I had to go in the midst of them with only the clothing on I have mentioned.

Accordingly, I put myself to contriving how I might get over to the other Indians, among whom matters turned somewhat more favorably for me. I set to trafficking, and strove to make my employment profitable in the ways I could best contrive, and by that means I got food and good treatment. The Indians would beg me to go from one quarter to another for things of which they have need; for in consequence of incessant hostilities, they cannot traverse the country, nor make many exchanges. With my merchandise and trade I went into the interior as far as I pleased, and traveled along the coast forty or fifty leagues. The principal wares were cones and other pieces of sea-snail, conches used for cutting, and fruit like a bean of the highest value among them, which they use as a medicine and employ in their dances and festivities. Among other matters were sea-beads. Such were what I carried into the interior; and in barter I got and brought back skins, ochre with which they rub and color the face, hard canes of which to make arrows, sinews, cement and flint for the heads, and tassels of the hair of deer that by dyeing they make red. This occupation suited me well, for the travel allowed me liberty to go where I wished, I was not obliged to work, and was not a slave. Wherever I went I received fair treatment, and the Indians gave me to eat out of regard to my commodities. My leading object, while journeying in this business, was to find out the way by which I should go forward, and I became well known. The inhabitants were pleased when they saw me, and I had brought them what they wanted; and those who did not know me sought and desired the acquaintance, for my reputation. The hardships that I underwent in this were long to tell, as well of peril and privation as of storms and cold. Oftentimes they overtook me alone and in the wilderness, but I came forth from them all by the great mercy of God, our Lord. Because of them I avoided pursuing the business in winter, a season in which the natives themselves retire to their huts and ranches, torpid and incapable of exertion.

I was in this country nearly six years,[1] alone among the Indians, and naked like them. The reason why I remained so long, was that I might take with me the Christian, Lope de Oviedo, from the island,

Alaniz, his companion, who had been left with him by Alonzo del Castillo, Andrés Dorantes and the rest, died soon after their departure; and to get the survivor out from there, I went over to the island every year, and entreated him that we should go, in the best way we could contrive, in quest of Christians. He put me off every year, saying in the next coming we would start. At last I got him off, crossing him over the bay, and over four rivers in the coast, as he could not swim. In this way we went on with some Indians, until coming to a bay a league in width, and everywhere deep. From the appearance we supposed it to be that which is called Espiritu Sancto.[2] We met some Indians on the other side of it, coming to visit ours, who told us that beyond them were three men like us, and gave their names. We asked for the others, and were told that they were all dead of cold and hunger, that the Indians farther on, of whom they were, for their diversion had killed Diego Dorantes, Valdevieso, and Diego de Huelva, because they left one house for another; and that other Indians, their neighbors with whom Captain Dorantes now was, had in consequence of a dream, killed Esquivel and Mendez.[3] We asked how the living were situated, and they answered that they were very ill used, the boys and some of the Indian men being very idle, out of cruelty gave them many kicks, cuffs and blows with sticks; that such was the life they led.

We desired to be informed of the country ahead, and of the subsistence: they said there was nothing to eat, and that it was thin of people, who suffered of cold, having no skins or other things to cover them. They told us also if we wished to see those three Christians, two days from that time the Indians who had them would come to eat walnuts a league from there on the margin of that river; and that we might know what they told us of the ill usage to be true, they slapped my companion and beat him with a stick, and I was not left without my portion. Many times they threw lumps of mud at us, and every day they put their arrows to our hearts, saying that they were inclined to kill us in the way that they had destroyed our friends. Lope Oviedo, my comrade, in fear said that he wished to go back with the women of those who had crossed the bay with us, the men having remained some distance behind. I contended strongly against his returning, and urged my objections; but in no way could I keep him. So he went back, and I remained alone with those savages. They are called Quevenes, and those with whom he returned, Deaguanes.

[1] From the year 1528 to 1533.

[2] These, and other words of like import in BIEDMA, perhaps refer to discoveries made in the first voyage of Pineda, who ran the northern shore of the Gulf of Mexico for Garay in the year 1519. That Alvar Nuñez was informed of the extent of northern explorations may be supposed from a document existing of record from the King, directing him to apply to the officers of the *Contratacion* in Sevilla "of whom, outside of this instruction, you will ask a relation of the notices that shall appear to them you ought to have knowledge of, and to possess touching the matters of that country."

In the Letter, of which two sections accompany the two next chapters to elucidate the text, some great sand hills are mentioned as betokening the position of Espiritu Santo, and it will appear that there was a river likewise of the same name not distant from the bay. This is an extract from the Report of the United States Coast Surveyor, year 1859, p. 325.

"The north west shore," of the bay of San Antonio (which is the northern bend of the Espiritu Santo bay), "is the delta of the Guadalupe, a low alluvial formation, scarcely raised above the level of the adjacent waters, and covered with a dense growth of cane grass, jungle and forest trees. On the west shore the elevated prairie also comes to the bay in a bluff or bank of twenty feet, and is likewise dotted over with the houses of settlers, and with oak or hackberry trees. The soil is fertile, the range for stock excellent, and the locality is said to be very healthy. At one place on this side a singular range of sand hills, known as the Sand mounds, approaches the shore. The highest peak is about seventy five feet above the bay. The mounds are covered with bushes and the valleys between them filled with trees, so that at a distance of five or six miles, the whole presents the appearance of a forest of live oak or similar timber, forming a marked feature in that otherwise level prairie region."

Should this point on the shores of Texas be recognized as the one to which the remnant of adventurers have now arrived, the highest peak of Sand mounds in latitude 28° 16' 34.08 North, in longitude 96° 47' 39.83 West, we may look with some confidence over the north eastern portion of the bay, as far as the entrance upon the bay of Matagorda, in latitude 28° 24' 06.95 North longitude 96° 24' 50.56 West, the distance in a direct line of twenty five statute miles, for the discovery of Malhado. There is, however, no island in this direction that appears to answer its description, nor any place with the conditions for the point that the Sand mounds unite. To the south are no hills on the shore of a bay near a river, nor any of particular mark, or height as far as where the river Bravo or Grand del Norte finds outlet.

² Mendez was one of the number who had been sent to Pánuco. Esquivel had belonged to the boat of Alonzo Enriquez, the Comptroller.

CHAPTER XVII

THE COMING OF INDIANS WITH ANDRÉS DORANTES, CASTILLO, AND ESTEVANICO.

Two days after Lope de Oviedo left, the Indians, who had Alonzo del Castillo and Andrés Dorantes, came to the place of which we had been told, to eat walnuts. These are ground with a kind of small grain, and this is the subsistence of the people two months in the year without any other thing; but even the nuts they do not have every season, as the tree produces in alternate years. The fruit is the size of that in Galicia; the trees are very large and numerous.

An Indian told me of the arrival of the Christians, and that if I wished to see them I must steal away and flee to the point of a wood to which he directed me, and that as he and others, kindred of his, should pass by there to visit those Indians, they would take me with them to the spot where the Christians were. I determined to attempt this and trust to them, as they spoke a language distinct from that of the others. I did so, and the next day they left, and found me in the place that had been pointed out, and accordingly took me with them.

When I arrived near their abode, Andrés Dorantes came out to see who it could be, for the Indians had told him that a Christian was coming. His astonishment was great when he saw me, as they had for many a day considered me dead, and the natives had said that I was. We gave many thanks at seeing ourselves together, and this was a day to us of the greatest pleasure we had enjoyed in life. Having come to where Castillo was, they inquired of me where I was going? I told them my purpose was to reach the land of Christians, I being then in search and pursuit of it. Andrés Dorantes said that for a long time he had entreated Castillo and Estevanico to go forward; but that they dared not venture, because they knew not how to swim, and greatly dreaded the rivers and bays they should have to cross, there being many in that country. Thus the Almighty had been pleased to preserve me through many trials and diseases, conducting me in the end to the fellowship of those who had abandoned me, that I might lead them over the bays and rivers that obstructed our progress. They advised me on no account to let the natives know or have a suspicion of my desire to go on, else they would destroy me, and that for success it would be necessary for me to remain quiet until the end of six months, when comes the season in which these Indians go to another part of the country to eat prickly pears. People would arrive from parts farther on, bringing bows to barter and for exchange, with whom, after making our escape, we should be able to go on their return. Having consented to this course, I remained. The prickly pear is the size of a hen's egg, vermilion and black in color, and of agreeable flavor. The natives live on it three months in the year, having nothing beside.

I was given as a slave to an Indian, with whom was Dorantes. He was blind of one eye, as were also his wife and sons, and likewise another who was with him, so that of a fashion they were all blind.[1] These are called Marianes. Castillo was with another neighboring people, called Yguases.

While here the Christians related to me how they had left the island of Malhado, and found the boat in which the Comptroller and the friars had sailed, bottom up on the sea shore, and that going along crossing the rivers, which are four, very large and of rapid current, their boats were swept away and carried to sea, where four of their number were drowned, that thus they proceeded until they crossed the bay, getting over it with great difficulty, and fifteen leagues thence they came to another. By the time they reached this, they had lost two companions in the sixty leagues they traveled, and those remaining were nearly dead, in all the while having eaten nothing but crabs and rockweed. Arrived at this bay, they found Indians eating mulberries, who, when they saw them, went to a cape opposite. While contriving and seeking for some means to cross the bay, there came over to them an Indian[2] and a Christian, whom they recognized to be Figueroa, one of the four we had sent forward from the Island of Malhado. He there recounted how he and his companions had got as far as that place, when two of them and an Indian died of cold and hunger, being exposed in the most inclement of seasons. He and Mendez were taken by the Indians, and while with them his associate fled, going as well as he could in the direction of Pánuco, and the natives pursuing, put him to death.

While living with these Indians, Figueroa learned from them that there was a Christian among the Mariames, who had come over from the opposite side, and he found him among the Quevenes. This was Hernardo de Esquivel, a native of Badajoz, who had come in company with the Commissary. From him Figueroa learned the end to which the Governor, the Comptroller and the others had come. Esquivel told him that the Comptroller and the friars had upset their boat at the confluence of the rivers, and that the boat of the Governor, moving along the coast, came with its people to land. Narváez went in the boat until arriving at that great bay, where he took in the people, and, crossing them to the opposite point, returned for the Comptroller, the friars and the rest. And he related that being disembarked the Governor had recalled the commission the Comptroller held as his lieutenant, assigning the duties to a captain with him named Pantoja; that Narváez stayed the night in his boat, not wishing to come on shore, having a coxswain with him and a page who was unwell, there being no water nor anything to eat on board; that at midnight the boat having only a stone for anchor, the north wind blowing strongly took her unobserved to sea, and they never knew more of their commander.³

The others then went along the coast, and as they were arrested by a wide extent of water, they made rafts with much labor, on which they crossed to the opposite shore. Going on, they arrived at a point of woods on the banks of the water where were Indians, who, as they saw them coming, put their houses into their canoes and went over to the opposite side. The Christians, in consideration of the season, for it was now the month of November, stopped at this wood, where they found water and fuel, some crabs and shell fish. They began, one by one, to die of cold and hunger; and, more than this, Pantoja, who was Lieutenant Governor, used them severely, which Soto-Mayor (the brother of Vasco Porcallo, of the Island of Cuba), who had come with the armament as campmaster, not being able to bear, had a struggle with him, and, giving him a blow with a club, Pantoja was instantly killed.⁴

Thus did the number go on diminishing. The living dried the flesh of them that died; and the last that died was Soto-Mayor, when Esquivel preserved his flesh, and, feeding on it, sustained existence until the first of March, when an Indian of those that had fled, coming to see if they were alive, took Esquivel with him. While he was in the possession of the native, Figueroa saw him, and learned all that had been related. He besought Esquivel to come with him, that together they might pursue the way to Pánuco, to which Esquivel would not consent, saying that he had understood from the friars that Pánuco had been left behind: so he remained there and Figueroa went to the coast where he was accustomed to live.

ADDENDUM.

Some circumstances are a little differently told in the *Letter* from what they are in the *Relation*, with additional particulars too important to be omitted. The text of OVIEDO is here tangled, but the facts, keeping in mind the *Relation*, are as follows:

" . . . . Cabeça de Vaca coming upon two Indians, they conducted him to Alonzo del Castillo and to Andrés Dorantes, who was there waiting the arrival of his slave.

" Asturiano the clergyman, with a negro, were living (*he just understood*) on an island where they went for subsistence, situated back of the one on which the boats were lost. The Indians brought them again across the bay in a canoe to the island where were Andrés Dorantes, Alonzo del Castillo, Diego Dorantes, Pedro Valdivieso, with six others who had survived cold and hunger. Together, on the first day of April, they took their departure, leaving two for want of strength to march, as also Cabeça de Vaca and another person inland, who could not be got at to bring away. In return for some things, the Indians passed them over another bay.

" The Christians travelled thence two leagues to a large river that was beginning to swell from freshets, and run, where they made rafts on which they crossed with much difficulty, there being few swimmers. Three leagues further they came to another river running powerfully from the same cause, and with so much impetuosity that the fresh water for a time extended a good way into the sea. They made rafts as before. The first one being assisted went over in safety; the other was driven to sea more than a league, for the men being emaciated and worn by the hard laps of the winter, had no strength. On the way they had eaten only of the abundant rock weed of which glass is made in Spain, and certain crabs hatched in crevices along shore, that are little else than shell. Two men were drowned, two escaped from the raft by swimming, and one who had remained sitting, finding himself beyond the current, got on the top, where the wind acting on him as a sail took him in the again and cast him on the shore in safety.

"The ten were now joined by another Christian, and after going four leagues came to a river, where they found a boat which was recognized to be that of the Comptroller Alonzo Enriquez and the Commissary, but nothing could be seen of the people. Having walked five or six leagues more, they arrived at another large river where were two ranches, out of which the tenants fled. Other Indians came from the side opposite, having before seen the men of that boat and others belonging to the one of the Governor, who knew who these were, and after assuring themselves took them over in canoes. There was nothing in their houses to eat; nevertheless the Christians got a little fish sufficient to sustain them through the night.

"The Spaniards left the next day, and on the fourth day arrived at a bay, having lost two of their number by hunger and fatigue. Nine only now remained. The bay was broad, nearly a league across. The side towards Pánuco forms a point running out nearly a quarter of a league, having on it some large white sand-sticks which it is reasonable to suppose can be descried from a distance at sea, and were consequently thought to mark the river Espiritu Sancto. Finding no way to pass, they were greatly embarrassed. At last they discovered a broken canoe, which, setting to rights in the best manner possible, they managed to get over in the two days they were there. Going on, much depressed by hunger, the greater number swollen by the seaweed they had eaten, with much exertion, at the end of twelve leagues they came to a small bay, not over the breadth of a river. They tarried over the day of their arrival. The next day, seeing an Indian on the opposite shore, they called to him, but he gave them no heed and went off. In the afternoon he returned, bringing with him one of the four who had been sent forward in the previous winter, to reach the Land of Christians. Presently the two came over, and Figueroa there recounted to them the fate of his three companions, two dying of hunger, the third killed by Indians.

"Figueroa stated that he had come upon a Christian named Esquivel, the sole survivor in the boats of the Governor and Alonzo Enriquez, who had with others subsisted on the flesh of those that died; that the boat of the Comptroller was wrecked where they saw her, and the Governor following along by the coast came upon those men, as he still kept the sea in his boat; that on discovering them he concluded to lighten his vessel by setting his people on shore, that they might travel together along the coast, they being weary of the voyage and without food, and that keeping in sight of them on coming to any river or bay, he would pass them over to the other shore. In this manner they arrived at a river supposed to be Espiritu Sancto, where the Governor crossed them to the other shore, remaining himself in the boat, unwilling to land, there being with him only a pilot, Antón Perez, and his page Campo. As the night set in, a strong wind came on to blow from the north, and from that hour nothing was ever heard of them. Narváez at the time was covered with spots, and as those with him were not robust, they may be considered to have been swallowed up by the sea. The people passing by certain pools and overflowed grounds, went inland, where, without resource, they all died during the winter of cold and hunger, while subsisting, some of them as has been related."

¹ Subsequently Cabeça de Vaca speaks of seeing a people disfigured in this manner, who were lighter in color than any other Indians he had found. See Chapter XXVIII, and note 1.

² One of the Quevenes.

³ BERNAL DIAZ portrays Pánfilo de Narváez from memory, after the lapse of half a century, as he saw him in New Spain in 1520, seven or eight years before his death.

"Narváez was in appearance about forty-two years of age, tall, very muscular, of full face, and he had a red beard. He reasoned well, and his presence was agreeable; he was leisurely in discourse, with a voice of great volume, like that of one speaking in a vault. He rode well, and was reputed to be courageous. The place of his nativity was Valladolid, or Tudela on the Duero. He was married to a lady, Maria de Valenzuela. He had been a captain in Cuba, was wealthy, and was said to be penurious. He had an eye put out at the time we overthrew him. He went to Castilla to complain of Cortes and us, and his Majesty conferred on him the government of Florida, in which country he expended all his treasure and was lost."—*Historia Verdadera de la Conquista de Nueva España*, Cap. CCX. 1632.

The recollection of the first Chronicler of the New World treats the reader to a little information of the family circle and private circumstances of the Governor, with the much good advice he threw away upon him.

"If Pámphilo de Narváez had not forgotten the manner of his treatment in New Spain, and how contrary to expectation his plans turned out, he would not have gone forth in quest of other whirlwinds and more fatigue, but rested content with being a hidalgo, who having come into these parts to gain a livelihood with sword and buckler, had won honor and renown besides a woman of virtue and rank, God giving him children and an estate with which he might easily enough pass his days in keeping with his condition. He was a man of accomplishments, gentle breeding and pure blood; on proper occasions he had shown himself brave in arms as a soldier and skillful as a captain. When he had conquered and pacified Cuba, he lived prosperously on the Island, having good possessions, and even afterward, when he got out of the prison and talons of Cortés, he found his wife, Maria de Valenzuela, then waiting upon him for some years, with the honor and reputation of Penelope, but instead of tangling and untangling, for any doubts or fears that her husband would not return, when informed of the capture and misfortunes of her Ulysses, she set about to improve and husband his estate as the means of his relief. In this state did Narváez find matters on returning to his house, for besides what he had left, and beyond the increase of his property, the wife had laid up for him thirteen or fourteen thousand dollars in gold dust, which she obtained from the washings by the labor of their slaves and Indians. These facts he told me himself in Toledo, in the year 1525, the Imperial Majesty of Charles at the time being there.

"While he was entreating for justice and single combat with Cortés, I counseled him as a friend that he should tranquilly retire to his house into the bosom of his family, giving thanks to God for the sufficiency he possessed to go through this stormy world so full of troubles, but as his desires took him rather to lead the sons of others than to guide his own, what I said must have appeared less to his purpose than what he thought. And thus ended his career, driven on to his own and others' destruction: nor did he lack age to need repose, having passed as many years as I had, if not more, and his person appeared to me not a little worn.[1] Although he thanked me for my advice, I saw it did not agree with him, which brought to memory what a husbandman asked upon a time, while I was yet a young man: 'Your Worships who are of the palace, I venture to say know not why the ass is struck with the stick the third time;' which I responded to, saying, 'It must be to make him get up.' The villager replied, 'that is not the reason, it is because the ass does not remember the first time, and because he did not amend with the second.' I, with the others who heard this, considered he spoke with good reason, and we thought the words well enough to bear in mind to be preserved for the benefit of men as well as mules, since such should those be considered who do not amend with many stripes, whom one, another and another peril does not suffice to teach. We will leave this.'

To these felicitous pictures from those who knew him, may be added one nearly as remarkable from the hand of an old acquaint-

[1] This was in 1525. At the time Narvaez was lost, 1528, Oviedo was in the fiftieth year of his life, having been born in August 1478.

ance, perhaps friend, the famous Bishop of Chiapa, who was a companion in his lesser enterprises some years earlier.

"This Pánfilo de Narváez was a man of commanding person, tall of stature, complexion fair inclining to red, honest, of good judgment, though not very discreet, agreeable in conversation, with pleasing address, brave against Indians and probably would have been against any people, had ever occasion offered for fighting them; but over every other fault he had, was that of being very careless."

Narváez had gone with his adherents from Santo Domingo to Cuba, where he was well received by Velasquez, became his principal captain, was respected and held the first position after the Governor on the Island; but accursed be any good that resulted to the Indians from his coming. Las Casas soon followed him thither, invited by Velasquez through ancient friendship, where he and Narváez were together nearly two years, pacifying the unsubdued portions of the country, to the injury, the writer declares, of the whole Island. — *General Historia de las Indias, escrita por Don Fray* BARTOLOME DE LAS CASAS, *de la Orden de Sto. Domingo.* Lib. III Cap. XXVI. MS.

Soon after Hernan Cortés had completed the conquest of Mexico, he turned his attention to the religious instruction of its people. He besought the king that persons might be sent thither whose purity of life should give no scandal to their religion, that the heathen might be won from their idolatry by example as well as teaching. The policy of the General, more extended in this regard than is worth while here to state, was favorably considered, and never lost sight of during the reign of Charles V. After long delay the General of the Order of Franciscan Friars, acting under the united authority of the King and the Pope, selected for the mission Martin de Valencia, a venerable prelate, who chose twelve persons to attend him. Six were styled learned preachers, two were priests and two lay brothers. Among the first, was Juan Xuárez of the list Juan de Palos. The latter TORQUEMADA speaks of as a person simple minded, pure and devout.

The respectful reception given by Cortés to these holy men at their entrance of the capital, earned their honest encomiums. Surrounded by his cavaliers, while he spread his rich mantle for the chief friar to walk upon, on bended knee he kissed the hands of the passing brothers. The humble bearing and poor covering of the Mendicants were in strange contrast to the gallant deportment and gay attire of the knights; and when the Indians saw this obeisance they thought a race had arrived superior to their turbulent conquerors. There were not wanting then those to tell Cortés that he had brought into the country an element of his ruin, and they forgot not to remind him of the occasion afterward. Torquemada considers the act to have been the greatest of his achievements in that he conquered himself, but admits that his downfall came in the course of the struggles made necessary for preserving the rights and liberty of the natives, which followed upon his own misconduct. The pencil of the age found a subject for its frequent employment in that reception, but none of its labor, we are told, remains with the tradition, while the grateful chronicle undergoes a scrutiny which no more allows humility and devotion to pass unquestioned, than that heroism to go unchallenged

Soon after the arrival of friar Juan Xuarez in New Spain he became Superior of the Convent of Huexotzinco, and subsequently hearing that a captain was about to undertake the conquest of Florida, his zeal for the conversion of its inhabitants took him with friar Juan Palos to join the army, and attending its vicissitudes, they ultimately perished together on the coast. *Monarchia Indiana* 3a P. GÓMARA *Cartas de* CORTÉS *Noticias Historicas de Nuño de Guzmán*, Mexico 1847 In the Convent of Tlaltelalco in a gallery of paintings in oil of personages who early came to Mexico, are the portraits here presented of the Friars, taken from copies obtained for me by my distinguished friend José Fernando Ramirez

CHAPTER XVIII.

THE STORY FIGUEROA RECOUNTED FROM ESQUIVEL.

This account was all given by Figueroa, according to the relation he received from Esquivel, and from him through the others it came to me; whence may be seen and understood the fate of the armament, and the individual fortunes of the greater part of the people. Figueroa said, moreover, that if the Christians should at any time go in that direction, it were possible they might see Esquivel, for he knew that he had fled from the Indian with whom he was, to the Mariames, who were neighbors. After Figueroa had finished telling the story, he and the Asturian made an attempt to go to other Indians farther on; but as soon as they who had the Christians discovered it, they followed, and beating them severely, stripped the Asturian and shot an arrow through his arm. They finally escaped by flight

The other Christians remained, and prevailed on the Indians to receive them as slaves. In their service they were abused as slaves never were, nor men in any condition have ever been. Not content with frequently buffeting them, striking them with sticks, and pulling out their beard for amusement, they killed three of the six for only going from one house to another These were the persons I have named before: Diego Dorantes, Valdivieso, and Diego de Huelva: and the three that remained looked forward to the same fate. Not to endure this life, Andrés Dorantes fled, and passed to the Mariames, the people among whom Esquivel tarried. They told him that having had Esquivel there, he wished to run away because a woman dreamed that a son of hers would kill him; and that they followed after, and slew him. They showed Dorantes his sword, beads and book, with other things that had been his.

Thus in obedience to their custom they take life, destroying even their male children on account of dreams. They cast away their daughters at birth, and cause them to be eaten by dogs. The reason of their doing this, as they state, is because all the nations of the country are their foes, and as they have unceasing war with them, if they were to marry away their daughters, they would so greatly multiply their enemies that they must be overcome and made slaves; thus they prefer to destroy all, rather than that from them should come a single enemy. We asked why they did not themselves marry them; and they said it would be a disgustful thing to marry among relatives, and far better to kill than to give them either to their kindred or to their foes.

This is likewise the practice of their neighbors the Yguazes, but of no other people of that country. When the men would marry, they buy the women of their enemies: the price paid for a wife is a bow, the best that can be got, with two arrows: if it happens that the suitor should have no bow, then a net a fathom in length and another in breadth. They kill their male children, and buy those of strangers. The marriage state continues no longer than while the parties are satisfied, and they separate for the slightest cause. Dorantes was among this people, and after a few days escaped.

Castillo and Estevanico went inland to the Yguazes. This people are universally good archers and of a fine symmetry, although not so large as those we left. They have a nipple and a lip bored. Their support is principally roots, of two or three kinds, and they look for them over the face of all the country. The food is poor and gripes the persons who eat it. The roots require roasting two days: many are very bitter, and withal difficult to be dug. They are sought the distance of two or three leagues, and so great is the want these people experience, that they cannot get through the year without them. Occasionally they kill deer, and at times take fish, but the quantity is so small and the famine so great, that they eat spiders and the eggs of ants, worms, lizards, salamanders, snakes, and vipers that kill whom they strike; and they eat earth and wood, and all that there is, the dung of deer, and other things that I omit to mention, and I honestly believe that were there stones in that land they would eat them. They save the bones of the fishes they consume, of snakes and other animals, that they may afterwards beat them together and eat the powder. The men bear no burthens, nor carry anything of weight; such are borne by women and old men who are of the least esteem. They have not so great love for their children as those we have before spoken of.* Some among them are accustomed to sin against nature. The women work very hard, and do a great deal; of the twenty-four hours they have only six of repose; the rest of the night they pass in heating the ovens to bake those roots they eat. At daybreak they begin to dig them, to bring wood and water to their houses and get in readiness other things that may be necessary. The majority of the people are great thieves; for though they are free to divide with each other, on turning the head, even a son or a father will take what he can. They are great liars, and also great drunkards, which they become from the use of a certain liquor.

These Indians are so accustomed to running, that without rest or fatigue they follow a deer from morning to night. In this way they kill many. They pursue them until tired down, and sometimes overtake them in the race. Their houses are of matting, placed upon four hoops. They carry them on the back, and remove every two or three days in search of food. Nothing is planted for support. They are a merry people, considering the hunger they suffer, for they never cease, notwithstanding, to observe their festivities and areytos. To them the happiest part of the year is the season of eating prickly pears, they have

* The people of Malhado.

hunger then no longer, pass all the time in dancing, and eat day and night. While these last, they squeeze out the juice, open and set them to dry, and when dry they are put in hampers like figs. These they keep to eat on their way back. The peel is beaten to powder.

It occurred to us many times while we were among this people, and there was no food, to be three or four days without eating, when they, to revive our spirits, would tell us not to be sad, that soon there would be prickly pears when we should eat a plenty and drink of the juice, when our bellies would be very big and we should be content and joyful, having no hunger. From the time they first told us this, to that at which the earliest were ripe enough to be eaten, was an interval of five or six months; so having tarried until the lapse of this period, and the season had come, we went to eat the fruit.

We found mosquitos of three sorts, and all of them abundant in every part of the country. They poison and inflame, and during the greater part of the summer gave us great annoyance. As a protection we made fires, encircling the people with them, burning rotten and wet wood to produce smoke without flame. The remedy brought another trouble, and the night long we did little else than shed tears from the smoke that came into our eyes, besides feeling intense heat from the many fires, and if at any time, we went out for repose to the seaside and fell asleep, we were reminded with blows to make up the fires. The Indians of the interior have a different method, as intolerable, and worse even than the one I have spoken of, which is to go with brands in the hand firing the plains and forests within their reach, that the mosquitos may fly away, and at the same time to drive out lizards and other like things from the earth for them to eat.

They are accustomed also to kill deer by encircling them with fires. The pasturage is taken from the cattle by burning, that necessity may drive them to seek it in places where it is desired they should go. They encamp only where there are wood and water; and sometimes all carry loads of these when they go to hunt deer, which are usually found where neither is to be got. On the day of their arrival, they kill the deer and other animals which they can, and consume all the water and all the wood in cooking and on the fires they make to relieve them of mosquitos. They remain the next day to get something to sustain them on their return: and when they go, such is their state from those insects that they appear to have the affliction of holy Lazarus. In this way do they appease their hunger, two or three times in the year, at the cost I have mentioned. From my own experience, I can state there is no torment known in this world that can equal it.

Inland are many deer, birds and beasts other than those I have spoken of. Cattle come as far as here. Three times I have seen them and eaten of their meat. I think they are about the size of those in Spain. They have small horns like the cows of Morocco; the hair is very long and flocky like the merino's. Some are tawny, others black. To my judgment the flesh is finer and fatter than that of this country. Of the skins of those not full grown the Indians make blankets, and of the larger they make shoes and bucklers. They come as far as the sea-coast of Florida, from a northerly direction, ranging through a tract of more than four hundred leagues, and throughout the whole region over which they run, the people who inhabit near, descend and live upon them, distributing a vast many hides into the interior country.

ADDENDUM

These sections, appropriate to the matter in the XVIII Chapter, are from the *Letter* written by Cabeça de Vaca and Dorantes incorporated in the work of OVIEDO.

Thus ended the account of Figueroa, without his being able to add more to it, than that Esquivel was about there in the possession of some natives, and they might see him in a little while; but a month afterwards it was known that he no longer lived, for having gone from the natives they had followed after and put him to death. Figueroa tarried a few moments, long enough to relate the sad news. The Indian who brought him would not permit him to remain. Asturiano the clergyman, and a young man being the only ones who could swim, accompanied them for the purpose of returning with fish which they were promised; as likewise that they should be brought back over that bay; but when the Indians found them at their houses they would neither bring them nor let them return: on the contrary, they put their houses into their canoes and took the two Christians with them, saying that they would soon come back.

"The eight companions remained that day to appease their hunger, and the next morning they saw two Indians of a rancho coming over the water to place their dwellings on the further side. The purpose was to live on blackberries that grow in some places along the coast, which they seek at a season they know full well, and although precarious they promise a food that supports life. They called to the

Indians, who came as to persons they thought lightly of, taking some part of what they possessed almost by force. The Christians besought the natives to set them over, which they did in a canoe, taking them to their houses near by, and at dark gave them a small quantity of fish. They went out the next day for more, and returned at night, giving them a part of what they had caught. The day following they moved off with the Christians and never after were the two seen whom the other Indians had taken away.

"At last the natives, weary of seeking food for their guests, turned away five, that they should go to some Indians who they said were to be found in another bay, six leagues farther on. Alonzo del Castillo went there with Pedro de Valdivieso, cousin of Andrés Dorantes, and another, Diego de Huelva, where they remained a long time; the two others went down near the coast, seeking relief, where they died, as Dorantes states, who found the bodies, one of whom, Diego Dorantes, was his cousin. The two hidalgos and the negro remaining in that rancho, sufficed for the use of the natives, to bring back loads of wood and water as slaves. After three or four days however these likewise were turned off, when for some time they wandered about lost without hope of relief; and going naked among marshes, having been previously despoiled one night of their clothing, they came upon those dead.

"They continued the route until they found some Indians with whom Andrés Dorantes remained. A cousin of his, one of the three who had gone on to the bay where they stopped, came over from the opposite shore, and told him that the swimmers who went from them, had passed in that direction, having their clothes taken from them, and they much bruised about the head with sticks because they would not remain: still though beaten and stripped, they had gone on for the sake of the oath they had taken, never to stop even if death stood in the path before coming to a country of Christians. Dorantes states that he saw in the rancho where he was, the clothes belonging to the clergyman and to one of the swimmers, with a breviary or prayer book. Valdivieso returned, and a couple of days afterwards was killed, because he wished to flee; and likewise in a little time Diego de Huelva, because he forsook one lodge house for another.

"The Christians were there made slaves, forced with more cruelty to serve than the Moor would have used. Besides going stark naked and bare-footed over the coast burning in summer like fire, their continual occupation was bringing wood and water on the back, or whatever the Indians needed, and dragging canoes over inundated grounds in hot weather.

"These natives eat nothing the year round but fish, and of that not much. They experience far less hunger however, than the inhabitants inland among whom the Spaniards afterwards lived. The food often fails, causing frequent removals, or otherwise they starve. They have finger nails that for any ordinary purpose are knives, and are their principal arms among themselves.

"The Spaniards lived here fourteen months, from May to the May ensuing of the year 1530, and to the middle of the month of August, when Andrés Dorantes, being at a point that appeared most favorable for going, commended himself to God and went off at mid day. Castillo tarried among that hard people a year and a half later, until an opportunity presented for starting; but on arriving he found only the negro. Dorantes, discovering that Indians unbearably cruel had gone back more than twenty leagues to a river near the bay of Espíritu Sancto, among those who had killed Esquivel, the solitary one that had escaped from the boats of the Governor and Alonzo Enriques slain as they were told because a woman had dreamed some absurdity. The people of this country have belief in dreams, their only superstition. On account of them they will even kill their children; and this had Igo Dorantes states that in the course of four years he had been a witness to the killing or burying alive of eleven or twelve young males, and rarely do they let a girl live.

Andrés Dorantes passed ten months among this people, enduring much privation with continual labor, and in such fear of being killed that——. Sometimes the Indians kill deer, setting fire to the land and savannahs, thus driving them thence. There are many rats about those rivers. The number killed is nevertheless small, as the natives go up and down stream the winter long in quest of food, they alarm and keep back the game. At times they eat fish killed in that river; the quantity however is small except during freshets which come yearly in April. When they occur oftener, a second time is in May. Large numbers of good quality are then killed which are dried in abundance on flakes, although the greater part is lost for want of salt in the preparation, nor can that be got anywhere. In the end of March the winter is gone, and the fish is eaten if any remain of what they take from the rivers in their flood and dry. Then they begin to travel for prickly pears, which are abundant in that country, eating them the while and occasionally killing a deer.

Sometimes it happens that a few persons will kill two or three hundred deer. Andrés Dorantes says he has known that many to be killed in eight days time by sixty Indians, though oftener than otherwise they do not kill any. The manner of hunting them is this.

As the animals stray towards the coast the Indians run inland where are many deer, no people ever living there, and these being collected are driven before them into the sea, and are kept there the day long until drowned, when the rise of the tide, with the wind, casts them ashore. They are not chased when the wind is off the land, as at such times they will return immediately. The animal will only run against the wind.

"After the practice of this exercise once or twice the Indians leaving the salt water take up their journey and go inland to eat prickly pears, which they begin upon as they ripen, about August. These last fifty or sixty days. It is the best part of the twelve months for these people, when, excepting some snails they pick up, they live entirely on this fruit, making merry over it day and night, so rejoiced are they in that season, while all the rest of the year they are suffering severe privation.

CHAPTER XIX

OUR SEPARATION BY THE INDIANS.

When the six months were over, I had to spend with the Christians to put in execution the plan we had concerted, the Indians went after prickly pears, the place at which they grew being thirty leagues off; and when we approached the point of flight, those among whom we were quarreled about a woman. After striking with fists, beating with sticks and bruising heads in great anger, each took his lodge and went his way, whence it became necessary that the Christians should also separate, and in no way could we come together until another year.

In this time I passed a hard life, caused as much by hunger as ill-usage. Three times I was obliged to run from my masters, and each time they went in pursuit and endeavored to slay me; but God our Lord in his mercy chose to protect and preserve me; and when the season of prickly pears returned, we again came together in the same place. After we had arranged our escape, and appointed a time, that very day the Indians separated and all went back. I told my comrades I would wait for them among the prickly pear plants until the moon should be full. This day was the first of September,* and the first of the moon; and I said that if in this time they did not come as we had agreed, I would leave and go alone. So we parted, each going with his Indians. I remained with mine until the thirteenth day of the moon, having determined to flee to others when it should be full.[1]

At this time Andrés Dorantes arrived with Estevanico and informed me that they had left Castillo with other Indians near by, called Lanegados,[2] that they had encountered great obstacles and wandered about lost; that the next day the Indians, among whom we were, would move to where Castillo was, and were going to unite with those who held him and become friends, having been at war until then, and that in this way we should recover Castillo.

We had thirst all the time we ate the pears, which we quenched with their juice. We caught it in a hole made in the earth, and when it was full we drank until satisfied. It is sweet, and the color of must. In this manner they collect it for lack of vessels. There are many kinds of prickly pears, among them some very good, although they all appeared to me to be so, hunger never having given me leisure to choose, nor to reflect upon which were the best.

Nearly all these people drink rain-water, which lies about in spots. Although there are rivers, as the Indians never have fixed habitations, there are no

* September 1.

familiar or known places for getting water. Throughout the country are extensive and beautiful plains with good pasturage; and I think it would be a very fruitful region were it worked and inhabited by civilized men. We nowhere saw mountains.

These Indians told us that there was another people next in advance of us, called Camones, living towards the coast, and that they had killed the people who came in the boat of Peñalosa and Tellez, who arrived so feeble that even while being slain they could offer no resistance, and were all destroyed. We were shown their clothes and arms, and were told that the boat lay there stranded. Thus, the fifth boat, had remained till then unaccounted for. We have already stated how the boat of the Governor had been carried out to sea, and the one of the Comptroller and the Friars had been cast away on the coast, of which Esquevel narrated the tale of the men. We have once told how the two boats in which Castillo, I and Dorantes came, foundered near the Island of Malhado

NATIONAL OBSERVATORY
WASHINGTON June 23d 50

'Dear Sir I send you a table showing both for Old and New Style the new moons that occurred nearest the first of September from 1530 to 1540

It is probable that Cabeça de Vaca dated new moon from the time he first saw it and when it probably might have been a day old If so, and if you take it that the full moon occurred on the 13th when he determined to &c it would bring the year 1532, though it may have been in 1533 if we suppose him not to be very particular as to the actual date of change days

However, I send you the tabular statement, which Professor Keith U. S. N., has prepared.

Respectfully, etc.,
M. F. MAURY.

Buckingham Smith, Esq.

☉ ☾ ○

A. D	Date Old Style	Date New Style	Hour Civil Time
1530	Aug 22	Sept 1	23.2
1531	Sept 10	" 20	20.5
1532	Aug 30	" 9	17.6
1533	" 20	Aug 30	8.4
1534	Sept 8	Sept 18	8.5
1535	Aug 28	Sept 7	17.1
1536	" 16	Aug 26	15.0
1537	Sept 24	Sept 14	11.1
1538	Aug 24	" 3	11.1
1539	Sept 12	" 22	6.2
1540	" 1	" 11	12.1

² In the second edition, Anagados, perhaps they were the Nacadoch

CHAPTER XX.

OF OUR ESCAPE.

The second day after we had moved, we commended ourselves to God and set forth with speed, trusting, for all the lateness of the season and that the prickly pears were about ending, with the mast which remained in the woods, we might still be enabled to travel over a large territory! Hurrying on that day in great dread lest the Indians should overtake us, we saw some smokes, and going in the direction of them we arrived there after vespers, and found an Indian. He ran as he discovered us coming, not being willing to wait for us. We sent the negro after him, when he stopped, seeing him alone. The negro told him we were seeking the people who made those fires. He answered that their houses were near by, and he would guide us to them. So we followed him. He ran to make known our approach, and at sunset we saw the houses. Before our arrival, at the distance of two cross-bow shots from them, we found four Indians, who waited for us and received us well. We said in the language of the Mariames, that we were coming to look for them. They were evidently pleased with our company, and took us to their dwellings. Dorantes and the negro were lodged in the house of a physician, Castillo and myself in that of another.

These people speak a different language, and are called Avavares. They are the same that carried bows to those with whom we formerly lived,* going to traffic with them, and although they are of a different nation and tongue, they understand the other language. They arrived that day with their lodges, at the place where we found them. The community directly brought us a great many prickly pears, having heard of us before, of our cures, and of the wonders our Lord worked by us, which, although there had been no others, were adequate to open ways for us through a country poor like this, to afford us people where oftentimes there are none, and to lead us through imminent dangers, not permitting us to be killed, sustaining us under great want, and putting into those nations the heart of kindness, as we shall relate hereafter.

* The Mariames
† The only persons whom the little band may have been leaving behind alive, were Theodoro and the negro, who went on shore at St. Andrew's or at Pensacola bay, Ovuedo, who returned towards Malhado, Figueroa and the Asturian, who had been last heard of as being on the coast, among the People of the Figs

CHAPTER XXI

OUR CURE OF SOME OF THE AFFLICTED.

That same night of our arrival, some Indians came to Castillo and told him that they had great pain in the head, begging him to cure them. After he made over them the sign of the cross, and commended them to God, they instantly said that all the pain had left, and went to their houses bringing us prickly pears, with a piece of venison, a thing to us little known. As the report of Castillo's performances spread, many came to us that night sick, that we should heal them, each bringing a piece of venison, until the quantity became so great we knew not where to dispose of it. We gave many thanks to God, for every day went on increasing his compassion and his gifts. After the sick were attended to, they began to dance and sing, making themselves festive, until sunrise; and because of our arrival, the rejoicing was continued for three days.

When these were ended, we asked the Indians about the country farther on, the people we should find in it, and of the subsistence there. They answered us, that throughout all the region prickly pear plants abounded; but the fruit was now gathered and all the people had gone back to their houses. They said the country was very cold, and there were few skins. Reflecting on this, and that it was already winter, we resolved to pass the season with these Indians.

Five days after our arrival, all the Indians went off, taking us with them to gather more prickly pears, where there were other peoples speaking different tongues. After walking five days in great hunger, since on the way was no manner of fruit, we came to a river and put up our houses. We then went to seek the product of certain trees, which is like peas. As there are no paths in the country, I was detained some time. The others returned, and coming to look for them in the dark, I got lost. Thank God I found a burning tree, and in the warmth of it passed the cold of that night. In the morning, loading myself with sticks, and taking two brands with me, I returned to seek them. In this manner I wandered five days, ever with my fire and load, for if the wood had failed me where none could be found, as many parts are without any, though I might have sought sticks elsewhere, there would have been no fire to kindle them. This was all the protection I had against cold, while walking naked as I was born. Going to the low woods near the rivers, I prepared myself for the night, stopping in them before sunset. I made a hole in the ground and threw in fuel which the trees abundantly afforded, collected in good quantity from those that were fallen and dry. About the whole I made four fires, in the form of a cross, which I watched and made up from time to time. I also gathered some bundles of the coarse straw that there abounds, with which I covered myself in the hole. In this way I was sheltered at night from cold. On one occasion while I slept, the fire fell upon the straw, when it began to blaze so rapidly that notwithstanding the haste I made to get out of it, I carried some marks on my hair of the danger to which I was exposed. All this while I tasted not a mouthful, nor did I find anything I could eat. My feet were bare and bled a good deal. Through the mercy of God, the wind did not blow from the north in all this time, otherwise I should have died.

At the end of the fifth day I arrived on the margin of a river, where I found the Indians who with the Christians, had considered me dead, supposing that I had been stung by a viper. All were rejoiced to see me, and most so were my companions. They said that up to that time they had struggled with great hunger, which was the cause of their not having sought me. At night all gave me of their prickly pears, and the next morning we set out for a place where they were in large quantity, with which we satisfied our great craving, the Christians rendering thanks to our Lord that he had ever given us his aid.

CHAPTER XXII

THE COMING OF OTHER SICK TO US THE NEXT DAY

The next day morning, many Indians came, and brought five persons who had cramps and were very unwell. They came that Castillo might cure them. Each offered his bow and arrows, which Castillo received. At sunset he blessed them, commending them to God our Lord, and we all prayed to Him the best we could to send health; for that He knew there was no other means, than through Him, by which this people would aid us, so we could come forth from this unhappy existence. He bestowed it so mercifully, that, the morning having come, all got up well and sound, and were as strong as though they never had a disorder. It caused great admiration, and inclined us to render many thanks to God our Lord, whose goodness we now clearly beheld, giving us firm hopes that He would liberate and bring us to where we might serve Him. For myself I can say that I ever had trust in His providence that He would lead me out from that captivity, and thus I always spoke of it to my companions.

The Indians having gone and taken their friends with them in health, we departed for a place at which others were eating prickly pears. These people are called Cuthalchuches¹ and Malicones, who speak different tongues. Adjoining them were others called Coayos and Susolas, and on the opposite side, others called Atayos,² who were at war with the Susolas, exchanging arrow-shots daily. As through all the country they talked only of the wonders which God our Lord worked through us, persons came from many parts to seek us that we might cure them. At the end of the second day after our arrival some of the Susolas came to us and besought Castillo that he would go to cure one wounded and others sick, and they said that among them was one very near his end. Castillo was a timid practitioner, most so in serious and dangerous cases, believing that his sins would weigh, and some day hinder him in performing cures. The Indians told me to go and heal them, as they liked me; they remembered that I had ministered to them in the walnut grove when they gave us nuts and skins, which occurred when I first joined the Christians.³ So I had to go with them, and Dorantes accompanied me with Estevanico. Coming near their huts, I perceived that the sick man we went to heal was dead. Many persons were around him weeping, and his house was prostrate, a sign that the one who dwelt in it is no more.³ When I arrived I found his eyes rolled up, and the pulse gone, he having all the appearances of death, as they seemed to me and as Dorantes said. I removed a mat with which he was covered, and suppli-

¹ They were Marames

cated our Lord as fervently as I could, that he would be pleased to give health to him and to the rest that might have need of it. After he had been blessed and breathed upon many times, they brought me his bow, and gave me a basket of pounded prickly pears.

The natives took me to cure many others who were sick of a stupor, and presented me two more baskets of prickly pears, which I gave to the Indians who accompanied us. We then went back to our lodgings. Those to whom we gave the fruit tarried, and returned at night to their houses, reporting that he who had been dead and for whom I wrought before them, had got up whole and walked, had eaten and spoken with them, and that all to whom I had ministered were well and much pleased. This caused great wonder and fear, and throughout the land the people talked of nothing else. All to whom the fame of it reached came to seek us that we should cure them and bless their children.

When the Cuthalchuches who were in company with our Indians, were about to return to their own country, they left us all the prickly pears they had, without keeping one; they gave us flints of very high value there, a palm and a half in length, with which they cut. They begged that we would remember them and pray to God that they might always be well, and we promised to do so. They left the most satisfied beings in the world, having given us the best of all they had.

We remained with the Avavares eight months, reckoned by the number of moons. In all this time people came to seek us from many parts and they said that most truly we were children of the sun. Dorantes and the negro to this time had not attempted to practice, but because of the great solicitation made by those coming from different parts to find us we all became physicians, although in being venturous and bold to attempt the performance of any cure, I was the most remarkable. No one whom we treated but told us he was left well, and so great was the confidence that they would become healed if we administered to them, they even believed that whilst we remained none of them could die. These and the rest of the people behind, related an extraordinary circumstance, and by the way they counted, there appeared to be fifteen or sixteen years since it occurred.

They said that a man wandered through the country whom they called Badthing; he was small of body and wore beard, and they never distinctly saw his features. When he came to the house where they lived, their hair stood up and they trembled. Presently a blazing torch shone at the door, when he entered and seized whom he chose, and giving him three great gashes in the side with a very sharp flint, the width of the hand and two palms in length, he put his hand through them drawing forth the entrails, from one of which he would cut off a portion more or less the length of a palm, and throw it on the embers. Then he would give three gashes to an arm, the second cut on the inside of an elbow, and would sever the limb. A little after this, he would begin to unite it, and putting his hands on the wounds, these would instantly become healed. They said that frequently in the dance he appeared among them, sometimes in the dress of a woman, at others in that of a man; that when it pleased him he would take a buhio, or house, and lifting it high, after a little he would come down with it in a heavy fall. They also stated that many times they offered him victuals but that he never ate; they asked him whence he came and where was his abiding place, and he showed them a fissure in the earth and said that his house was there below. These things they told us of, we much laughed at and ridiculed; and they, seeing our incredulity, brought to us many of those they said he had seized; and we saw the marks of the gashes made in the places according to the manner they had described.[4] We told them he was an evil one, and in the best way we could, gave them to understand that if they would believe in God our Lord and become Christians like us, they need have no fear of him, nor would he dare to come and inflict those injuries, and they might be certain he would not venture to appear while we remained in the land. At this they were delighted and lost much of their dread. They told us that they had seen the Asturian and Figueroa with people farther along the coast, whom we had called those of the figs.

They are all ignorant of time, either by the sun or moon; nor do they reckon by the month or year; they better know and understand the differences of the seasons when the fruits come to ripen, where the fish resort,[5] and the position of the stars, at which they are ready and practiced. By these we were ever well treated. We dug our own food and brought our loads of wood and water. Their houses and also the things we eat, are like those of the nation from which we came, but they suffer far greater want, having neither maize, acorns nor nuts. We always went naked like them, and covered ourselves at night with deer-skins.

Of the eight months we were among this people six we supported in great want, for fish are not to be found where they are. At the expiration of the time, the prickly pears began to ripen, and I and the negro went, without these Indians knowing it, to others further on a day's journey distant, called Mahacones. At the end of three days, I sent him to bring Castillo and Dorantes, and they having arrived, we all set out with the Indians who were going to get the small fruit of certain trees on which they support themselves ten or twelve days whilst the prickly pears are maturing. They joined others called Arbadaos, whom we found to be very weak, lank and swollen, so much so as to cause us great astonishment. We told those with whom we came, that we wished to stop with these people, at which they showed regret and went back by the way they came, so we remained in the field near the houses of the Indians, which when they observed, after talking among themselves, they came up together, and each of them taking one of us by the hand, led us to their dwellings. Among them we underwent greater hunger than with the others, we ate daily not more than two handfulls of the prickly pears which were green and so milky they burned our mouths. As there was lack of water, those who ate suffered great thirst. In our extreme want we bought two dogs, giving in exchange some nets, with other things, and a skin I used to cover myself.

I have already stated that throughout all this country we went naked, and as we were unaccustomed to being so, twice a year we cast our skins like serpents. The sun and air produced great sores on our breasts and shoulders, giving us sharp pain, and the large loads we had being very heavy, caused the cords to cut into our arms. The country is so broken and thickset, that often after getting our wood in the forests, the blood flowed from us in many places, caused by the obstruction of thorns and shrubs that tore our flesh wherever we went. At times, when my turn came to get wood, after it had cost me much blood I could not bring it out either on my back or by dragging. In these labors my only solace and relief were in thinking of the sufferings of our Redeemer, Jesus Christ, and in the blood he shed for me, in considering how much greater must have been the torment he sustained from the thorns, than that I there received.

I bartered with these Indians in combs that I made for them, and in bows, arrows and nets. We made mats, which are their houses, that they have great necessity for; and although they know how to make them, they wish to give their full time to getting food, since when otherwise employed they are pinched with hunger. Sometimes the Indians would set me to scraping and softening skins, and the days of my greatest prosperity there, were those in which they gave me skins to dress. I would scrape them a very great deal and eat the scraps, which would sustain me two or three days. When it happened among these people, as it had likewise among others whom we left behind, that a piece of meat was given us, we ate it raw; for if we had put it to roast, the first native that should come along would have taken it off and devoured it; and it appeared to us not well to expose it to this risk; besides we were in such condition it would have given us pain to eat it roasted, and we could not have digested it so well as raw. Such was the life we spent there; and the meagre subsistence we earned by the matters of traffic which were the work of our hands.

¹ Spelled Cutalches in the second edition.

² The Adayes or Adaize lived in the year 1805 according to the report of Dr. John Sibley, about forty miles from Nachitoches.— *Documents accompanying the President's Message,* year 1806. At a much earlier day the *Hadaies* were in a town between the Nachitoches and Sabine rivers, north of 32° at which the Spaniards erected a fort.—*M.S.*

³ The same custom prevails among the Navajo Indians who either burn or pull down the lodge in which a person dies. *The Spanish Conquest of New Mexico by W. W. H. Davis.*

⁴ The treatment of prisoners by a *paracoussi* of Florida, in which practice he was perhaps not alone, may be thought in explanation of the origin of these wounds shown in evidence of the truth of this marvelous Indian story. The statement made by René Laudonnière who received it from a native king is to be found in his account of the *Second Voyage* made by the French to Florida in the year 1564.

⁵ ...... then he named three others no less puissant than Satouriova, whereof the first dwelt two days journey from his lord Olata

Ouae Utina, and ordinarily made warre but pittifull in the execution of his furie. For he tooke the prisoners to mercy, being content to marke them on the left arme with a great marke like unto a seale, and so imprinted as if it had bene touched with an hote yron, then he let them goe without any more hurt." Translation in 3d volume of HAKLUYT's *Voyages and Discoveries*. The residence of Utina appears to have been about midway between the mouth of Santa Fé river and the harbor of St. Augustine.

⁵ "en tiempo que muere el Pescado." Some persons incline to understand this passage, "the times at which the fishes die," as when in cold weather on the shoal waters of Texas they freeze and come to the surface.

CHAPTER XXIII

OF OUR DEPARTURE AFTER HAVING EATEN THE DOGS

After eating the dogs, it seemed to us we had some strength to go forward, and so commending ourselves to God our Lord, that he would guide us, we took our leave of the Indians. They showed us the way to others, near by, who spoke their language. While on our journey rain fell, and we traveled the day in wet. We lost our way and went to stop in an extensive wood. We pulled many leaves of the prickly pear, which we put at night in an oven we made, and giving them much heat by the morning they were in readiness. After eating, we put ourselves under the care of the Almighty and started. We discovered the way we had lost. Having passed the wood, we found other houses, and coming up to them, we saw two women with some boys walking in the forest, who were frightened at the sight of us and fled, running into the woods to call the men. These arriving, stopped behind trees to look at us. We called to them and they came up with much timidity. After some conversation they told us that food was very scarce with them; that near by were many houses of their people to which they would guide us. We came at night where were fifty dwellings. The inhabitants were astonished at our appearance, showing much fear. After becoming somewhat accustomed to us, they reached their hands to our faces and bodies, and passed them in like manner over their own.

We stayed there that night, and in the morning the Indians brought us their sick, beseeching us that we would bless them. They gave us of what they had to eat, the leaves of the prickly pear and the green fruit roasted. As they did this with kindness and good will, and were happy to be without anything to eat, that they might have food to give us, we tarried some days. While there, others came from beyond, and when they were about to depart, we told our entertainers that we wished to go with those people. They felt much uneasiness at this, and pressed us warmly to stay: however, we took our leave in the midst of their weeping for our departure weighed heavily upon them.

CHAPTER XXIV

CUSTOMS OF THE INDIANS OF THAT COUNTRY.

From the Island of Malhado to this land, all the Indians whom we saw have the custom from the time in which their wives find themselves pregnant, of not sleeping with them until two years after they have given birth. The children are suckled until the age of twelve years, when they are old enough to get support for themselves. We asked why they reared them in this manner; and they said because of the great poverty of the land, it happened many times, as we witnessed, that they were two or three days without eating, sometimes four, and consequently, in seasons of scarcity, the children were allowed to suckle, that they might not famish; otherwise those who lived would be delicate having little strength.

If any one chance to fall sick in the desert, and cannot keep up with the rest, the Indians leave him to perish, unless it be a son or a brother; him they will assist, even to carrying on their back. It is common among them all to leave their wives when there is no conformity, and directly they connect themselves with whom they please. This is the course of the men who are childless; those who have children, remain with their wives and never abandon them.

When they dispute and quarrel in their towns, they strike each other with the fists, fighting until exhausted, and then separate. Sometimes they are parted by the women going between them: the men never interfere. For no disaffection that arises do they resort to bows and arrows. After they have fought, or had out their dispute, they take their dwellings and go into the woods, living apart from each other until their heat has subsided. When no longer offended and their anger is gone, they return. From that time they are friends as if nothing had happened; nor is it necessary that any one should mend their friendships, as they in this way again unite them. If those that quarrel are single, they go to some neighboring people, and although these should be enemies, they receive them well and welcome them warmly, giving them so largely of what they have, that when their animosity cools, and they return to their town, they go rich.

They are all warlike, and have as much strategy for protecting themselves against enemies as they could have were they reared in Italy in continual feuds. When they are in a part of the country where their enemies may attack them, they place their houses on the skirt of a wood, the thickest and most tangled they can find, and near it make a ditch in which they sleep. The warriors are covered by small pieces of stick through which are loop holes; these hide them and present so false an appearance that if come upon they are not discovered. They open a very narrow way, entering into the midst of the wood, where a spot is prepared on which the women and children sleep. When night comes they kindle fires in their lodges, that should spies be about, they may think to find them there; and before daybreak they again light those fires. If the enemy comes to assault the houses, they who are in the ditch make a sally, and from their trenches do much injury without those who are outside seeing or being able to find them. When there is no wood in which they can take shelter in this way, and make their ambuscades, they settle on open ground at a place they select, which they invest with trenches covered with broken sticks, having apertures whence to discharge arrows. These arrangements are made for night.

While I was among the Aguenes, their enemies coming suddenly at midnight, fell upon them, killed three and wounded many, so that they ran from their houses to the fields before them. As soon as these ascertained that their assailants had withdrawn, they returned to pick up all the arrows the others had shot, and following after them in the most stealthy manner possible, came that night to their dwellings without their presence being suspected. At four o'clock in the morning the Aguenes attacked them, killed five and wounded numerous others, and made them flee from their houses, leaving their bows with all they possessed. In a little while came the wives of the Quevenes to them and formed a treaty whereby the parties became friends. The women, however, are sometimes the cause of war. All these nations, when they have personal enmities, and are not of one family, assassinate at night, waylay, and inflict gross barbarities on each other.

CHAPTER XXV

VIGILANCE OF THE INDIANS IN WAR

They are the most watchful in danger of any people I ever knew. If they fear an enemy they are awake the night long, each with a bow at his side and a dozen arrows. He that would sleep tries his bow, and if it is not strung, he gives the turn necessary to the cord. They often come out from their houses, bending to the ground in such manner that they cannot be seen, looking and watching on all sides to catch every object. If they perceive anything about, they are at once in the bushes with their bows and arrows, and there remain until day, running from place to place where it is needful to be, or where they think their enemies are. When the light has come, they unbend their bows until they go out to hunt. The strings are the sinews of deer.

The method they have of fighting is bending low to the earth, and whilst shot at they move about, speaking and leaping from one point to another, thus avoiding the shafts of their enemies. So effectual is their manœuvering that they can receive very little injury from cross-bow or arquebus; they rather scoff at them, for these arms are of little value employed in open field where the Indians move nimbly about. They are proper for defiles and in water; everywhere else the horse will best subdue, being what the natives universally dread. Whosoever would fight them must be cautious to show no fear, or desire to have anything that is theirs. While war exists they must be treated with the utmost rigor; for if they discover any timidity or covetousness, they are a race that well discern the opportunities for vengeance, and gather strength from any weakness of their adversaries. When they use arrows in battle and exhaust their store, each returns his own way, without the one party following the other, although the one be many and the other few, such being their custom. Oftentimes the body of an Indian is traversed by the arrow: yet unless the entrails or the heart be struck, he does not die but recovers from the wound.

I believe these people see and hear better, and have keener senses than any other in the world. They are great in hunger, thirst, and cold, as if they were made for the endurance of these more than other men, by habit and nature.

Thus much I have wished to say, beyond the gratification of that desire men have to learn the customs and manners of each other, that those who hereafter at some time find themselves amongst these people, may have knowledge of their usages and artifices, the value of which they will not find inconsiderable in such event.

CHAPTER XXVI.

OF THE NATIONS AND TONGUES.

I desire to enumerate the natives and tongues that exist from those of Malhado to the farthest Cuchendados¹ there are. Two languages are found in the island: the people of one are called Cahoques, of the other, Han. On the tierra-firme, over against the island is another people, called Chorruco who take their names from the forests where they live. Advancing by the shores of the sea, others inhabit who are called the Doguenes, and opposite them others by the name of Mendica. Farther along the coast are the Quevenes, and in front of them on the main, the Mariames; and continuing by the coast are other called Guaycones, and in front of them, within on the main the Yguazes. At the close of these are the Atayos, and in their rear others, the Acubadaos and beyond them are many in the same direction. By the coast live those called Quitoks, and in front inward on the main are the Chavavares, to whom adjoin the Mahacones, the Cultalchulches and others called Susolas, and the Comos and by the coast farther on are the Camoles, and on the same coast in advance are those whom we called People of the Figs.

They all differ in their habitations, towns and tongues. There is a language in which calling to a person, for "look here" they say "Arre aca," and to a dog "Xo." Everywhere they produce stupefaction with a smoke, and for that they will give whatever they possess. They drink a tea made from leaves of a tree like those of the oak, which they toast in a pot; and after these are parched, the vessel, still remaining on the fire, is filled with water. When the liquor has twice boiled, they pour it into a jar, and in cooling it use the half of a gourd. So soon as it is covered thickly with froth, it is drunk as warm as can be supported; and from the time it is taken out of the pot until it is used they are crying aloud "Who wishes to drink?" When the women hear these cries, they instantly stop, fearing to move, and although they may be heavily laden they dare do nothing further. Should one of them move, they dishonor her, beating her with sticks, and greatly vexed, throw away the liquor they have prepared; while they who have drunk eject it, which they do readily and without pain. The reason they give for this usage is, that when they are about to drink if the women move from where they hear the cry, something pernicious enters the body in that liquid, shortly producing death. At the time of boiling the vessel must be covered; and if it should happen to be open when a woman passes, they use no more of that liquid but throw it out. The color is yellow. They are three days taking it, eating nothing in the time, and daily each one drinks an arroba and a half.

When the women have their indisposition, they seek food only for themselves, as no one else will eat of what they bring. In the time I was thus among these people I witnessed a diabolical practice: a man living with another, one of those who are emasculate and impotent. These go habited like women, and perform their duties, use the bow, and carry heavy loads. Among them we saw many mutilated in the way I describe. They are more muscular than other men and taller; they bear very weighty burthens.

CHAPTER XXVII.

WE MOVED AWAY AND WERE WELL RECEIVED

After parting with those we left weeping,* we went with the others to their houses and were hospitably received by the people in them. They brought their children to us that we might touch their hands, and gave us a great quantity of the flour of mezquiquez. The fruit while hanging on the tree, is very bitter and like unto the carob; when eaten with earth it is sweet and wholesome. The method they have of preparing it is this: they make a hole of requisite depth in the ground, and throwing in the fruit, pound it with a club the size of the leg, a fathom and a half in length, until it is well mashed. Besides the earth that comes from the hole, they bring and add some handfulls, then returning to beat it a little while longer. Afterward it is thrown into a jar, like a basket, upon which water is poured until it rises above and covers the mixture. He that beats it tastes it, and if it appears to him not sweet, he asks for earth to stir in, which is added until he finds it sweet. Then all sit round, and each putting in a hand, takes out as much as he

* The Arbadaos: see Chapter XXIII.

can. The pits and hulls are thrown upon a skin, whence they are taken by him who does the pounding, and put into the jar whereon water is poured as at first, whence having expressed the froth and juice, again the pits and husks are thrown upon the skin. This they do three or four times to each pounding. Those present, for whom this is a great banquet, have their stomachs greatly distended by the earth and water they swallow. The Indians made a protracted festival of this sort on our account, and great areitos during the time we remained.¹

When we proposed to leave them, some women of another people came there who lived farther along. They informed us whereabout were their dwellings, and we set out for them, although the inhabitants entreated us to remain for that day, because the houses whither we were going were distant, there was no path to them, the women had come tired, and would the next day go with us refreshed and show us the way. Soon after we had taken our leave, some of the women, who had come on together from the same town, followed behind us. As there are no paths in the country we presently got lost, and thus traveled four leagues, when stopping to drink we found the women in pursuit of us at the water, who told us of the great exertion they had made to overtake us. We went on taking them for guides, and passed over a river towards evening, the water reaching to the breast. It might be as wide as that at Seville; its current was very rapid.²

At sunset we reached a hundred Indian habitations. Before we arrived, all the people who were in them came out to receive us, with such yells as were terrific, striking the palms of their hands violently against their thighs. They brought us gourds bored with holes and having pebbles in them, an instrument for the most important occasions, produced only at the dance or to effect cures, and which none dare touch but those who own them. They say there is virtue in them, and because they do not grow in that country, they come from heaven; nor do they know where they are to be found, only that the rivers bring them in their floods. So great were the fear and distraction of these people, some to reach us sooner than others, that they might touch us, they pressed us so closely that they lacked little of killing us; and without letting us put our feet to the ground carried us to their dwellings. We were so crowded upon by numbers, that we went into the houses they had made for us. On no account would we consent that they should rejoice over us any more that night. The night long they passed in singing and dancing among themselves; and the next day they brought us all the people of the town, that we should touch and bless them in the way we had done to others among whom we had been. After this performance they presented many arrows to some women of the other town who had accompanied theirs.

The next day we left, and all the people of the place went with us; and when we came to the other Indians we were as well received as we had been by the last. They gave us of what they had to eat, and the deer they had killed that day. Among them we witnessed another custom, which is this: they who were with us took from him who came to be cured, his bow and arrows, shoes and beads if he wore any, and then brought him before us that we should heal him. After being attended to, he would go away highly pleased, saying that he was well. So we parted from these Indians, and went to others by whom we were welcomed. They brought us their sick, which, we having blessed, they declared were sound: he who was healed, believed we could cure him, and with what the others to whom we had administered would relate, they made great rejoicing and dancing, so that they left us no sleep.

---

¹ The mezquite is of the family of the *mimosa*. The tree is not found to the east of the Mississippi river, and is first seen in going west on drawing near the Rio Bravo del Norte. At times they, the Indians of Sonora, says Padre Rivas, also avail themselves of the fruit of the Tepeguages or Mezquites, a small kind of Algorrova abundant in that country. It is crushed in large mortars of wood; the flour is somewhat sweet and well flavored, affording both drink and nutriment. — *Historia de los Triumphos de nuestra Santa Fe*.

² The expanse of the Guadalquiver is here a hundred paces, a few feet more or less, as one may find above *Toro del Oro*, in walking across it on the iron bridge that connects Seville and Triana. The river nowhere appears to have changed or enlarged its bed in many ages.

CHAPTER XXVIII.

OF ANOTHER STRANGE CUSTOM

Leaving these Indians, we went to the dwellings of numerous others. From this place began another novel custom, which is, that while the people received us very well, those who accompanied us began to use them so ill as to take their goods and ransack their houses, without leaving anything. To witness this unjust procedure gave us great concern, inflicted too, on those who received us hospitably: we feared also that it might provoke offense, and be the cause of some tumult between them: but, as we were in no condition to make it better, or to dare chastise such conduct, for the present we had to bear with it, until a time when we might have greater authority among them. They, also, who lost their effects, noticing our dejection, attempted to console us by saying that we should not be grieved on this account, as they were so gratified at having seen us, they held their properties to be well bestowed, and that farther on they would be repaid by others who were very rich.

On all the day's travel we received great inconvenience from the many persons following us. Had we attempted to escape we could not have succeeded, such was their haste in pursuit, in order to touch us. So great was the importunity for this privilege, we consumed three hours in going through with them that they might depart. The next day all the inhabitants were brought before us. The greater part were clouded of an eye, and others in like manner were entirely blind,¹ which caused in us great astonishment. They are a people of fine figure, agreeable features, and whiter than any of the many nations we had seen until then.

Here we began to see mountains; they appeared to come in succession from the North sea,² and, according to the information the Indians gave us, we believe they rise fifteen leagues from the sea. We set forth in a direction towards them with these Indians, and they guided us by the way of some kindred of theirs, for they wished to take us only where were their relations, and were not willing that their enemies should come to such great good, as they thought it was to see us. After we arrived they that went with us plundered the others; but as the people there knew the fashion, they had hidden some things before we came, and having welcomed us with great festivity and rejoicing, they brought out and presented to us what they had concealed. These were beads, ochre and some little bags of silver.³ In pursuance of custom, we directly gave them to the Indians who came with us, which, when they had received, they began their dances and festivities, sending to call others from a town near by, that they also might see us.

In the afternoon they all came and brought us beads and bows, with trifles of other sort, which we also distributed. Desiring to leave the next day, the inhabitants all wished to take us to others, friends of theirs, who were at the point of the ridge, stating that many houses were there, and people who would give us various things. As it was out of our way, we did not wish to go to them, and took our course along the plain near the mountains, which we believed not to be distant from the coast where the people are all evil disposed, and we considered it preferable to travel inland; for those of the interior are of a better condition and treated us mildly, and we felt sure that we should find it more populous and better provisioned. Moreover, we chose this course because in traversing the country we should learn many particulars of it, so that should God our Lord be pleased to take any of us thence, and lead us to the land of Christians, we might carry that information and news of it. As the Indians saw that we were determined not to go where they would take us, they said that in the direction we would go, there were no inhabitants, nor any prickly pears nor other thing to eat, and begged us to tarry there that day; we accordingly did so. They directly sent two of their number to seek for people in the direction that we wished to go; and the next day we left, taking with us several of the Indians. The women went carrying water, and so great was our authority that no one dared drink of it without our permission.

Two leagues from there we met those who had gone out, and they said that they had found no one, at which the Indians seemed much disheartened, and began again to entreat us to go by way of the mountains. We did not wish to do so, and they, seeing our disposition, took their leave of us with much regret, and returned down the river to their houses while we ascended along by it. After a little time we came upon two women with burthens, who put them down as they saw us, and brought to us, of what they carried. It was the flour of maize. They told us that farther up on that river we should find dwellings, a plenty of prickly pears and of that meal. We bade them farewell; they were going to those whom we had left.

We walked until sunset and arrived at a town of some twenty houses, where we were received with weeping and in great sorrow, for they already knew that wheresoever we should come, all would be pillaged and spoiled by those who accompanied us. When they saw that we were alone, they lost their fear, and gave us prickly pears with nothing more. We remained there that night, and at dawn, the Indians who had left us the day before, broke upon their houses. As they came upon the occupants unprepared and in supposed safety, having no place in which to conceal anything, all they possessed was taken from them, for which they wept much. In consolation the plunderers told them that we were children of the sun and that we had power to heal the sick and to destroy; and other lies, even greater than these, which none knew how to tell better than they when they find it convenient. They bade them conduct us with great respect, advised that they should be careful to offend us in nothing, give us all they might possess, and endeavor to take us where people were numerous, and that wheresoever they arrived with us, they should rob and pillage the people of what they have, since this was customary.

¹ The story has its parallel. This passage is from a traveler who was at a town of the Shoccories in the year 1701. "Most of these Indians have but one Eye, but what Mischance or Quarrel has bereaved them of the other I could not learn." *New Voyage to Carolina*, etc., by JOHN LAWSON, Gent., Surveyor General of North Carolina. London, 1709.

² The ocean as seen from Bisca was the North sea, and that name for the maritime people there, extended over the Atlantic; the discovery of another ocean, the Pacific, as seen to the southward from Panama, became in contradistinction for Spaniards, the South sea.

The travelers now approach the San Saba mountains to follow at the foot along their course westward.

³ This is in error of the printer, and should read "little bags of small pearls" instead of silver.—OVIEDO.

CHAPTER XXIX

THE INDIANS PLUNDER EACH OTHER.

After the Indians had told and shown these natives well what to do, they left us together and went back. Remembering the instruction, they began to treat us with the same awe and reverence that the others had shown. We traveled with them three days, and they took us where were many inhabitants. Before we arrived, these were informed of our coming by the others, who told them respecting us all that the first had imparted, adding much more, for these people are all very fond of romance, and are great liars, particularly so where they have any interest. When we came near the houses all the inhabitants ran out with delight and great festivity to receive us. Among other things, two of their physicians gave us two gourds, and thenceforth we carried these with us, and added to our authority a token highly reverenced by Indians. Those who accompanied us rifled the houses, but as these were many and the others few, they could not carry off what they took, and abandoned more than the half.

From here we went along the base of the ridge, striking inland more than fifty leagues, and at the close we found upwards of forty houses. Among the articles given us, Andrés Dorantes received a hawk bell of copper, thick and large, figured with a face, which the natives had shown, greatly prizing it. They told him that they had received it from others, their neighbors; we asked them whence the others had obtained it, and they said it had been brought from the northern direction, where there was much copper, which was highly esteemed. We concluded that whencesoever it came there was a foundery, and that work was done in hollow form.[1]

We departed the next day, and traversed a ridge seven leagues in extent. The stones on it are scoria of iron. At night we arrived at many houses seated on the banks of a very beautiful river. The owners of them came half way out on the road to meet us, bringing their children on their backs. They gave us many little bags of marquesite and pulverized galena with which they rub the face. They presented us many beads, and blankets of cowhide, loading all who accompanied us with some of every thing they had. They eat prickly pears and the seed of pine. In that country are small pine trees, the cones like little eggs, but the seed is better than that of Castilla, as its husk is very thin, and while green is beat and made into balls, to be thus eaten. If the seed be dry, it is pounded in the husk, and consumed in the form of flour.

Those who there received us, after they had touched us, went running to their houses and directly returned, and did not stop running, going and coming, to bring us in this manner many things for support on the way. They fetched a man to me and stated that a long time since he had been wounded by an arrow in the right shoulder, and that the point of the shaft was lodged above his heart, which, he said, gave him much pain, and in consequence, he was always sick. Probing the wound I felt the arrow-head, and found it had passed through the cartilage. With a knife I carried, I opened the breast to the place, and saw the point was aslant and troublesome to take out. I continued to cut, and, putting in the point of the knife, at last with great difficulty I drew the head forth. It was very large. With the bone of a deer, and by virtue of my calling, I made two stitches that threw the blood over me, and with hair from a skin I stanched the flow. They asked me for the arrow-head after I had taken it out, which I gave, when the whole town came to look at it. They sent it into the back country that the people there might view it. In consequence of this operation they had many of their customary dances and festivities. The next day I cut the two stitches and the Indian was well. The wound I made appeared only like a seam in the palm of the hand. He said he felt no pain or sensitiveness in it whatsoever. This cure gave us control throughout the country in all that the inhabitants had power or deemed of any value or cherished. We showed them the hawk-bell we brought, and they told us that in the place whence that had come, were buried many plates of the same material; it was a thing they greatly esteemed, and where it came from were fixed habitations. The country we considered to be on the South sea, which we had ever understood to be richer than the one of the North.

We left there, and traveled through so many sorts of people, of such diverse languages, the memory fails to recall them.² They ever plundered each other, and those that lost, like those that gained, were fully content. We drew so many followers that we had not use for their services. While on our way through these vales, every Indian carried a club three palms in length, and kept on the alert. On raising a hare, which animals are abundant, they surround it directly and throw numerous clubs at it with astonishing precision.³ Thus they cause it to run from one to another; so that, according to my thinking, it is the most pleasing sport which can be imagined, as oftentimes the animal runs into the hand. So many did they give us that at night when we stopped we had eight or ten back-loads apiece. Those having bows were not with us; they dispersed about the ridge in pursuit of deer; and at dark came bringing five or six for each of us, besides quail, and other game. Indeed, whatever they either killed or found, was put before us, without themselves daring to take anything until we had blessed it, though they should be expiring of hunger, they having so established the rule, since marching with us.

The women carried many mats, of which the men made us houses, each of us having a separate one, with all his attendants. After these were put up, we ordered the deer and hares to be roasted, with the rest that had been taken. This was done by means of certain ovens made for the purpose. Of each we took a little and the remainder we gave to the principal personage of the people coming with us, directing him to divide it among the rest. Every one brought his portion to us that we might breathe upon and give it our benediction, for not until then did they dare eat any of it. Frequently we were accompanied by three or four thousand persons, and as we had to breathe upon and sanctify the food and drink for each, and grant permission to do the many things they would come to ask, it may be seen how great was the annoyance. The women first brought us prickly pears, spiders, worms, and whatever else they could gather; for even were they famishing, they would eat nothing unless we gave it them.

In company with these we crossed a great river coming from the north,¹ and passing over some plains thirty leagues in extent, we found many persons coming a long distance to receive us, who met us on the road over which we were to travel, and welcomed us in the manner of those we had left.

¹ From the Province of Tiguex, Coronado writes to the King on the 20th of October 1541 respecting Quivira: "The natives there gave me a piece of copper which a principal Indian wore hanging from his neck. I sent it to the Viceroy of New Spain. I have seen no other metal in the country except this sample, and what is more, tin hawk bells of copper I sent with a little metal that appears like gold."

² A multitude of small bands of warring savages are stated to have been found originally scattered over Texas, speaking a diversity of tongues. The friar Bartholomé Garcia, in a *Manual para administrar*

where it came from were fixed habitations. The country we considered to be on the South sea, which we had ever understood to be richer than the one of the North.

We left there, and traveled through so many sorts of people, of such diverse languages, the memory fails to recall them. They ever plundered each other, and those that lost, like those that gained, were fully content. We drew so many followers that we had not use for their services. While on our way through these vales, every Indian carried a club three palms in length, and kept on the alert. On raising a hare, which animals are abundant, they surround it directly and throw numerous clubs at it with astonishing precision. Thus they cause it to run from one to another, so that, according to my thinking, it is the most pleasing sport which can be imagined, as oftentimes the animal runs into the hand. So many did they give us that at night when we stopped we had eight or ten back-loads apiece. Those having bows were not with us; they dispersed about the ridge in pursuit of deer, and at dark came bringing five or six for each of us, besides quail, and other game. Indeed whatever they either killed or found, was put before us, without themselves daring to take anything until we had blessed it, though they should be expiring of hunger, they having so established the rule, since marching with us.

The women carried many mats of which the men made us houses, each of us having a separate one, with all his attendants. After these were put up we ordered the deer and hares to be roasted, with the rest that had been taken. This was done by means of certain ovens made for the purpose. Of each we took a little and the remainder we gave to the principal personage of the people coming with us, directing him to divide it among the rest. Every one brought his portion to us, that we might breathe upon and give it our benediction, for not until then did they dare eat any of it. Frequently we were accompanied by three or four thousand persons, and as we had to breathe upon and sanctify the food and drink for each, and grant permission to do the many things they would come to ask, it may be seen how great was the annoyance. The women first brought us prickly pears, spiders, worms, and whatever else they could gather; for even were they famishing, they would eat nothing unless we gave it them.

In company with these we crossed a great river coming from the north,¹ and passing over some plains thirty leagues in extent we found many persons coming a long distance to receive us, who met us on the road over which we were to travel and welcomed us in the manner of those we had left.

¹ From the Province of Tiguex Coronado writes to the King on the 20th of October 1541, respecting Quivira. "The natives there gave me a piece of copper which a principal Indian wore hanging from his neck. I sent it to the Viceroy of New Spain. I have seen no other metal in the country except this sample and what is uncertain, hawk bells of copper I sent with a little metal that appears like gold."

² A multitude of small bands of wandering savages are stated to have been found originally scattered over Texas, speaking a diversity of tongues. The first BAPTH ROMÉ GOMEZ in a *Visita para adunar*

privation and labor they had undergone in the passage of those ridges, which are sterile and difficult in the extreme. They conducted us to certain plains at the base of the mountains, where people came to meet us from a great distance, and received us as the last had done, and gave so many goods to those who came with us, that the half were left because they could not be carried. I told those who gave, to resume the goods that they might not be there and be lost; but they answered they could in no wise do so, as it was not their custom after they had bestowed a thing to take it back: so considering the articles no longer of value, they were left to perish.

We told these people that we desired to go where the sun sets; and they said inhabitants in that direction were remote. We commanded them to send and make known our coming; but they strove to excuse themselves the best they could, the people being their enemies, and they did not wish to go to them. Not daring to disobey, however, they sent two women, one of their own, the other a captive from that people; for the women can negotiate even though there be war. We followed them and stopped at a place where we agreed to wait. They tarried five days; and the Indians said they could not have found anybody.

We told them to conduct us towards the north, and they answered, as before, that except afar off there were no people in that direction, and nothing to eat, nor could water be found. Notwithstanding all this, we persisted and said we desired to go in that course.

They still tried to excuse themselves in the best manner possible. At this we became offended, and one night I went out to sleep in the woods apart from them, but directly they came to where I was, and remained all night without sleep, talking to me in great fear, telling me how terrified they were, beseeching us to be no longer angry, and said that they would lead us in the direction it was our wish to go, though they knew they should die on the way.

Whilst we still feigned to be displeased lest their fright should leave them, a remarkable circumstance happened, which was, that on the same day many of the Indians became ill, and the next day eight men died. Abroad in the country wheresoever this became known, there was such dread, and it seemed as if the inhabitants would die of fear at sight of us. They besought us not to remain angered, nor require that more of them should die. They believed we caused their death by only willing it, when in truth it gave us so much pain that it could not be greater; for beyond their loss we feared they might all die or abandon us of fright, and that other people thenceforward would do the same, seeing what had come to these. We prayed to God, our Lord, to relieve them; and from that time the sick began to get better.

We witnessed one thing with great admiration, that the parents, brothers and wives of those who died had great sympathy for them in their suffering, but when dead they showed no feeling, neither did they weep nor speak among themselves, make any signs, nor dare approach the bodies until we commanded these to be taken to burial.

While we were among these people, which was more than fifteen days, we saw no one speak to another, nor did we see an infant smile. the only one that cried they took off to a distance, and with the sharp teeth of a rat, they scratched it from the shoulders down nearly to the end of the legs. Seeing this cruelty, and offended at it, I asked why they did so: they said for chastisement, because the child had wept in my presence.² These terrors they imparted to all those who had lately come to know us, that they might give us whatever they had, for they knew we kept nothing and would relinquish all to them. This people were the most obedient we had found in all the land, the best conditioned, and in general, comely.

The sick having recovered, and three days having passed since we came to the place, the women whom we sent away returned, and said they had found very few people: nearly all had gone for cattle, being then in the season. We ordered the convalescent to remain and the well to go with us, and that at the end of two days' journey, those women should go with two of our number to fetch up the people, and bring them on the road to receive us. Consequently the next morning the most robust started with us. At the end of three days' travel we stopped, and the next day Alonzo del Castillo set out with Estevanico the negro, taking the two women as guides. She that was the captive led them to the river which ran between some ridges, where was a town at which her father lived; and these habitations were the first seen, having the appearance and structure of houses.

Here Castillo and Estevanico arrived, and after talking with the Indians, Castillo returned at the end of three days to the spot where he had left us, and brought five or six of the people. He told us he had found fixed dwellings of civilization, that the inhabitants lived on beans and pumpkins, and that he had seen maize. This news the most of anything delighted us, and for it we gave infinite thanks to our Lord. Castillo told us the negro was coming with all the population to wait for us in the road not far off. Accordingly we left, and having traveled a league and a half, we met the negro and the people coming to receive us. They gave us beans, many pumpkins, calabashes, blankets of cowhide and other things. As this people and those who came with us were enemies, and spoke not each other's language, we discharged the latter, giving them what we received, and we departed with the others. Six leagues from there, as the night set in we arrived at the houses, where great festivities were made over us. We remained one day, and the next set out with these Indians. They took us to the settled habitations of others who lived upon the same food.

From that place onward was another usage. Those who knew of our approach did not come out to receive us on the road as the others had done, but we found them in their houses, and they had made other for our reception. They were all seated with their faces turned to the wall, their heads down, the hair brought before their eyes, and their property placed in a heap in the middle of the house. From this place they began to give us many blankets of skin; and they had nothing they did not bestow. They have the finest persons of any people we saw, of the greatest activity and strength, who best understood us and intelligently answered our inquiries. We called them the Cow nation, because most of the cattle killed are slaughtered in their neighborhood, and along up that river for over fifty leagues, they destroy great numbers.

They go entirely naked after the manner of the first we saw. The women are dressed with deer skin, and some few men, mostly the aged, who are incapable of fighting. The country is very populous. We asked how it was they did not plant maize: they answered it was that they might not lose what they should put in the ground; that the rains had failed for two years in succession, and the seasons were so dry the seed had everywhere been taken by the moles, and they could not venture to plant again until after water had fallen copiously. They begged us to tell the sky to rain, and to pray for it, and we said we would do so. We also desired to know whence they got the maize and they told us from where the sun goes down; there it grew throughout the region, and the nearest was by that path. Since they did not wish to go thither, we asked by what direction we might best proceed and bade them inform us concerning the way; they said the path was along up by that river towards the north, for otherwise in a journey of seventeen days, we should find nothing to eat, except a fruit they call chacan that is ground between stones, and even then it could with difficulty be eaten for its dryness and pungency, which was true. They showed it to us there, and we could not eat it. They informed us also that whilst we traveled by the river upward, we should all the way pass through a people that were their enemies, who spoke their tongue, and though they had nothing to give us to eat they would receive us with the best good will, and present us with mantles of cotton, hides, and other articles of their wealth. Still it appeared to them we ought by no means to take that course.

Doubting what it would be best to do, and which way we should choose for suitableness and support, we remained two days with these Indians who gave us beans and pumpkins for our subsistence. Their method of cooking is so new, that for its strangeness I desire to speak of it; thus it may be seen and remarked how curious and diversified are the contrivances and ingenuity of the human family. Not having discovered the use of pipkins to boil what they would eat, they fill the half of a large calabash with water, and throw on the fire many stones of such as are most convenient and readily take the heat. When hot they are taken up with tongs of sticks and dropped into the calabash until the water in it boils from the fervor of the stones. Then whatever is to be cooked is put in, and until it is done they continue taking out cooled stones and throwing in hot ones. Thus they boil their food.

ADDENDUM

Southward of this line of travel for the last few days, ANTONIO DE ESPEJO led a troop to the north in November of the year 1582, from the mines of Santa Bárbara in the valley of San Bartolomé. The second day he came upon the Conchos who in good numbers were living over an extensive tract of country, in houses of grass, subsisting by agriculture and the chase. After passing among them a distance of more than twenty-four leagues, he came to the Passaguates, a similar people.

At the end of other four days Espejo found the Tobosos, who go naked and use the bow. Twelve miles farther were the Jumanos, whom the Spaniards call Patarabueyes. Their country is broad and populous, containing many towns, well laid out. The houses are of stone and lime, with flat roofs. Both males and females have the face, arms and legs marked with lines. They were of greater civility than any people seen until then, and more robust. Food was abundant, both meat and grain; fish was taken in the streams flowing southward. One great river like the Guadalquivir runs into the North sea. Salt is got in its season from the lakes.

Following the shore of the great river for twelve days, Espejo passed through a constant succession of towns, one cacique after another coming forth without arms to meet him offering food and presents, chiefly buckskins. They were warlike, and their persons entirely clothed. Men, women and children sought the friar and soldiers for their blessing, and to have the sign of the cross made over them, spoke of *Apalito*, looked up into the heavens and pointed thither. They were asked whence came their knowledge, and they said from three white men who went through there with a black, and tarried some days with them.

Journeying a few days longer Espejo arrived at a large town, where he was presented articles of many colored feather work, and numerous cotton shawls with blue and white bars. Without an interpreter he could not ascertain the name of the place. *Itinerario del Nuevo Mundo* por MENDOZA, 1595. The Report of Espejo is extant in the *Patronato of the Lonja*, Sevilla.

From the narration, Alvar Nuñez and his companions appear to have struck the river Bravo del Norte where the Conchos flows into it, coming from the west, the Jumanos being to the right of them as they approached from the east, and the Tobosos on the left.

Of the four nations, we know a little of the Tobosos only; they were a barbarous people whose arms were seldom out of their hands, who constantly committed depredations on all sides, and were little influenced by teaching. OROZCO Y BERRA writes that they were of the kin and tongue of the Apaches, and stood in the way of their progress south; but after the extermination of that tribe, which was in the last third of the last century, the Tobosos extended their incursions thitherward, particularly over the desert of Magrana.

We may infer that the Cow nation spoken of by Alvar Nuñez was probably a tribe of the Cumanche, or perhaps of the Apaches, of whom there is a comprehensive account written in 1796 by Lt. Col. ANTONIO CORDERO. He reports their knowledge of the existence of a supreme being whom they call *Yastasitasitanne* Chief of the heavens. They consist of nine principal bands, speak a common language, and roam over that region of the continent between 30 and 38 of North latitude and between 264 and 277 of longitude west from Teneriffe, waging war with the Cumanche from antiquity, for supremacy over the grounds of the bison.—*Geografia de las Lenguas y Carta Etnografica de Mexico.*

The earliest mention of the nation of Apaches I have found is made by JUAN DE OÑATE, at San Juan of Nuevo Mexico, 2d day of March, in the year 1599, who reports:

'We have seen other nations, the Querechos and Vaqueros, living in tents of dressed skin among the herds of cibola. Their numbers are infinite. The Apaches of whom we have also seen, some are in towns. There is one not many leagues distant with fifteen squares. They have not yet given in their obedience to His Majesty as the other Provinces have done, by instrument of writing which has been brought about at the cost of notable labor, diligence, and care, with long journeys, and no little circumspection, vigilance and caution.'

An accompanying map shows San Juan to be on the east side of the river Bravo, northward of Socorro and south of the valley of Quarra. A chief of that country in our time says the town is called by the people *Okpa*. Jaramillo, a captain under Coronado in the year 1542, states that on first coming to the plains he found Indians among the bison who called others Querechos, or People of the flat roof houses.

*M. Ino HARIOT gives a like instance of the effect of fear and superstition on the minds of the Indians that occurred during his stay in Virginia in the years 1585-6.

'There could at no time happen any strange sicknesse, losses, hurts, or any other crosse unto them but what they would impute to us the cause or meanes thereof for offending or not pleasing us. One other rare and strange accident leaving others will I mention before I end, which moved the whole Countrey that either knew or heard of us, to have us in wonderfull admiration.

'There was no towne where wee had any subtile devise practised against us, wee leaving it unpunished or not revenged (because we sought by all meanes possible to win them by gentlenesse), but that within a few dayes after our departure from every such Towne the people began to die very fast, and many in short space, in some Townes about twentie, in some fourtie, and in one sixe score, which in trueth was very many in respect of their numbers. This happened in no place that we could learne but where we had bin, where they used some practise against us, and after such time. The disease also was so strange, that they neither knewe what it was, nor how to cure it; the like by report of the oldest men in the Countrey never happened before time out of minde. A thinge specially observed by us, as also by the naturall inhabitants themselves. Insomuch that when some of the inhabitants which were our friends, and especially the Wiroans Wingina, had observed such effects in foure or five Townes to followe their wicked practises, they were persuaded that it was the worke of our God through our meanes, and that we by him might kill and slay whom we would without weapons, and not come neere them. And thereupon when it had happened that they had understanding that any of their enemies had abused us in our iourneys, hearing that we had wrought no revenge with our weapons, and fearing upon some cause the matter should so rest, did come and intreate us that we would bee a meanes to our God that they, as others that had dealt ill with us might in like sort doe, alledging how much it would bee for our credite and profite, as also theirs, and hoping furthermore that we would doe so much at their requests in respect of the friendship we professed them. * * *

* * * * * * * *

' This marvellous accident in all the Countrey wrought so strange opinions of us, that some people could not tell whether to thinke us gods or men, and the rather because that all the space of their sicknes, there was no man of ours knowen to die, or that was specially sicke.'—HAKLUYT'S *Voyages and Discoveries*, vol III, p 278.

² This practice, as existing among the Muskokes, is spoken of by ROMANS. They make their boys ' frequently undergo scratching from head to foot through the skin with broken glass or garfish teeth, so as to make them all in a gore of blood, and then wash them in

cold water; this is with them the *arcanum* against all diseases; but when they design it as punishment to the boys, they dry scratch them, (i. e.), they apply no water for the operation, which renders it very painful."

In the same manner Major CALEB SWAN writes of the practice of that people: "Their mode of correction is singular: if a child require punishment, the mother scratches its legs and thighs with the point of a pin or needle, until it bleeds; some keep the jaw bone of a gar fish, having two teeth, entirely for that purpose.—*Schoolcraft's Indian Tribes*, vol. v.

³ The slowness with which some American fruits and vegetables have come into use among Europeans, contrasts with the rapidity with which some from there have spread into the remotest Indian fields of this country. Supposing the pumpkin an exotic to the new world, to have been brought to the coast of Mexico by the first discoverers, and introduced into the interior from Veracruz by the most probable route, through the capital northward to the river Conchos, down to its junction with the Rio Grande, near the site of Presidio del Norte, where we now deem ourselves to be in this narrative, and in the month of March, 1536, the seed will be found to have traveled, notwithstanding wars, hostile nations and barbarous tribes, through eight degrees of longitude and ten and a half of latitude, at the rate sixty miles a year. Eight summers before, the vegetable had been found in abundance by the soldiers of Narváez at Aute, and not improbably it was known at that time to the natives in nearly every part of the northern continent where the earth was tilled and the vine would grow. The army that the Viceroy sent from Mexico to Cibola in the year 1542, found the melon already there.

CHAPTER XXXI.

OF OUR TAKING THE WAY TO THE MAIZE.

Two days being spent while we tarried, we resolved to go in search of the maize. We did not wish to follow the path leading to where the cattle are, because it is towards the north, and for us very circuitous, since we ever held it certain, that going towards the sunset we must find what we desired.

Thus we took our way, and traversed all the country until coming out at the South sea. Nor was the dread we had of the sharp hunger through which we should have to pass, (as in verity we did, throughout the seventeen days' journey of which the natives spoke,) sufficient to hinder us. During all that time, in ascending by the river, they gave us many coverings of cowhide, but we did not eat of the fruit. Our sustenance each day was about a handful of deer-suet, which we had a long time been used to saving for such trials. Thus we passed the entire journey of seventeen days, and at the close we crossed the river and traveled other seventeen days.

As the sun went down, upon some plains that lie between chains of very great mountains, we found a people who for the third part of the year eat nothing but the powder of straw,¹ and that being the season when we passed, we also had to eat of it until reaching permanent habitations, where was abundance of maize brought together. They gave us a large quantity in grain and flour, pumpkins, beans and shawls of cotton. With all these we loaded our guides, who went back the happiest creatures on earth. We gave thanks to God, our Lord, for having brought us where we had found so much food.

Some houses are of earth, the rest all of cane mats. From this point we marched through more than a hundred leagues of country, and continually found settled domicils with plenty of maize and beans. The people gave us many deer and cotton shawls better than those of New Spain, many beads and certain corals found on the South sea, and fine turquoises that come from the North.² Indeed they gave us every thing they had. To me they gave five emeralds made into arrow-heads, which they use at their singing and dancing. They appeared to be very precious. I asked whence they got these, and they said the stones were brought from some lofty mountains that stand towards the north, where were populous towns and very large houses, and that they were purchased with plumes and the feathers of parrots.

Among this people the women are treated with more decorum than in any part of the Indies we had visited. They wear a shirt of cotton that falls as low as the knee, and over it half sleeves with skirts reaching to the ground, made of dressed deer-skin. It opens in front and is brought close with straps of leather. They soap this with a certain root that cleanses well, by which they are enabled to keep it becomingly. Shoes are worn. The people all came to us that we should touch and bless them, they being very urgent, which we could accomplish only with great labor, for sick and well all wished to go with a benediction. Many times it occurred that some of the women who accompanied us gave birth, and so soon as the children were born the mothers would bring them to us that we should touch and bless them.

These Indians ever accompanied us until they delivered us to others, and all held full faith in our coming from heaven. While traveling we went without food all day until night, and we ate so little as to astonish them. We never felt exhaustion, neither were we in fact at all weary, so inured were we to hardship. We possessed great influence and authority to preserve both we seldom talked with them. The negro was in constant conversation, he informed himself about the ways we wished to take, of the towns there were, and the matters we desired to know.

We passed through many and dissimilar tongues. Our Lord granted us favor with the people who spoke them, for they always understood us, and we them. We questioned them and received their answers by signs, just as if they spoke our language and we theirs, for although we knew six languages, we could not everywhere avail ourselves of them, there being a thousand differences.

Throughout all these countries the people who were at war immediately made friends, that they might come to meet us, and bring what they possessed. In this way we left all the land at peace, and we taught all the inhabitants by signs, which they understood, that in heaven was a Man we called God, who had created the sky and the earth: him we worshiped and had for our master; that we did what he commanded and from his hand came all good; and would they do as we did, all would be well with them. So ready of apprehension we found them, that could we have had the use of language by which to make ourselves perfectly understood, we should have left them all Christians. Thus much we gave them to understand the best we could. And afterward, when the sun rose, they opened their hands together with loud shouting towards the heavens, and then drew them down all over their bodies. They did the same again when the sun went down. They are a people of good condition and substance, capable in any pursuit.¹

¹ "The Apaches make likewise a kind of *esmola* (cracked wheat) or *pinole*, the seed of straw or grass which they tediously gather at harvest time and in small quantities, they not being husbandmen."—*Report of Lt. Col. Cordero in the year 1796.*

The plains spoken of according to the latest maps must be the region between the Sierra of Barragan and the Cordillera of the Andes. According to the ethnographic map of Mexico by Orozco y Berra, the Spaniards in going westward from Presidio del Norte had traversed the northern portion of the territory of the Concho Indians, the southern edge of the Apache, the northern of the Tarauma, the southern of the Opata, and are now entering on the north-eastern end of the Pima Bajo of whom the writer has begun to speak. The route is curving south westwardly, they will soon be upon an extreme branch of the river Yakime

*The *American Journal of Science and Art* for March, 1858, contains an account of the interesting region whence probably came these turquoises, the character of the stone in which such are found, and their chemical elements. The writer, W. P. BLAKE, states that they are got by digging in sandstone or granular porphyry among Los Cerillos, a group of conical peaks in a mountainous tract, lying twenty miles south east of Santa Fé, to the north of the Placer ridges, from which they are separated by the intervening valley of the Galisteo. The Professor describes seemingly the most ancient of the cavities whence are derived these Indian gems, to be much the greatest, and "the work of the aborigines long before the conquest and settlement of the country," and apparently two hundred feet deep with three hundred or more in diameter. The sides around of projecting crag, bear in their fissures a growth of shrubs and trees on the fragments at the bottom, gray with age, are standing pines, the development of a century. Thousands of tons of stone bearing no indication of containing ore, have been broken out of the solid mass and removed.

The largest piece of this "chalchuite," as it is called by the Navajos, picked up by the explorer, measured three-quarters of an inch in length by one in thickness. It is generally found in the lining of seams, though discoverable in nodules and also in the body of the rock; the color is in shades of apple or pea green, passing into blue, the latter perhaps the result of decomposition. The mineral is apparently the result of infiltration. The constituents are nearly the same as those of the Persian turquoise.

Beneath the towering rocks, which on one side overhang the excavation forming a recess where lie an accumulation of ashes that mark numberless camp-fires made by the Indians who still resort there for the coveted gem, is the spot whence the traveler overlooks the great pit covered with ancient growth. Turning north eastwardly, the expanse of plain slopes towards Santa Fé, beyond it rise the lofty peaks of the Stony mountains; on the west and south west the country opens towards the Rio Bravo del Norte, the monotony of the extensive area between, being relieved by the solitary eminences of Zandia and Albuquerque.

Tlaçotetl is the Nahual or Mexican word for precious stone from *tlaçotl* strung and *tell*, stone; but *chalchuitl* defined by MOLINA to be *course or false emerald*, "emeralda basta," appears to be the word in use for stones in general of value. Thus *chalchiuhximalqui* signifies lapidary. The meaning of *chalchi* being nowhere discoverable, it may be thought to be of foreign origin. *Xiuitl*, besides grass, means turquoise; *xiuhtic*, color of turquoise. *Quetzalitzli*, emerald, is from *quetzalli* a rich green plume and *ytz tli* knife-stone, obsidian.

³ Pitchlynn once said in conversation respecting usages existing among Indians similar to those spoken of by Alvar Nuñez:

"In December of the year 1828, then in my twenty-second year, I was sent a commissioner from the Chahtas to the Osages Washasha, to make peace at White hair's village, west of Missouri state, on the Neosho, Clear-water river. A state of war had existed between our nations from time immemorial. There I noticed this method of singing and weeping every morning and eve, a species of worship performed by the men. They sing a mournful melancholy song, growing louder and louder, breaking into a full wild cry. In the same way they sing on going into battle. That such is the custom of the Osages is proverbial everywhere among Indians, and they are the only people I have ever heard of as practicing it. So far as I know their history they have never lived south of the Arkansas though in their war and hunting excursions they may have roamed to Red river, the Okchoma of the Chahta.

"I found the language of signs all over the plains west of the Mississippi, but to the east of the river I do not know that it has ever been in use. It appears to be an almost natural system in which the Indians however strangers to each other express themselves when they meet with great rapidity and fullness.

"From all I have seen and can understand of the Indians who once inhabited the portions of country covered by the southern states of the Union they appear to have been originally worshipers of the sun. The Chahta when he is greatly misbehaved utters the ejaculations: 'When the sun forsakes a man he will do things he never thought to do!' 'The sun is turned against me, therefore have I come to this!' On the garments and tents of some Comanches I once met in an excursion to the western prairies were pictures of the hand, the symbol to me of friendship and greeting. The band had an image of the sun with them which they presented to him when he rose, turned it as he advanced and withdrew at his setting. A speech in council among us was apt to be begun in this way: 'We have come together from different parts and clasped hands.' Over the doors of deserted edifices about the Stony mountains I am told the hand is sometimes found drawn and colored red. I, as an Indian, understand that sign to mean salutation to the sun, and suppose those who placed it there to have been its worshipers.

CHAPTER XXXII.

THE INDIANS GIVE US THE HEARTS OF DEER

In the town where the emeralds were presented to us, the people gave Dorantes over six hundred open hearts of deer.¹ They ever keep a good supply of them for food, and we called the place Pueblo de los Corazones. It is the entrance into many provinces on the South sea.² They who go to look for them and do not enter there, will be lost. On the coast is no maize; the inhabitants eat the powder of rush and of straw, and fish that is caught in the sea from rafts not having canoes. With grass and straw the women cover their nudity.³ They are a timid and dejected people.

We think that near the coast by way of those towns through which we came, are more than a thousand leagues of inhabited country, plentiful of subsistence. Three times the year it is planted with maize and beans. Deer are of three kinds, one the size of the young steer of Spain. There are innumerable houses, such as are called bahios. They have poison from a certain tree the size of the apple. For effect, no more is necessary than to pluck the fruit and moisten the arrow with it, or if there be no fruit, to break a twig and with the milk do the like. The tree is abundant and so deadly that if the leaves be bruised and steeped in some neighboring water, the deer and other animals drinking it soon burst.⁴

We were in this town three days. A day's journey farther was another town, at which the rain fell heavily while we were there, and the river became so swollen we could not cross it, which detained us fifteen days. In this time Castillo saw the buckle of a sword-belt on the neck of an Indian and stitched to it the nail of a horse shoe. He took them, and we asked the native what they were: he answered that they came from heaven. We questioned him further, as to who had brought them thence: they all responded, that certain men who wore beards like us, had come from heaven and arrived at that river; bringing horses, lances, and swords, and that they had lanced two Indians. In a manner of the utmost indifference we could feign, we asked them what had become of those men: they answered us that they had gone to sea, putting their lances beneath the water, and going themselves also under the water; afterwards that they were seen on the surface going towards the sunset. For this we gave many thanks to God our Lord. We had before despaired of ever hearing more of Christians. Even yet we were left in great doubt and anxiety, thinking those people were merely persons who had come by sea on discoveries. However, as we had now such exact information, we made greater speed, and as we advanced on our way, the news of the Christians continually grew. We told the natives that we were going in search of that people, to order them not to kill nor make slaves of them, nor take them from their lands, nor do other injustice. Of this the Indians were very glad.

We passed through many territories and found them all vacant: their inhabitants wandered fleeing among the mountains, without daring to have houses or till the earth for fear of Christians. The sight was one of infinite pain to us, a land very fertile and beautiful, abounding in springs and streams, the hamlets deserted and burned, the people thin and weak, all fleeing or in concealment. As they did not plant, they appeased their keen hunger by eating roots, and the bark of trees. We bore a share in the famine along the whole way; for poorly could these unfortunates provide for us, themselves being so reduced they looked as though they would willingly die. They brought shawls of those they had concealed because of the Christians, presenting them to us; and they related how the Christians, at other times had come through the land destroying and burning the towns, carrying away half the men, and all the women and the boys, while those who had been able to escape were wandering about fugitives. We found them so alarmed they dared not remain anywhere. They would not, nor could they till the earth, but preferred to die rather than live in dread of such cruel usage as they received. Although these showed themselves greatly delighted with us, we feared that on our arrival among those who held the frontier and fought against the Christians, they would treat us badly, and revenge upon us the conduct of their enemies; but when God our Lord was pleased to bring us there, they began to dread and respect us as the others had done, and even somewhat more, at which we no little wondered. Thence it may at once be seen, that to bring all these people to be Christians and to the obedience of the Imperial Majesty, they must be won by kindness, which is a way certain, and no other is.

They took us to a town on the edge of a range of mountains, to which the ascent is over difficult crags. We found many people there collected out of fear of the Christians. They received us well and presented us all they had. They gave us more than two thousand back-loads of maize, which we gave to the distressed and hungered beings who guided us to that place. The next day we dispatched four messengers through the country, as we were accustomed to do, that they should call together all the rest of the Indians at a town distant three days' march. We set out the day after with all the people. The tracks of the Christians and marks where they slept were continually seen. At midday we met our messengers, who told us they had found no Indians, that they were roving and hiding in the forests, fleeing that the Christians might not kill nor make them slaves; the night before, they had observed the Christians from behind trees, and discovered what they were about, carrying away many people in chains.

Those who came with us were alarmed at this intelligence; some returned to spread the news over the land that the Christians were coming; and many more would have followed, had we not forbidden it, and told them to cast aside their fear, when they reassured themselves and were well content. At the time, we had Indians with us belonging a hundred leagues behind, and we were in no condition to discharge them, that they might return to their homes. To encourage them, we staid there that night, the day after we marched and slept on the road. The following day, those whom we had sent forward as messengers, guided us to the place where they had seen Christians. We arrived in the afternoon, and saw at once that they told the truth. We perceived that the persons were mounted, by the stakes to which the horses had been tied.

From this spot, called the river Petutan, to the river to which Diego de Guzmán came, where we heard of Christians,[6] may be as many as eighty leagues; thence to the town, where the rains overtook us, twelve leagues, and that is twelve leagues from the South sea. Throughout this region, wheresoever the mountains extend, we saw clear traces of gold and lead, iron, copper, and other metals. Where the settled habitations are, the climate is hot; even in January, the weather is very warm. Thence toward the meridian, the country unoccupied to the North sea, is unhappy and sterile. There we underwent great and incredible hunger. Those who inhabit and wander over it, are a race of evil inclination and most cruel customs. The people of the fixed residences and those beyond, regard silver and gold with indifference, nor can they conceive of any use for them

¹ These passages are translated from an unpublished work by FRIAR BARTOLOMÉ DE LAS CASAS

"The hearts I incline to think are used by the people of these Provinces as offerings rather than for food. It is stated by those who have written, though not by Cabeça de Vaca in his personal narrative, that when the Spaniards arrived at the town, the people of the village were making merry in the celebration of a festival thus described

"They bring numerous deer, wolves, hares and birds before a great idol, playing on many flutes with other instruments they have, and opening the animals through the middle take out the hearts, which they suspend about the neck of the image, wetting it with the flowing blood. It is certain that in all this Province of the Valley of Sonora the only offering made, was the hearts of brutes. There are two occasions of festivity, one at seedtime, the other at harvest, when such hearts are offered with great rejoicing, ceremonial and devotion * * *

A friar, whom I knew well, Marcos de Niça of the Order of Saint Francis, on coming to Sonora entered the chief and principal town, where the lord of the valley came out to receive him, and extending his hands towards him rubbed them everywhere over his own person. Passing that place, in another town of the Valley, six leagues distant, in the direction of Civola was the principal oratory where Chicamasth, king and lord of the country went to make his offerings. In a very high temple of stone laid in mortar (of which we made mention when writing of temples) was a statue covered with blood, having the hearts of numerous animals about its neck. Near the stone image were many bodies of men placed about the walls, with the brains and entrails taken out. These must have been the persons of the former lords of the valley, and that place their sepulchre." *Historia Apologetica de las Indias Occidentales.* Tomo III Cap 168.

² BENAVIDES thus writes of this Town of Hearts in the year 1630

Leaving the town of Chiametla and journeying eighty leagues to the north coasting and keeping ever next to the South sea, the traveler strikes the Valley of Señora which is sixty leagues long by ten wide. Through the midst passes a very broad river, having upon its banks a country of fruitful fields and many towns. The first town is called Corazones, for the many hearts of deer that the people there *upon a time* gave to ours. The place consists of seven hundred well arranged houses the temperature is delightful." *Memorial* p 101.

The Indian name of the town is Tekora. The people are the Névome, a nation of the Pima. The language they speak is the Heve or Eudeve, in which a grammar and dictionary exist, composed by a Spanish missionary.

Father Alegre in writing of the march of Coronado from the south to invade Cíbola says

"In May the force left Culiacán, and in four days' journey arrived at the river Petatlán thence in three at the Zuaque, called then Cinaloa From here the General sent ten cavalry, that with double speed they should come to the Arroyo de Cedros, (Cedar stream) whence they should go to the north-east by an opening there is through the mountains in that direction. Following this course they arrived at the stream and valley of Corazones, a name given by the companions of Alvaro Nuñez. This rivulet we think may be that which running from west to east, empties into a stream known as Mulatos on the bank of which is now the town of Tecora. What is certain is, the valley of Corazones, and the river were on the confines of Sinaloa and Sonora, as all accounts state. In the manuscripts we read that a town was here founded with forty seven Spaniards, which was called Pueblo de los Corazones, of which Diego de Alcaraz was Alcalde and Chief magistrate, a man haughty and inhuman." *Historia de la Compañia de Jesus en Nueva España por el Padre* FRANCISCO JAVIER ALEGRE Tomo I, p 237.

"Gen Carlos P Stone has made for me an elaborate map of a wide extent of this country, from his personal observations and surveys From his letters, full of exact information, I take the liberty to offer excerpta

"The coast of Sonora, from a short distance north of Guaymas to the mouth of the Colorado, is a picture of barrenness. The only vegetable substances that I know of growing in that region are a root called by the natives *sava* somewhat resembling the Jerusalem artichoke, and some species of the cactus. The Indians referred to were the Ceris. They are now much reduced in numbers and live almost exclusively on fish. They build very curious rafts, forming them of bundles of wild cane lashed together skillfully, giving them the shape of a long canoe, but making them solid in order to avail themselves as much as possible of the buoyancy of the cane. The women cover their nakedness by mats of grass. The grass is twisted into cords. They wear two mats, one before and one behind, held in place by a cord run through the two and fastened over the hips

Since the historian of Cinaloa a century later than Alvar Nuñez, has represented that these inhabitants of the coast of Sonora, the Ceri doubtless, were in a state of savagery greater than that of the human race anywhere else, it may be well to repeat briefly what he describes, as a comparison of their condition with that of the Mariame with whom we have just been made acquainted on the shores of Texas, under nearly the same parallels.

These people of the western shore lived among the sands, subsisting on little animals, locusts and reptiles, with the grass seed that grows below tide water. Fish is their bread, which dried with salt, is their sole food the greater part of the year. The pitahaya covers districts two, four and even six leagues in extent. The best fruit comes in dry soil, like the coast, where rain seldom falls. The season of this prickly pear lasts two months.

If the native should desire shelter from rain, he gathers an armful of long straw or stalks, ties it at the top, then seating himself, opens and puts it over his head so that it covers his person like a thatch roof. This for him is an impervious cap, coat, and field camp, though the rain should pour the night through. His protection is no better against the burning rays of the sun as they fall in this climate. A few branches of trees driven into the ground afford a shade under which these Indians live. There is no contrivance for the naked body against winds. In some severe nights of December and January they make fires, sitting near on the cold ground. In this way they travel the desert building fires in row a little way apart, and reposing a while at each. If a single person only have this fancy to journey four or six leagues of a night however rigorous the weather, he uses a burning brand applying it near the stomach while the rest of the body goes free to the air.

This remarkable people as well as those living in the rough districts among briars and bushes, or in much smaller number than the husbandmen of the country, to whose towns they resort in common, to exchange fish for maize when it is in season. Although they live in this manner, they are of greater stature than any of the people of New Spain or even of Europe, are quick and nimble in their movement, and, what appears strange, are very corpulent. On that poor diet they survive even into decrepitude; yet are they more content than if they possessed the abundance and accommodation of palaces. Such is the early testimony of Ribas, Lib. 1. Cap. II. p. 7.

Alvar Nuñez remarked the symmetry and great size of the natives among whom he resided on the coast of Texas even the comeliness of one of the nations as well as their extraordinary hardihood and capa-bits of abstaining from food. These result he believes both from nature and habit. In their circumstances he declares them to be a cheerful people. With more limited resources for obtaining aliment, they undoubtedly experienced a greater extremity of hunger than those of the west. Like them they went entirely naked, and got intoxicated together, with every opportunity.

Destroying female children at birth, obtaining wives from the enemy, waging continual war, wearing no clothes, gaining a precarious subsistence by unceasing exertion, with the single superstition of dreams, preeminently entitle the Mariame and the Yeguaz, who appear to be their congeners, to represent the state characterized as the most savage. They acknowledged no kin but mother and brother, perhaps they discovered none, though they held that the relationship was too close within the nation to permit sexual intercourse, even had female infants been permitted to live. It was a nation with a full knowledge, it seems, of that organization which holds a community of red men together, and which it respected.

No improvement could take place in the condition of these people without a change of territory, or an invention which should increase the resources for food. When this stage is attained and to an extent that renders a wandering life no longer imperative, the inhabitants gravitate into villages at a source of supply, perhaps, for the convenience of a brook, a good landing place from a canoe, shelter from high winds, or a sufficiency of fuel. Principal men must appear. The first superfluous food will be in their cabins, the first female babe that is spared will be a chief's. The affections assert their power. We have read that they are supreme in the island of Malhado.

The daughter in the beginning finds the natural protector and tutor of her children in her brother; his line is perpetuated through the only safe channel from their common mother through her, and takes his name as that of the clan of which she and her female posterity are the stock, the males being absorbed in other stocks of the nation. At the different villages the course of affairs is alike. Corn plant, tortoise and White Buck are severally the guardians by blood, each of his sister's children. Thus the earliest form of society might be established. In this dawn of change, should another sister exist and another brother, we may suppose a second stock to arise again under a natural protector. The lines cannot mingle, for the female affinity, and the stocks are deemed brothers.

How few and how slight the ties that held together the Mariame! Differences of language may have kept the nation from joining other people the love of strife may have hindered them, even the share of contiguous dwellings, in the absence of better reason, may have been sufficiently abhorrent to each other to keep them asunder. Nevertheless, look where we may, we shall not find an instance of a republic more simple and free than this wild one that, in the first condition of society, sprang up by the mud marshes and chaparals of the Texan lagoons.

"The paragraph just closed appears to be in advance of the journey and to belong farther on.

Four nations of the Zuaque are spoken of by Rivas as being the principal seated on its shores. At the upper end, where the river flows from the mountains of Topia, the confine of Florida with the west, are the Cinoloa, six leagues below them lies to us the wild and dreaded Jeguas with their allies, begin to occupy the country farther down, the Terce Cuzque commence, having settlements along for ten leagues and, finally four leagues below them, and there eleven leagues to the sea, are the mild and gentle Ahome with their neighbors. The river takes its names from those of the nations by which it passes.

Besides their enjoyment of the water, the natives take abundance of mullet from it, bream and other fish that breed there, as well as kinds more numerous that ascend from the sea. They come over the bar by the mouth in the season proper to them for casting their spawn, remaining to sport in fresh water until about summer when the river goes down. This is the principal fishing season. Then the people of the towns, bringing great bundles of bushes, gather about the holes and pools, beat the water; when the fishes in the depths becoming intoxicated from the sap, ascend to the surface, and are taken. Persons receive no harm from the poison in eating them.'

In Corizones says TARAHITO is gently poison used on arrows. From what was witnessed of its operation and effects no worse can be found. We understand it to be the milk of a small tree like mastich, growing in flats and sterile ground.

"This account appears to confound the arrival of two expeditions of Spaniards at the river Petatchitla, twenty leagues north of the Petatlan. When Guzman crossed there in the year 1532 on his way to the north, the natives were observed to wear iron nails strung about the neck and arms for ornament and to possess the blades of knives and swords. On investigation it was ascertained that Hurtado who had been sent by Cortes on discoveries had here been killed with his party of twenty men while they slept, those only in the vessel being supposed to escape.—HERRERA, D. N. Ld. 1 Cap. 7

The Temochula or Temotchala on modern maps is the river Ahome, the Petatlán is the Cinaloa.

⁶ In the year 1532, the Governor of New Galicia marched northward in quest of seven cities of which he had heard, and a great river four or five leagues in width that emptied into the South sea. He came to the river Yakémi, crossed it, and having tried the valor of the in habitants, he returned to Colicán.—HERRERA, *Dec* V, *Lib* I, *Cap* 8

CHAPTER XXXIII.

WE SEE TRACES OF CHRISTIANS

When we saw sure signs of Christians, and heard how near we were to them, we gave thanks to God our Lord, for having chosen to bring us out of a captivity so melancholy and wretched. The delight we felt let each one conjecture when he shall remember the length of time we were in that country, the suffering and perils we underwent. That night I entreated my companions that one of them should go back three days' journey after the Christians who were moving about over the country, where we had given assurance of protection. Neither of them received this proposal well, excusing themselves because of weariness and exhaustion; and although either might have done better than I, being more youthful and athletic, yet seeing their unwillingness, the next morning I took the negro with eleven Indians, and following the Christians by their trail, I traveled ten leagues, passing three villages, at which they had slept.

The day after I overtook four of them on horseback, who were astonished at the sight of me, so strangely habited as I was, and in company with Indians. They stood staring at me a length of time, so confounded that they neither hailed me nor drew near to make an inquiry¹ I bade them take me to their chief: accordingly we went together half a league to the place where was Diego de Alcaraz, their captain.

After we had conversed, he stated to me that he was completely undone; he had not been able in a long time to take any Indians, he knew not which way to turn, and his men had well begun to experience hunger and fatigue. I told him of Castillo and Dorantes, who were behind, ten leagues off, with a multitude that conducted us. He thereupon sent three cavalry to them, with fifty of the Indians who accompanied him. The negro returned to guide them, while I remained. I asked the Christians to give me a certificate of the year, month and day, I arrived there, and of the manner of my coming, which they accordingly did. From this river to the town of the Christians, named San Miguel, within the government of the province called New Galicia, are thirty leagues

¹ "They found Captain Lazaro de Çebreros with three mounted men in the Oneclos on the road to Tzinaloa by the river Petatlán." Padre BEAUMONT. He mistook the captain and doubtless meant to write the name of Alcaraz.

CHAPTER XXXIV.

OF SENDING FOR THE CHRISTIANS

Five days having elapsed, Andrés Dorantes and Alonzo del Castillo arrived with those who had been sent after them. They brought more than six hundred persons of that community, whom the Christians had driven into the forests, and who had wandered in concealment over the land. Those who accompanied us so far, had drawn them out, and given them to the Christians, who thereupon dismissed all the others they had brought with them. Upon their coming to where I was, Alcaraz begged that we would summon the people of the towns on the margin of the river, who straggled about under cover of the woods, and order them to fetch us something to eat. This last was unnecessary, the Indians being ever diligent to bring us all they could. Directly we sent out messengers to call them, when there came six hundred souls, bringing us all the maize in their possession. They fetched it in certain pots, closed with clay, which they had concealed in the earth. They brought us whatever else they had; but we, wishing only to have the provision, gave the rest to the Christians, that they might divide among themselves. After this we had many high words with them; for they wished to make slaves of the Indians we brought.

In consequence of the dispute, we left at our departure many bows of Turkish shape we had along with us and many pouches. The five arrows with the points of emerald were forgotten among others, and we lost them. We gave the Christians a store of robes of cowhide and other things we brought. We found it difficult to induce the Indians to return to their dwellings, to feel no apprehension and plant maize. They were willing to do nothing until they had gone with us and delivered us into the hands of other Indians, as had been the custom; for if they returned without doing so, they were afraid they should die, and going with us, they feared neither Christians nor lances. Our countrymen became jealous at this, and caused their interpreter to tell the Indians that we were of them, and for a long time we had been lost; that they were the lords of the land who must be obeyed and served, while we were persons of mean condition and small force. The Indians cared little or nothing for what was told them; and conversing among themselves said the Christians lied: that we had come whence the sun rises, and they whence it goes down; we healed the sick, they killed the sound; that we had come naked and barefooted, while they had arrived in clothing and on horses with lances; that we were not covetous of anything, but all that was given to us, we directly turned to give, remaining with nothing; that the others had the only purpose to rob whomsoever they found, bestowing nothing on any one

In this way they spoke of all matters respecting us, which they enhanced by contrast with matters concerning the others, delivering their response through the interpreter of the Spaniards. To other Indians they made this known by means of one among them through whom they understood us. Those who speak that tongue we discriminately call Primahaitu, which is like saying Vasconyados.[1] We found it in use over more than four hundred leagues of our travel, without another over that whole extent. Even to the last, I could not convince the Indians that we were of the Christians; and only with great effort and solicitation we got them to go back to their residences. We ordered them to put away apprehension, establish their towns, plant and cultivate the soil.

From abandonment the country had already grown up thickly in trees. It is, no doubt, the best in all these Indias, the most prolific and plenteous in provisions. Three times in the year it is planted. It produces great variety of fruit, has beautiful rivers, with many other good waters. There are ores with clear traces of gold and silver. The people are well disposed: they serve such Christians as are their friends, with great good will. They are comely, much more so than the Mexicans. Indeed, the land needs no circumstance to make it blessed.

The Indians, at taking their leave told us they would do what we commanded, and would build their towns, if the Christians would suffer them; and this I say and affirm most positively, that if they have not done so, it is the fault of the Christians.

After we had dismissed the Indians in peace, and thanked them for the toil they had supported with us, the Christians with subtlety sent us on our way under charge of Zeburos, an Alcalde, attended by two men. They took us through forests and solitudes, to hinder us from intercourse with the natives, that we might neither witness nor have knowledge of the act they would commit. It is but an instance of how frequently men are mistaken in their aims; we set about to preserve the liberty of the Indians and thought we had secured it, but the contrary appeared, for the Christians had arranged to go and spring upon those we had sent away in peace and confidence. They executed their plan as they had designed, taking us through the woods, wherein for two days we were lost, without water and without way. Seven of our men died of thirst, and we all thought to have perished. Many friendly to the Christians in their company, were unable to reach the place where we got water the second night, until the noon of next day. We traveled twenty-five leagues, little more or less, and reached a town of friendly Indians. The Alcalde left us there, and went on three leagues farther to a town called Culiaçan where was Melchior Diaz, principal Alcalde and Captain of the Province.

¹ This name seemingly comes from these words, taken from a dictionary in MS of the Hève or Eudeve, a dialect of the Pima, and

nearest of kin to the Ópata, composed by a Spanish missionary. No, *pima* nothing, *pima haitu* Ques What, Ai? Ans *Pima haitu*, (nihil) Time has shown the wide extent of country over which the Pima and its affinities were spoken. For an Andaluz to make such concession to the original diffusion of the Vascuence is no little, and has come near to equaling the patriotic pretensions since made for the language by Larramendi.

CHAPTER XXXV

THE CHIEF ALCALDE RECEIVES US KINDLY THE NIGHT WE ARRIVE

The Alcalde Mayor knew of the expedition, and hearing of our return, he immediately left that night and came to where we were. He wept with us, giving praises to God our Lord for having extended over us so great care. He comforted and entertained us hospitably. In behalf of the Governor, Nuño de Guzmán and himself, he tendered all that he had, and the service in his power. He showed much regret for the seizure, and the injustice we had received from Alcaraz and others. We were sure, had he been present, what was done to the Indians and to us would never have occurred.

The night being passed, we set out the next day for Anhacan.[1] The chief Alcalde besought us to tarry there, since by so doing we could be of eminent service to God and your Majesty; the deserted land was without tillage and everywhere badly wasted, the Indians were fleeing and concealing themselves in the thickets, unwilling to occupy their towns; we were to send and call them, commanding them in behalf of God and the King, to return to live in the vales and cultivate the soil.

To us this appeared difficult to effect. We had brought no native of our own, nor of those who accompanied us according to custom, intelligent in these affairs. At last we made the attempt with two captives, brought from that country, who were with the Christians we first overtook. They had seen the people who conducted us, and learned from them the great authority and command we carried and exercised throughout those parts, the wonders we had worked, the sick we had cured, and the many things besides we had done. We ordered that they with others of the town, should go together to summon the hostile natives among the mountains and of the river Petachan,² where we had found the Christians, and say to them they must come to us, that we wished to speak with them. For the protection of the messengers, and as a token to the others of our will, we gave them a gourd of those we were accustomed to bear in our hands, which had been our principal insignia and evidence of rank, and with this they went away.

The Indians were gone seven days, and returned with three chiefs of those revolted among the ridges, who brought with them fifteen men, and presented us beads, turquoises, and feathers. The messengers said they had not found the people of the river where we appeared, the Christians having again made them run away into the mountains. Melchior Diaz told the interpreter to speak to the natives for us, to say to them we came in the name of God, who is in heaven, that we had traveled about the world many years,¹ telling all the people we found that they should believe in God and serve him; for he was the master of all things on the earth, benefiting and rewarding the virtuous, and to the bad giving perpetual punishment of fire, that when the good die, he takes them to heaven, where none ever die, nor feel cold, nor hunger, nor thirst, nor any inconvenience whatsoever, but the greatest enjoyment possible to conceive: that those who will not believe in him nor obey his commands, he casts beneath the earth into the company of demons, and into a great fire which is never to go out, but always torment: that, over this, if they desired to be Christians and serve God in the way we required, the Christians would cherish them as brothers and behave towards them very kindly: that we would command they give no offense nor take them from their territories, but be their great friends. If the Indians did not do this, the Christians would treat them very hardly, carrying them away as slaves into other lands.

They answered through the interpreter that they would be true Christians and serve God. Being asked to whom they sacrifice and offer worship, from whom they ask rain for their corn-fields and health for themselves, they answered of a man that is in heaven. We inquired of them his name, and they told us Aguar; and they believed he created the whole world, and the things in it. We returned to question them as to how they knew this: they answered their fathers and grandfathers had told them, that from distant time had come their knowledge, and they knew the rain and all good things were sent to them by him. We told them that the name of him of whom they spoke we called Dios; and if they would call him so, and would worship him as we directed, they would find their welfare. They responded that they well understood, and would do as we said. We ordered them to come down from the mountains in confidence and peace, inhabit the whole country and construct their houses: among these they should build one for God, at its entrance place a cross like that which we had there present; and when Christians came among them, they should go out to receive them with crosses in their hands, without bows or any arms, and take them to their dwellings, giving of what they have to eat, and the Christians would do them no injury, but be their friends; and the Indians told us they would do as we had commanded.

The Captain having given them shawls and entertained them, they returned, taking the two captives who had been used as emissaries. This occurrence took place before the Notary, in the presence of many witnesses.

---

¹ The two last words are omitted in the second edition.

Spelled Petatan in the second edition. A region of country on the south nearly to this river Petatlan had formed a part of the extreme northern dominion of Montezuma, and where the Mexican was spoken. The name appears to be made from *petate*, in that language a sort of matting, or better, it is a contraction of *petatlan*, among mats. Anciently tribute appears to have been paid in this commodity to the metropolis.

² In the first edition, nine years.

CHAPTER XXXVI.

OF BUILDING CHURCHES IN THAT LAND.

As soon as these Indians went back all those of that province who were friendly to the Christians and had heard of us, came to visit us, bringing beads and feathers. We commanded them to build churches and put crosses in them: to that time none had been raised, and we made them bring their principal men to be baptized.

Then the Captain made a covenant with God, not to invade nor consent to invasion, nor to enslave any of that country and people, to whom we had guarantied safety, that this he would enforce and defend until your Majesty and the Governor Nuño de Guzmán, or the Viceroy in your name, should direct what would be most for the service of God and your Highness.

When the children had been baptized, we departed for the town of San Miguel. So soon as we arrived, April 1,* 1536, came Indians, who told us many people had come down from the mountains and were living in the vales, that they had made churches and crosses, doing all we had required. Each day we heard how these things were advancing to a full improvement.

* April 1

Fifteen days of our residence having passed, Alcaraz got back with the Christians from the incursion, and they related to the Captain the manner in which the Indians had come down and peopled the plain; that the towns were inhabited which had been tenantless and deserted, the residents, coming out to receive them with crosses in their hands, had taken them to their houses, giving of what they had, and the Christians had slept among them over night. They were surprised at a thing so novel, but as the natives said they had been assured of safety, it was ordered that they should not be harmed, and the Christians took friendly leave of them.

God of his infinite mercy is pleased that in the days of your Majesty, under your might and dominion, these nations should come to be thoroughly and voluntarily subject to the Lord, who has created and redeemed us. We regard this as certain, that your Majesty is he who is destined to do so much, not difficult to accomplish; for in the two thousand leagues we journeyed on land and in boats on water, and in that we traveled unceasingly for ten months after coming out of captivity, we found neither sacrifices nor idolatry.

In the time, we traversed from sea to sea; and from information gathered with great diligence there may be a distance from one to another at the widest part of two thousand leagues, and we learned that on the coast of the South sea there are pearls and great riches, and the best and all the most opulent countries are near there.

We were in the village of San Miguel until the fifteenth day of May.* The cause of so long a detention was, that from thence to the city of Compostela, where the Governor Nuño de Guzmán resided, are a hundred leagues of country, entirely devastated and filled with enemies, where it was necessary we should have protection. Twenty mounted men went with us for forty leagues, and after that six Christians accompanied us, who had with them five hundred slaves. Arrived at Compostela, the Governor entertained us graciously and gave us of his clothing for our use. I could not wear any for some time, nor could we sleep anywhere else but on the ground. After ten or twelve days we left for Mexico, and were all along on the way well entertained by Christians. Many came out on the roads to gaze at us, giving thanks to God for having saved us from so many calamities. We arrived at Mexico on Sunday, the day before the vespers of Saint Iago,† where we were handsomely treated by the Viceroy and the Marquis del Valle, and welcomed with joy. They gave us clothing and proffered whatsoever they had. On the day of Saint Iago was a celebration, and a joust of reeds with bulls-

* May 15 † July 25 1536

¹ The distance these Christians traveled in going from one sea to the other, at the place they came out appeared to them two hundred leagues, which they so declared at the town of San Miguel, with the other matter here stated, on oath before a notary, the 15th day of May.—HERRERA

CHAPTER XXXVII.

OF WHAT OCCURRED WHEN I WISHED TO RETURN.

When we had rested two months in Mexico, I desired to return to these kingdoms; and being about to embark in the month of October, a storm came on capsizing the ship and she was lost. In consequence I resolved to remain through the winter, because in those parts it is a boisterous season for navigation. After that had gone by Dorantes and I left Mexico, about Lent, to take shipping at Vera Cruz. We remained waiting for a wind until Palm Sunday, when we went on board, and were detained fifteen days longer for a wind. The ship leaked so much that I quitted her, and went to one of two other vessels that were ready to sail, but Dorantes remained in her.

On the tenth day of April* the three ships left the port, and sailed one hundred and fifty leagues. Two of them leaked a great deal, and one night the vessel I was in lost their company. Their pilots and masters, as afterwards appeared, dared not proceed with the other vessels so without telling us of their intentions, or letting us know aught of them, put back to the port they had left. We pursued our voyage, and on the fourth day of May† we entered the harbor of Havana, in the island of Cuba. We remained waiting for the other vessels, believing them to be on their way, until the second of June,* when we sailed, in much fear of falling in with Frenchmen, as they had a few days before taken three Spanish vessels. Having arrived at the Island of Bermuda, we were struck by one of those storms that overtake those who pass there, according to what they state who sail thither. All one night we considered ourselves lost; and we were thankful that when the morning was come, the storm ceased, and we could go on our course.

At the end of twenty-nine days after our departure from Havana, we had sailed eleven hundred leagues, which are said to be thence to the town of the Azores. The next morning, passing by the Island called Cuervo, we fell in with a French ship. At noon she began to follow, bringing with her a caravel captured from the Portuguese, and gave us chase. In the evening we saw nine other sail; but they were so distant we could not make out whether they were Portuguese or of those that pursued us. At night the Frenchman was within shot of a lombard from our ship, and we stole away from our course in the dark to evade him, and this we did three or four times. He approached so near that he saw us and fired. He might have taken us, or, at his option could leave us until the morning. I remember with gratitude to the Almighty when the sun rose, and we found ourselves close with

* June 2   1537

the Frenchman, that near us were the nine sail we saw the evening before, which we now recognized to be of the fleet of Portugal. I gave thanks to our Lord for escape from the troubles of the land and perils of the sea. The Frenchman, so soon as he discovered their character, let go the caravel he had seized with a cargo of negroes and kept as a prize, to make us think he was Portuguese, that we might wait for him. When he cast her off, he told the pilot and the master of her, that we were French and under his convoy. This said, sixty oars were put out from his ship, and thus with these and sail he commenced to flee, moving so fast it was hardly credible. The caravel being let go, went to the galleon, and informed the commander that the other ship and ours were French. As we drew nigh the galleon, and the fleet saw we were coming down upon them, they made no doubt we were, and putting themselves in order of battle, bore up for us, and when near we hailed them. Discovering that we were friends, they found that they were mocked in permitting the corsair to escape, by being told that we were French and of his company.

Four caravels were sent in pursuit. The galleon drawing near, after the salutation from us, the commander Diego de Silveira, asked whence we came and what merchandise we carried; when we answered that we came from New Spain, and were loaded with silver and gold. He asked us how much there might be; the Captain told him we carried three hundred thousand Castillanos. The Commander replied: "Boa fee, que venis muito ricos, pero traçedes muy ruin Navio y muyto ruin Antilleria, ó fide puta can á reneyado Frāces, y que bon bocado perdio, bota deus. Ora sus pois vos avedes escapado, seguime, y non vos apartedes de mi, que cō ajuda de deus en vos porne en Castila."[1]

After a little time, the caravels that pursued the Frenchman returned, for plainly he moved too fast for them; they did not like either, to leave the fleet, which was guarding three ships that came laden with spices. Thus we reached the island of Terceira, where we reposed fifteen days, taking refreshment and awaiting the arrival of another ship coming with a cargo from India, the companion of the three of which the armada was in charge. The time having run out, we left that place with the fleet, and arrived at the port of Lisbon on the ninth of August,[k] in the afternoon of the day of our master Saint Lawrence, in the year one thousand five hundred and thirty-seven.

That what I have stated in my foregoing narrative is true, I subscribe with my name.

*August 8   1537

The relation whence this is taken, is signed with the name of Cabeça de Vaca, and bears the impress of his escutcheon

¹ The words are in Portuguese "In honest truth you come very rich, although you bring a very sorry ship and a still poorer artillery. By Heaven, that renegade whoreson Frenchman has lost a good mouthful. Now that you have escaped, follow me, and do not leave me that I may, with God's help, deliver you in Spain."

CHAPTER XXXVIII.

OF WHAT BECAME OF THE OTHERS WHO WENT TO INDIAS.

Since giving this circumstantial account of events attending the voyage to Florida, the invasion, and our going out thence, until the arrival in these realms, I desire to state what became of the ships and of the people who remained with them. I have not before touched on this, as we were uninformed until coming to New Spain, where we found many of the persons, and others here in Castilla, from whom we learned everything to the latest particular.

At the time we left, one of the ships had already been lost on the breakers, and the three others were in considerable danger, having nearly a hundred souls on board and few stores. Among the persons were ten married women, one of whom had told the Governor many things that afterwards befel him on the voyage. She cautioned him before he went inland not to go, as she was confident that neither he nor any going with him could ever escape; but should any one come back from that country, the Almighty must work great wonders in his behalf, though she believed few or none would return. The Governor said that he and his followers were going to fight and conquer nations and countries wholly unknown, and in subduing them he knew that many would be slain; nevertheless, that those who survived would be fortunate, since from what he had understood of the opulence of that land, they must become very rich. And further he begged her to inform him whence she learned those things that had passed, as well as those she spoke of, that were to come: she replied that in Castilla a Moorish woman of Hornachos had told them to her, which she had stated to us likewise before we left Spain, and while on the passage many things happened in the way she foretold.

After the Governor had made Caravallo, a native of Cuenca de Huete, his lieutenant and commander of the vessels and people, he departed, leaving orders that all diligence should be used to repair on board, and take the direct course to Pánuco, keeping along the shore closely examining for the harbor, and having found it, the vessels should enter there and await our arrival. And the people state, that when they had betaken themselves to the ships, all of them looking at that woman, they distinctly heard her say to the females, that well, since their husbands had gone inland, putting their persons in so great jeopardy, their wives should in no way take more account of them, but ought soon to be looking after whom they would marry, and that she should do so. She did accordingly: she and others married, or became the concubines of those who remained in the ships.

After we left, the vessels made sail, taking their course onward; but not finding the harbor, they returned. Five leagues below* the place at which we debarked, they found the port, the same we discovered when we saw the Spanish cases containing dead bodies, which were of Christians. Into this haven and along this coast, the three ships passed with the other ship that came from Cuba, and the brigantine, looking for us nearly a year, and not finding us, they went to New Spain.

The port of which we speak is the best in the world. At the entrance are six fathoms of water and five near the shore. It runs up into the land seven or eight leagues. The bottom is fine white sand. No sea breaks upon it nor boisterous storm, and it can contain many vessels. Fish is in great plenty. There are a hundred leagues to Havana, a town of Christians in Cuba, with which it bears north and south. The north-east wind ever prevails and vessels go from one to the other, returning in a few days, for the reason that they sail either way with it on the quarter.

As I have given account of the vessels, it may be well that I state who are, and from what parts of these kingdoms come, the persons whom our Lord has been pleased to release from these troubles. The first is Alonzo del Castillo Maldonado, native of Salamanca, son of Doctor Castillo and Doña Aldonça Maldonado; the second is Andrés Dorantes, son of Pablo Dorantes, native of Béjar, and citizen of Gibraleon. The third is Alvar Nuñez Cabeça de Vaca, son of Francisco de

---

* This "below" should be "above."

Vera, and grandson of Pedro de Vera who conquered the Canaries, and his mother was Doña Tereça Cabeça de Vaca, native of Xeréz de la Frontera. The fourth, called Estevanico, is an Arabian black, native of Açamor.[1]

The End

The present tract was imprinted in the very magnificent, noble and very ancient City of Zamora, by the honored residents Augustin de Paz and Juan Picardo, partners, printers of books, at the cost and outlay of the virtuous Juan Pedro Musetti, book merchant of Medina del Campo, having been finished the sixth day of the month of October, in the year one thousand five hundred and forty two of the birth of our Saviour Jesus Christ.

[1] The reader who follows this strange tale to its conclusion, will desire to learn more of those who had escaped the final disaster. After they reached Mexico, and before their separation the survivors united in giving an account to the *Audiencia* of Española respecting the loss of the army and what attended the individuals who survived it. They laid before the Viceroy at his request a map of the country and the course they had traversed.

Following upon this, a single trace can be discovered of Captain Castillo. Among the cedulas for the government of New Spain is one issued the 25th day of July 1540* to the Viceroy on the memorial of Alonso Castillo Maldonado, resident of the city of Mexico. He having stated that one half the town of Teguacan is held by him in *encomi-*

* *Recopila. en Mejico* 1 63

cada, and the other half is in the king and that the Indians might well enough pay a higher tribute than the one at which they are rated asks that it may be increased, the Royal Council thereupon recommend that the tribute be assessed anew, and conformed to the state and condition of the inhabitants.

In April of the year 1537 Andrés Dorantes sailed for Spain. The ship in which he took passage being found unseaworthy put back, and Mendoça hearing of the return to Veracruz, invited him to the capital. The captain on his arrival was offered a mounted troop, to go in company with some religious fathers and retrace on discoveries the region of country from which he had issued the season before. On hearing the project of Mendoça, and discovering that the object was for the divine as well as the royal service he joyfully received the appointment. The slave Estevanico whom the owner had parted with to the Viceroy before going down to the coast, was to be employed in exploring for the advance of an enterprise then in the course of preparation for the north.*

A letter in the *Historia de los Indias de Nueva España* by Padre Motolinia dated the 24th day of February of the year 1541, dedicating the work to Pimentel, fifth count of Benevente introduces the bearer as one of those who had escaped the destruction attending the army of Narváez, and could inform him more at large in respect of a wandering and houseless race of men, the Chichimecas, about whom the writer speaks.

* Letter of Mendoça to the king 10th of December 1537.

APPENDIX

I

PETITIONS OF NARVAEZ TO THE KING OF SPAIN WITH NOTES OF CONCESSIONS MADE TO HIM BY THE COUNCIL OF INDIAS FOR THE CONQUEST OF FLORIDA

Originals in the Archivo de Indias at Sevilla

SACRED CÆSAREAN CATHOLIC MAJESTY

I, Pamfilo de Narváez, kiss the royal hands and declare, what may be known to Your Highness, that being ordered to go to New Spain, the greater part of my property was lost, and I was imprisoned and detained five years. Since for twenty-six years I have borne arms in the conquest of all those regions. I entreat Your Majesty will be well pleased to requite me in New Spain, in the manner that is customary with those who have long served. In so doing Your Highness will confer much good and favor on one who has in view the royal interest.

S C C M

Inasmuch as I, Pamfilo de Narváez, have ever had and still have the intention of serving God and Your Majesty, I desire to go in person with my means to a certain country on the main of the Ocean Sea. I propose chiefly to traffic with the natives of the coast, and to take thither religious men and ecclesiastics approved of your royal Council of the Indias, that they may make known and plant the Christian Faith. I shall observe fully what your Council require and ordain to the ends of serving God and Your Highness, and for the good of your subjects. I will carry new persons thither from these your realms of Castilla, Aragon and Germany, without unpeopling other isles of Spaniards and Indians.

I entreat Your Majesty may please to order the Very Reverend President and Council of Indias to take into early consideration the heads and conditions which I venture to suggest, and that they approve them with the emendations and assents which they find most conducive to the service of God and to your own. A grave responsibility rests on the royal conscience, if by delay the conversion of those natives to our holy Catholic Faith should be suspended, and the fruit withheld that is due to the royal patrimony and to your subjects.

I propose to undertake this in person, with my experience in those countries, and when the occasion shall present itself, to the extent of my property, which, to God be the praise, I have to employ in that enterprise, and am ready to make manifest when that shall become necessary.

S. C. C. M.

I, Panfilo Narvaez, native of these your kingdoms, and resident of the Island of Fernandina, presented a petition to your very high Council in Toledo, proposing to serve Your Majesty by the exploration, conquest and populating of certain lands in the Ocean Sea, asking that the subjugation of the countries there are from the Rio de Palmas to Florida might be given me, where I would explore, conquer, populate and discover all there is to be found of Florida in those parts, at my cost, and to that end I beg Your Highness to bestow on me as follows: 1.

Your Majesty be pleased to make me Governor and Chief Justice for my term of life, and Captain General, with adequate salary for each. 2.

More. I entreat Your Majesty to confer on me the High Constabulary of said lands I shall people in your royal name, for me, my heirs and successors. 3.

More. I beg Your Majesty to bestow on me the custody

of lands for fortifications Your Majesty may require to have erected in those parts in your royal name, for me and my heirs 4.

More I entreat Your Majesty to grant me the tenth of all that you may have of royal rents forever 5

More I solicit Your Majesty that whatsoever I take unto those parts for sustaining those lands, such as horses, arms and all other things, shall pay no duty while I live 6

More I entreat Your Majesty to confer on me twenty leagues square in the country I shall colonize and pacify wheresoever I may choose them, with civil and criminal jurisdiction, for me, my heirs and successors 7

More I ask Your Majesty to grant permission that mares be taken there from the Islands, horses and all other herds 8

More I ask Your Majesty that all I shall expend in exploring, subjugating and populating, be ordered to be paid me out of the royal revenue from those lands 9

More I entreat Your Majesty to confer on the conquerors of that country the favors following, written apart from this

More I ask that Your Majesty will make me Adelantado of those territories for me, my heirs and successors 10

The tenth of the gold to be given as has been done in the other countries, and this from barter as well as from mines 11

That to the first conquerors be given the two cavallerias* of land and two lots, which after four years residence, they may dispose of as their property 12

That neither residents nor those who should become so, pay duties for ten years 13

That they do not pay duties on salt for ten years 14.

More That Indians who shall be rebellious after being well admonished and comprehending, may be made slaves 15

More That the Indians held by the Caciques as slaves, may be bought and used as slaves paying full satisfaction justly and in presence of witnesses 16

---

* The *caballeria* contains about thirty three and a third acres. Dictionary of Velazquez

More   That Your Majesty confer on those lands, all the gifts, exemptions and liberties that other lands and islands have * 17

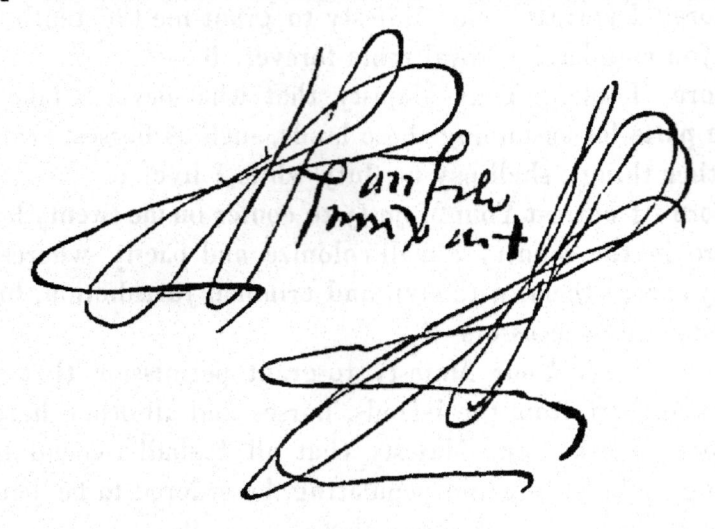

* Across the last three paragraphs is written the requirement·
He must populate

On the back of a leaf of paper that serves to enclose the previous petition from Narváez, is this memorandum of orders made in Council of the Indias, the figures corresponding to those on the concessions he asks

1 That his majesty concede to him the conquest and colonization of the countries from   to the cape of Florida, on condition that he be obliged to take from these realms of Castilla, persons and their families, who are not prohibited from being colonists, making two or more towns, as to him shall appear best, at the places he shall see proper, and for every one of these settlements he shall take at least one hundred men, and in the same country there should and shall be made two fortresses, all at his cost, and he shall leave Spain with at least CC men the first voyage, within a year from date, and give security that he do accordingly

2 *Fiat*   with salary of 100,050 *maravedies* for Governor, and 50,000 for Captain General

3 *Fiat*   for his life time, and one more

4 *Fiat*   for him and one successor of his, with salary of 60,000 for each he proposes to build

5 *Fiat*   This is not right nor fair, for what he either has served or is to serve or shall spend in this, should be given him fourfold the

advantages, after deducting costs and the salaries belonging to His Majesty.

6. *Fiat*, not being for merchandise and exchange, but for his house and person.

7. Ten leagues square and land to populate, not being of the best, nor the worst, to be selected and indicated by him and the royal officials, including no city or town *with jurisdiction that can conflict with that supreme*.

8. *Fiat*.

9. This is not proper: the King will grant him other favors for what he will expend in this.

10. *Fiat*.

11. The tithe of the gold from mines for the first three years, and thence lowering to the five per centum, but from barter always the five.

12. *Fiat*.

13. Those who should be of the first voyage, and those afterwards for five years that were not, as respects disposal of merchandise.

14. *Fiat*.

15. *Fiat*: observing the instructions that will be given him.

16. *Fiat*: being slaves according to the instructions to be given.

17. The favors will be granted, not adverse to the country, but favorable, which he will specify.

II.

INSTRUCTIONS TO THE FACTOR OF FLORIDA

Original in the *Archivo General de Indias*, at Seville, in the package inscribed "Nueva España, *Descubrimientos, Descripciones y Poblaciones*, Leg. 1, año 1520-1527." It appears to be a draft in blank for a formal authorization, with the signature of Charles V. No appointment to the office seems ever to have been made.

THE KING

What you, _____, are to do in the office you take with you as our Factor of the Rio de las Palmas and land which Pamphilo de Narvaez,—whom we have provided with the government thereof,—goes to settle, is as follows:

First. In the City of Sevilla you will present our provision, which you bear for that station,—to our officials in the House of Contratacion of the Indias, residing in said City, of whom you will ask an account of the notices that appear to them you should learn and have of the matters of that land, and beyond this instruction, of the manner in which you should discharge the duties of that office for the perfect security of our Exchequer.

Likewise. In that land you will receive into possession all merchandise and property that at the present time are there, or shall be sent there under our order, from the officials of said City of Sevilla, as well as from the officials of the Islands of Española, San Juan, Fernandina and Santiago, for expenditure and distribution in those lands, equally the things that appertain to our service, as those for sale and exchange, all which you are to do under our Comptroller of that land.

So likewise. All the things of our Exchequer that shall be in your charge, you will barter and sell and utilize in the manner most for the growth of the public treasure, and distribute by the orders and drafts signed by our Comptroller, whom we direct to take account and specification of the transactions, as well the time as the place thereof, that in our Exchequer there be proper security.

Also. the things that you have in possession, not necessary for our service and that shall be for sale, you must acquaint thereof our Governor of the country, and our officers residing therein, that you all collectively determine what should be sold and at what price, and you shall try to dispose of them to the greatest advantage possible, but, since it might happen, as has been known, that at the time things are appraised, they are worth the price at which they are valued and then cannot be sold, they come incontinently so to depreciate, that if kept to be sold for the price at which they are valued, they would become injured, then in such event you will attempt and strive to dispose of such things at the highest rate that you can, in the opinion of said Governor and officers, and keep your specification and account of the price of each article sold, that when asked, you may be able to state, as is reasonable and your duty to do

Again: You will go, with all the money that may arise from such articles in your charge as you shall sell, to ,
our Treasurer in that land, so soon as they are sold, without any deduction from the money or price at which they may have been sold while in your possession and control, all which you thus deliver to be entered in the book of our Comptroller, that in it may exist the particulars and amounts of all

So likewise You will have great care and diligence in protecting and preserving our Exchequer to the extent it may be in your charge, and improve and benefit it to the extent possible, giving all the good care and solicitude requisite, and for which I confide in you

Likewise You must take account, and in general particulars, of all the things that are sent or given to you, and of those you sell or deliver, each article by itself apart, that whenever worth while, the entire account may be seen and understood More than this, you will have a care to inform us of the profits there may be on each article, and likewise those said officers at Sevilla, and of the Island of Española, of San Juan, or Cuba and of Jamaica, that the advantages, if any, on each article may be known, and whether it will be for our interest to send such merchandise or otherwise

Also You will be vigilant and make much effort to learn what things are most profitable and necessary to be sent to that land, as much for barter as for sale and contract, first holding advisement with our said Governor and officers, and then informing us with particularity of all, as well those said officers at Sevilla and of the mentioned Islands, that they may provide therefor

And in as much as the offices of our Governor, Treasurer, Comptroller and Factor of that land are separate, each in its sphere having for object whatever may be for the good of our royal revenue and well populating and pacification of that land, every one, consequently, should consider the offices of the rest as his, and on this account you should communicate and converse of all matters touching your office that are for our service, and whatever else, with said Governor and officers, joining with them, that collectively you may see and commune respecting what in every instance should be done, as well for matters there, as to serve and inform us respecting all

So, likewise. You must have great care that whatever occurs touching your charge and office, wherein it may be necessary to resolve and determine by judicial proceeding, by free decision of a true man, or by agreement of friends, you will converse and communicate upon with our said Governor and our other said officers

And, for the fulfillment of the foregoing and safety of our Exchequer, I command our said officials at Sevilla to take and receive of you, the said   , before they allow you to depart in the exercise of the office, securities ample and approved, and, since it may be difficult for you to give such in Sevilla, before our said officials our will and disposition are that you give them in any part of our kingdoms, before the Board of Magistrates of the Province where you shall so offer them, and whom we command to receive them of you, full and sufficient, in   ducats, which we order, with the evidences and obligations of the bonds you shall give, to be put and kept in the archive, among the papers of said House, and, thus executed, they permit you to go freely to the exercise of said office, though you may not have given the securities in said city

And, that in our Exchequer there may be the requisite security, I command that all the gold, pearls and seed-pearl that shall come into the possession of our Treasurer of that land, as well our fifths as those of excise and dues of every other kind, be put in a chest with three different keys, of which you shall have one, and the two others, our Treasurer and Comptroller of said land, that no gold be taken from that chest save by hand of the three, obviating by this arrangement the inconveniences and frauds that otherwise might ensue and recur, and thus may be sent to us at the times we have required, which we order you to observe and comply with, likewise our said Treasurer and Comptroller, under pain of forfeiture of your offices and goods to our tribunals and treasury, in which pains we will condemn you, and hold you condemned, the contrary doing.

Done at   , on   day of the month of   , of the year One thousand five hundred and twenty

I THE KING

III.

PROCLAMATION TO, AND REQUIREMENT TO BE MADE OF, THE INHABITANTS OF THE COUNTRIES AND PROVINCES THAT THERE ARE FROM RIO DE PALMAS TO THE CAPE OF FLORIDA

Translated from an entry made in a book entitled *Traslados de la Florida, Capitulaciones Asientos,* * * * *de Gobernadores desde el año 1517 hasta 1578,* existing in the *Archivo de Indias* at Sevilla

In behalf of the Catholic Cæsarean Majesty of Don Carlos, King of the Romans and Emperor ever Augustus, and Doña Juana his mother, Sovereigns of Leon and Castilla, Defenders of the Church, ever victors, never vanquished, and rulers of barbarous nations, I, Panfilo de Narvaez, his servant, messenger and captain, notify and cause you to know in the best manner I can, that God our Lord, one and eternal, created the heaven and the earth, and one man and one woman of whom we and you and all men in the world have come, are descendants and the generation as well will those be who shall come after us but because of the infinity of offspring that followed in the five thousand years and more since the world was created, it has become necessary that some men should go in one direction and others in another, dividing into many Kingdoms and Provinces, since in a single one they could not be subsisted nor kept:

All these nations God our Lord gave in charge to one person called Saint Peter, that he might be Master and Superior over mankind, to be obeyed and be head of all the human race, wheresoever they might live and be, of whatever law, sect or belief, giving him the whole world for his kingdom, lordship and jurisdiction.

And He commanded him to place his seat in Rome, as a point most suited whence to rule the world, so He likewise permitted him to have and place his seat on any part of the earth to judge and govern all people, Christians, Moors, Jews, Gentiles and of whatever creed beside they might be: him they call Papa, which means admirable, greatest father and preserver, since he is father and governor of all men.

This Saint Peter was obeyed and taken for King, Lord and Superior of the Universe by those who lived at that time, and so likewise have all the rest been held, who to the Pontificate were afterward elected; and thus has it continued until now, and will continue to the end of things.

One of the Popes who succeeded him, to that seat and dignity of which I spake, as Lord of the world, made a gift of these islands and main of the Ocean Sea, to the said Emperor and Queen, and their successors, our Lords, in these kingdoms, with all that is in them, as is contained in certain writings that thereupon took place, which may be seen if you desire. Thus are their Highnesses King and Queen of these islands and continent, by virtue of said gift, and as Sovereigns and Masters, some other islands, and nearly all where they have been proclaimed, have received their Majesties, obeyed and served, and do serve them as subjects should, with good will and no resistance, and immediately without delay, directly as they were informed, obeying the religious men whom their Highnesses sent to preach to them and teach our Holy Faith, of their entire free will and pleasure, without reward or condition whatsoever, becoming Christians which they are, and their Highnessess received them joyfully and benignly, ordering them to be treated as their subjects and vassals were, and you are held and obliged to act likewise.

Wherefore, as best you can, I entreat and require you to understand this well which I have told you, taking the time for it that is just you should, to comprehend and reflect, and that you recognize the Church as Mistress and Superior of the universe, and the High Pontiff, called Papa, in its name, the Queen and King, our masters, in their place as Lords, Superiors and Sovereigns of these islands and the main by virtue of said gift, and you consent and give opportunity that these fathers and religious men, declare and preach to you as stated. If you shall do so you will do well in what you are held and obliged, and their Majesties, and I, in their royal name, will receive you with love and charity, relinquishing in freedom your women, children and estates without service, that with them and yourselves you may do with perfect liberty all you wish and may deem well, you shall not be required to become Christians, except when, informed of the truth, you desire to be converted to our Holy Catholic Faith, as nearly all the inhabitants of the other islands have done, and when His Highness will confer on you numerous privileges and instruction, with many favors.

If you do not this, and of malice you be dilatory, I protest to you, that, with the help of Our Lord, I will enter with force, making war upon you from all directions and in every manner that I may be able, when I will subject you to obedience to the Church and the yoke of their Majesties; and I will take the persons of yourselves, your wives and your children to make slaves, sell and dispose of you, as Their Majesties shall think fit, and I will take your goods, doing you all the evil and injury that I may be able, as to vassals who do not obey but reject their master, resist and deny him. And I declare to you that the deaths and damages that arise therefrom, will be your fault and not that of His Majesty, nor mine, nor of these cavaliers who come with me.

And so as I proclaim and require this, I ask of the Notary here that he give me a certificate, and those present I beseech that they will hereof be the witnesses.

FRCO. DE LOS COBOS.

IV.

INSTRUCTIONS GIVEN TO CABEÇA DE VACA FOR HIS OBSERVANCE AS TREASURER TO THE KING OF SPAIN IN THE ARMY OF NARVÁEZ FOR THE CONQUEST OF FLORIDA

Transcript in the *Archivo de Indias*, in the volume entitled *Libro de la Florida de Capitulaciones, Asientos*, desde el año 1517 hasta el de 1578

What you, Alvar Nuñez Cabeça de Vaca will perform in the office you fill as our Treasurer of *Rio de las Palmas* and the lands which Pánfilo de Narváez goes to people, on whom we have conferred the government thereof, is as follows.

First, in Sevilla, you will present the provision you bear for that position, to our officials in the House of *Contratacion* of Indias in that city, of whom, outside of this instruction, you will ask a narration of such notices as shall appear to them that you ought to be informed of and should have respecting the things of that country and of the manner in which you should discharge the duties of said office.

And when you arrive at said River of the Palmas, you will seek the Governor we have provided for that land, to whom you will show the authorization you have for that, your office, and, this done, you will inform yourself of the diligence used in the collection of our revenues, of the five per centum and duties appertaining to us, and of the persons appointed to take charge thereof, from whom you will receive account of what they have, and collect it of them and out of their goods, to the rightful extent that they are owing from what they have received, according to the instructions we have ordered to be sent to our Governor and officers in that country. Also, you will have a separate book, wherein shall be entered the account kept by our Comptroller in those lands, of what you may receive of those officers to the extent that may have been due, as well as what should newly come into your possession by reason of the duties belonging to us in said land, stating and setting down each matter specifically, what it is and when you received it, the full sum you received for it, each class of things separately, as by usage should be expressed

Also, you will ask account of every person and of all who in our name have received and collected the five per centum and other duties to us belonging, from whatsoever gold guañines* and other things which have been had in that land since its discovery, through barter or in any other manner, and, that account being taken, you will cause those persons to bring to you and pay the amount they should, which you shall take account of in your books before our Comptroller of that land, whom I require to enter it there, and make mention of all accordingly in the manner and order which by our instruction to that end he bears, and who shall sign with you in that book and in his own, the matter in account each class of things by itself, and this self same order I require that you observe in the collection of fines, which have been or shall be imposed in that land to the use of our tribunal

Likewise you will collect all the rents belonging to us in any manner in that land the five per centum duty on all gold and silver that shall be melted there, or got or had in any way, as has been customary to pay in the Island of Española

Also you will have to collect the rents which may henceforth arise, or have arisen in that land until now, on salt works and of any other character belonging to us as paid by custom in the Island of Española

Likewise, you will collect the seven and half per centum of import duty, and all others that have arisen or shall belong to us, and which should be paid on all merchandise and articles that to the said Rio de las Palmas and its Provinces, have been or henceforth shall be taken from here whilst that *almoxarifadgo* shall not be rented, and when it is so, you will collect the amount for which it is rented

---

*Guañin was an impure gold valued by the Indians of the Antilles in part for its color

Likewise, you will collect the five per centum and other dues belonging to us on all and every kind of exchange that has been or shall hereafter be made in that land, as well slaves and guañines, as pearls, precious stones and the other articles whatsoever they may be, upon which should be duty of any sort belonging to us, of which you shall take account as required before our said Comptroller

Also, you will give great care and attention to collecting all fines that have been or may be applied to our Tribunal by our said Governor and his *Lieutenants-governor* and by other justices whatsoever or persons, of which you will have separate account in your book, by the hand of our Comptroller

Likewise, when we shall have incomes, fields and live-stock in that land and those Provinces, you will take full care and keep account of the management of them with all the attention necessary for the interest and good of our Treasury, as has been done and is the custom to do in Española and other islands where we hold estate and have incomes, as shall appear to you best for the benefit and advantage of our Treasury

You will have to pay to our officers of that land and yourself, the salaries, balances and perquisites of outlay, according to, and in the manner that we order the disbursement in the triannual payments conformably with requirement, and the orders and drafts of other sort should any by our direction be issued

So likewise, in sending the gold, guañines, pearls and other things of our rents and duties to accrue, or which shall come into your hands in any way and you hold for us, you will observe this order, to put them in good condition on board the ships departing for, and coming to these kingdoms, directed to our officials residing in Sevilla the quantity in each ship that shall appear proper to our Governor and officials of that land, to be given to the captain or master, of whom you will take receipt, stating the manner of delivery and how by them received, thereby you may remain without responsibility for the gold, pearls and other articles you shall so send and they stand to your credit

Also, whenever you write to us and send gold, or when not sending, you will forward a particular statement of all our gold and property remaining in your possession, that we may have full knowledge of everything.

Also, you will take great care of, and be diligent to look after everything that may tend to our service and which should be done in that country or the neighboring islands, for their peopling and pacification, informing us extensively and particularly of every matter, especially of how our commands are obeyed and executed in those lands and provinces, of how the natives are treated, our instructions observed, and other of the things respecting their liberties that we have commanded; especially the matters touching the service of our Lord and divine worship, the teachings of the Indians in the Holy Faith and in many other things of our service, as well as all the rest you see, and I should be informed of.

Also, you will send report of the gold in foundry in that land and the provinces, the quantity submitted to casting at a time, and the amount that comes therefrom, as well what is for us as for other persons, which report should be in great detail and very specific.

Likewise, you will receive and collect of our Factor of that land, the gold and moneys he shall collect for us on articles and of the rents belonging to our Treasury in such manner that nothing be kept by him, neither the said gold nor money that may have been received belonging to the Treasury, nor things sent to him.

Again, although the offices of our Governor and Captain-general, Treasurer, Comptroller, and Factor of the land are separate in regard to everything that appertains to their duties, yet as respects our interests, the good and increase of our royal rents, the well peopling and pacification of that land and the Provinces, each should concern himself with what appertains to the duties of the rest, and to that end, you should communicate and converse upon all the topics of our service in your charge, or of others' concernment, with the Governor and Captain of said land and Provinces, and with the officers thereof, coming together with them in the manner and form we require, that you all unitedly may see and consult as to what in each case should be done, as much for that occasion as our service, and to report whatsoever else shall appear

In all the matters foregoing, and each one of them, you will have care and be diligent, and I trust you as well over those contained in this instruction, as over all others that shall there present themselves, and herein are not provided for.

And for the fulfillment of the foregoing and the security of our Treasury, I command that our said officials at Sevilla, take and receive of you, the said Alvar Nuñez Cabeça de Vaca, before they permit you to pass hence to exercise said office, good and sufficient securities, but as such may be difficult to give in Sevilla before our said officials, it is our pleasure and will, that you give them in any part of our kingdoms before the magistrates of the Provinces wherein you shall have them, and I order that they receive of you good and sufficient in two thousand ducats, and we direct our officials aforesaid to receive the evidence and obligations of the securities you present, and that they place and keep them in the archive with the documents of said House, and thereupon allow you to proceed freely to exercise your said office, though you may not have so executed them in said city

And that in our Treasury there should be proper vigilance, I command you that all the gold, pearls and those things inferior, coming to your possession as our fifths of excise and dues, as well as in all other ways, be placed in a chest with three different keys, one to be kept by you, and the others by our Comptroller and Factor of said land, in order that no gold be taken thence except by hands of the three, avoiding frauds thereby and the irregularities that might otherwise occur, enabling you to send to us periodically in the manner we have given instructions, commanding that you observe and comply with them, you and our said Comptroller and Factor under penalty of the forfeiture of your offices and goods to our Tribunal and Exchequer, in which we condemn you and hold you sentenced, the contrary doing.

Signed at Valladolid, the 15th day of February, of the year 1527

I THE KING

By command of His Majesty
FRANCISCO DE LOS COVOS.

V.

LETTER FROM A MISSIONARY TO THE PROVINCIAL OF NEW SPAIN RESPECTING THE ARRIVAL OF INDIANS IN CINALOA FROM THE PIMERIA BAJA, IN QUEST OF FRIENDS WHO EIGHTY YEARS BEFORE HAD FOLLOWED ALVAR NUÑEZ AND HIS COMRADES.

Taken from a transcript in the *Orden Real* existing in the Department of State Mexico

Among the many nations that there are in this Province of Sinaloa, omitting now to speak of such as are taught the catechism and are baptized, the information we have of the Nevomes is the earliest and most accurate. The nearest of that numerous people live eighty leagues northward from this Province. They are gentle and virtuous, and have always kept good faith with the Spaniards. They have never laid waste this country, nor made war on it; and this much is positively known to a time as far back as when Cabeça de Vaca passed out through it, when he arrived with three soldiers and a Moor from the ill-starred expedition into Florida. The Christians then for the first time coming among this people, were most hospitably received, and were escorted by a large number of men and women with their children, the whole community of a great town rising to follow them, without one person remaining behind. That the Spaniards might not be killed by those nations through which they should have to pass on their way to Mexico before coming to a peaceful country, these Indians accompanied them until they were brought to this river Petlatlan. On its banks they erected a house with fort for safety, until a favorable moment should arrive for their departure. They have ever since remained here, where they live and are established, without any having gone back to the ancient home and horde a long way off from the place in which they now dwell. Such is the evidence of the early attachment of these people; they also continue to manifest it, being always on the side of the Spaniards in whatever conflicts chance to arise with unfriendly nations.

According to late and precise information, the Nevome constitute ninety large settlements or towns of industrious husbandmen. They are modest of person, particularly the women, who without exception, wear skirts of buckskin elaborately colored with ingenious figures, having such length with fullness that even the toes are not seen. So nice is the female delicacy, that the little girls of a day old have petticoats put on them reaching to the feet, in which they are reared and are continually kept covered. This precious quality is rare among the inhabitants of these countries, where commonly it is of little value and honesty is not more prized.

Our Lord has been pleased in the first of this year, mercifully to permit a great beginning in the conversion of this nation, bringing to us the inhabitants of a town and settlement, who like deer thirsting at the fountains for their waters, ask, through the door of the church, peace and holy baptism. The nations are won by our uniform kind treatment, and the assistance they receive of Diego Martinez de Urdaide the Captain of the Province, who, besides favors confers, useful gifts, the chief support, however, being from the powerful hand of our Master.

A matter to me well known and notorious is, that this community, living eighty leagues to the northward from this town of Spaniards by the river Petlatlan, desiring quiet and to enjoy the protection that is extended over friendly nations, came to beg holy baptism and to reside among us. There can be no higher evidence of their sincere attachment. The number of persons is three hundred and fifty, one hundred and fifty having remained behind. These I expect to be here in the beginning of cold weather, with others who are to join them. Being persons of more age and advanced life, they will set out in a season not so unfavorable as the last. It was a year of scarcity when the others came, although out of the whole number only three died on the way.

I believe that the compassion of our Lord supplied what was wanting for the sustenance of this people that came with good intention and the desire of baptism, they having already knowledge of our holy faith and of its mysteries. At night while they encamped on their march one who was thoroughly instructed in every thing and long lived in this town, being likewise of the number who escorted Cabeça de Vaca and his companions hither, prayed aloud as temastian* and master teaching them as he said, that on their arrival they might be baptized, for what he taught their relatives who were baptized believed and venerated. So soon as they got here they went to call on the Captain of the Province saluting him with peace and friendship. He received them with great kindness and gifts making promises of aid that he now performs.

At the close of the interview the people went to call on the Father Martin Perez, then Visitant to these Missions, who likewise greeted them benevolently, giving them food and proffering the help they might need. After he had bestowed his blessing, they retired greatly delighted to Bamoa a town of their own community, belonging as I have stated to this Mission where I in robes, with the inhabitants awaited them. They were received under great arches with the sound of bells, instruments of music and the voice of fine singers, the people of the place forming a grand procession as on holidays. The new comers having intelligently fallen into line with the two great bodies as

* Temastli in [?] shorter a Mexican word

if they had been so trained, we moved on thence, taking them to the church amidst all that celebration and festivity.

When I had rendered thanks to our Lord for having brought these persons to his Holy Church and flock, and after the *Te Deum Laudamus*, singing and some appropriate prayers, I told them in a short discourse, while they knelt, that all these solemnities were expressive of the delight and satisfaction we felt at receiving them, of our desire to lend them aid, that they too living among their relations might be happy in a country that was equally theirs, where they should find no trouble, since in all things they would have the assistance of the Fathers the Captain, and of their own kindred, that the Great God of Heaven and Maker of man and things created, was He who had brought them hither, secretly whispering to their hearts for their immense benefit. Then I said to them, that in evidence of their coming in a right spirit, they should all advance, and kneeling, do reverence to the golden cross in my hands, as to the great emblem of Christianity, which by the baptized was held in the highest esteem and veneration, arranging my speech to their early perception and heathenism. They came forward and on their knees kissed the cross, putting it on their heads. None failed to do so, even the little children at the breast being brought, that it might be placed on theirs; and when any were passed over, the mothers would entreat for it to be done to them, lest it should show, as they thought, the appearance of a false heart.

The adoration of the cross being over, I caused this people to go out into the cemetery or churchyard, where I divided them by families to lodge among their kindred, who asked emulously for two or three families each on whom to confer their love and hospitality. All having been put in quarters and provided for, food was distributed to them in plenty by me and their friends.

The next day I baptized the children, one hundred and fourteen in number, to the joy of those just come, as well as to that of the denizens of the town, who saw in these persons and their offspring the wide increase of the Church. Such being their happiness, consider Your Reverence, what must be that of the Father Priest Minister, at finding himself unexpectedly with so many souls your already counted and marked for the fold of the Church, with the great hope by the favor of our Lord of gaining over the entire nation. To my Father Provincial I declare such to have been the gladness of my spirit that it appeared to me our Lord withdrew from my mind in that one day the years I had been in the mission, and the many more sufferings I must undergo in the same career, though they might be continued through a protracted life.

The children having been baptized, I presently gave orders for instructing the adults, dividing them into tens, the males and females apart, with their temistianes. They were delighted to find that we began at once to teach and catechize, in order to prepare them for the baptism they desired. The day after the order was given good lands were divided among them such as are found in Bamoa, to which many Indians have heretofore come in circumstances similar to these. I caused fourteen fanegas of maize to be distributed that they might cultivate for they well know how to plant and till the earth. They have now homes of their own and are content and cheerful. I go on baptizing them in *facie ecclesiæ* they coming in to every arrangement with alacrity and satisfaction feeling no kind of repugnance.

From this my Father Provincial may learn what he desires to know of the Nevames and moreover that this people have come near to asking the holy baptism as a matter of right. For their rapid and effectual progress I will state what appears necessary to be done that Your Reverence may take the proper steps to place it in the way for consummation.

The principal thing is that Your Reverence be pleased to procure a Father with all possible haste for this district to give me opportunity of putting the entire language into form. There is no work of the sort and sometime since I attempted the task of forming one. Having this preparation and with some one to take and fill my place, by the favor of our Lord a mission may be directly set on foot. The disposition of the people encourages it, and the pity is that it has been so long deferred. I proffer myself for the undertaking, though it prove to be the labor of a life and at the cost of my blood. The need warrants the attempt, the people unprompted desire it, and on account of their high moral condition they are worthy.

If I am not aided as I suggest, it will be impossible for me to do anything in this way, because of my occupation in other languages, and having no vocabulary or thing written, the undertaking will be delayed and not performed as it should be with the necessary preparation; but allowing me leisure, and with what I have mastered of the tongue, much may be advantageously done in a short time. Although it appears to be the will of our Lord that the business of Mayo should have no result owing perhaps to my not being destined to perform it, may be in mercy I am brought here to remain, that I may enter upon a task for the benefit of this nation and the glory of the Divine Majesty. I shall go on with the vocabulary, doing the best I can until Your Reverence shall send me a companion, when for its very great importance it can be my sole occupation.

With the object of gaining over this people and whole nation, I recommend a liberal course. Let Your Reverence be pleased to obtain two things from the Viceroy as incentives to their inclination, pressing them by additional objects and inducements. The one is, to grant to those who are here of their own free choice to live among Spaniards, and for being ever opposed to the nations hostile to us, as well as for the other reasons fairly declared, and, more than all, for having journeyed hither in a season of scarcity from a distant region, with confident hearts asking the sacred baptism, that they be set free from the *repartimentos*, and be equally excluded from the tribute of *encomienda*. These exemptions will be very important to the other nations that hear of them and shall desire peace, who will be thus led as with a halter to the Holy Evangelists. Although many come, all will not, neither is it possible nor politic they should, forbidden by the long distance between and the rich soil they possess. It were better to colonize among them, and thence communicate with adjoining nations. I would that a decree be issued giving to this people and their posterity the rights conferred on the Indians of Tlascála, who I am not sure are as deserving as they. If the one were true, aiding Cortés against Montezuma, the other unites with fidelity great qualities worthy of consideration and reward. I have made this matter known to the Father Visitant, to the other Fathers and to the Captain. All appears to them well designed and very proper for attaining the proposed object.

My other desire is that the Viceroy may present swords to the two principal persons who have conducted these Indians, and good woolen for each of them a suit of clothing, since it is they who make this great beginning with *tlatole** and arguments which they must go over with the remaining part of the nation, to bring them together in settlements, strengthened by offering a *coa†* or axe spared from the tools necessary for gaining my subsistence, that I too in something may contribute.

I look for no little from your great charity, from the zeal of Your Reverence for the honor of our Lord in the saving of souls and the promotion of this great cause, and that you will earnestly move in this behalf with the dignitaries and gentlemen who have the charge of providing for this want.

May God our Lord give happy success in all that we attempt. If he do so, since it is the great cause of Divine Majesty, my life is as nothing in so holy an enterprise. Had I a thousand lives, a thousand would I give in the cause that I might bring this broad spread people to the Holy Evangelists.

---

* *Tlatol*, a Mexican word meaning speech.

† The word given to a stick hardened in fire for moving the soil. In the dictionary of the Mexican language by Alonso de Molina, printed in 1571, it is used in the Spanish for hoe, and the same is done by Torquemada.

To Him I devote myself if it be His will, that he preserve Your Reverence a thousand years is my wish. To be remembered in your prayer and devotion, very humbly I commend me

From Sinaloa, 29 of September of 1629.

DIEGO DE GUZMAN.

There are several discrepancies in this letter. Passing lightly over them, as some of the transcripts in the collection whence it comes bear marks of carelessness, we refer for a correction of date to the history of Cinaloa, where the account has so close a likeness to the present one as to leave no doubt of the common original. At the time of the occurrence that is treated of, the station of RIBAS the missionary and author, was within twenty leagues of the town of Cinaloa; and he states the arrival of the Nevomes to have been on the 1st day of February 1615, which was the year of his removal northward from Guasaves after having passed sixteen years in the Mission, a circumstance that would steady his memory to the point of time. He also states in his *Triumphos* that Father Martin Perez who is mentioned in this letter as present on the occasion of the entry, died the 24th day of April, 1626, a fact repeated two years after his book was printed in the fourth volume of the *Varos Ejemplares* of JUAN EUSEBIO NIEREMBERG, who knew that work. This date makes the Temastian seventy eight years of age instead of ninety four supposing him to have been an infant among the multitude of Pima, who in 1536, led the way for the returning soldiers of Narvaez.

Padre Diego de Guzman is spoken of as a great missionary, and an ancient one, for having been in the country many years. He appears to have received the permission he solicited, and understanding their language perfectly, he went among the Nevomes who were seated, at the nearest point, within a dozen leagues of the Huaquis. Having baptized the young, he returned, his place remaining vacant. These, his first footsteps were soon followed by the Father Vanderspi, who became the founder of the new mission.

Urdaide having been made captain of the Province while in Mexico, he returned in 1599 to Cinaloa. The town had been settled by five Spaniards attended by a few natives. Here he presided many years with a company of thirty-six soldiers, exercising civil and military jurisdiction among the natives so far as he could make his power felt, and with such judgment and disinterestedness as to receive the warmest encomiums of the Fathers.

VI

PETITION OF CABEÇA DE VACA GOVERNOR OF LA PLATA TO THE COUNCIL OF INDIAS

Original in the *Archivo de Indias*, Sevilla

VERY POWERFUL LORDS:

I, Alvar Nuñez Cabeça de Vaca, having been informed that Pedro Dorantes against whom I made complaint was not at fault in my seizure nor for its consequences, neither did it stand him in hand to prevent it, making use of the permission granted me by your council of Indias I withdraw the complaint and accusation lodged against him. And I require and pray Your Lordships that neither because of my petition nor on any other account he be proceeded against for the reason foregoing, and to that effect I beg your superior interposition.

ALV° CABEÇA DE VACA

VERY POWERFUL LORDS:

I Alvar Nuñez Cabeça de Vaca Governor and Adelantado of the Provinces of Rio de la Plata remind Your Lordships of the length of time you are aware I have been detained at this court without means of support or wherewith to seek justice. I am deeply in debt for what I have laid out on the armada carrying succors to those countries where the officers seized me and took all my property, bringing me destitute and a prisoner. I beg and entreat for relief; and that I may seek out support and find maintenance, that you will terminate the imprisonment imposed; and as I cannot offer security, let me take the oath of faith and homage, to present myself when and as often as Your Lordships shall command. And I swear by God and this cross I have no person and know of no one who will trust me, so notorious is my poverty, in which may our Lord be served and may I receive justice and favor.

ORDER OF COUNCIL

In the Town of Valladolid, 11th day of the month of April, of the year 1551, Alvar Nuñez Cabeça de Vaca presented this petition in His Majesty's Council of the Indias, and the Lords of the Council ordered unanimously:

That he abide by the imprisonment imposed.

ANOTHER ORDER

What is asked for and required by Alvar Nuñez Cabeça de Vaca in this petition, should not and cannot be conceded and should be and is refused.

In Valladolid, 15th May of the year 1551.

SANTANDER.

VII

ALVA NUÑEZ CABEÇA DE VACA

Everything in the life of Alva Nuñez Cabeça de Vaca seemed destined to occur out of the ordinary course; and to be either clouded by the perversity of fortune, or obscured by a mystery impossible to penetrate. Notwithstanding the most zealous devotion of scholars, and the ceaseless delving of antiquaries, the place and period both of his birth and his decease, have evaded their research. His family was so eminent and ancient, that its dignity has been recorded in a Chronological History[1] of formidable dimensions, yet the name of the only member whose renown will preserve it from oblivion is dismissed with the briefest record.

The patronymic of his ancestors was Vera, whose lineage the author traces back to the 12th century, but from some caprice not at all explained, the grandson of the conqueror of the Canaries assumed the name of his mother's house — Cabeça de Vaca or cow's head. The origin of this unpoetical name is discussed by the family genealogist at great length, adducing in the course of his speculations eight hypotheses, maintained by as many learned antiquaries. The author finds evidence of two of the name of Vaca having fought at the battle of Navas,[2] in 1099.

M. Ternaux, in the preface to his French version of the Commentaries[2] narrates a traditionary origin of the name, which at least redeems it from vulgarity. His account, tinged as it is with the rich mediæval glow with which Spanish annalists seldom fail to color their histories, states

---

[1] *Genealogia de la noble y antigua de Cabeza de Vaca.* En Madrid 1652.

[2] Vol. 6 of *Voyages, Relations et Memoires de l'Amerique.* Paris, 1837.

'In the month of July, 1212, the Christian army, commanded by the Kings of Castile, Aragon and Navarre advanced against the Moors and arriving at Castro-Ferrel found all the passes occupied by the enemy. The Christians were about to return on their steps, when a berger named Martin Alhaja presented himself to the King of Navarre and offered to indicate a route by which the army could pass without obstacles. The King sent with him Don Diego Lopez de Naro and Don Garcia Romeu. In order that they might recognize the pass, Alhaja placed at the entrance the skeleton of the head of a cow (Cabeça de Vaca). The 12th of the same month the Christians gained the battle of Navas de Tolosa, which assured forever their supremacy over the Moors. The King recompensed Martin Alhaja by ennobling him and his descendants, and to commemorate the event by which he had merited the honor changed his name to Cabeça de Vaca.'

Three centuries have brought but little more to light, regarding Alvar Nuñez than he himself vouchsafes to us in his Relacion and Commentaries. What motives induced him to accompany the ill-fated Narvaez in his expedition to Florida, as Treasurer for the King, he leaves us to conjecture.

Of the occurrences during the six years he spent in wandering among the tribes near the Bay of Espiritu Sancto he is very reticent, as he is of the periods of the events he does narrate, and generally neglects to record the direction of his journeyings. The terrible severity of his sufferings may be judged from the fact that himself and his three companions were the only survivors of the force of three hundred men who accompanied Pamphilo Narvaez into Florida.

In consequence of his neglect in the particulars mentioned, it is now impossible to trace his route, or identify the places he mentions with any degree of certainty, until he struck the head waters of the Arkansas. To his first translation of the Relacion, Mr Smith appended some maps upon which were traced lines, doubtless intended to mark the supposed route of Cabeça de Vaca's wanderings. These represent the expedition to have

APPENDIX. 235

landed in Tampa Bay, on the eastern coast of Florida from whence it marched north on a route parallel to the coast until it turned westward near the northern boundary of the present state of Florida, passing near the site of Tallahassee, until it reached Apalache at the head of the bay of the same name, where they found the locality named Aute.

At the mouth of the Apalachicola river the ill fated explorers, now reduced to two hundred and fifty-one persons embarked in the boats they had built. In his former edition Mr Smith also appears to have decided that Mobile Bay was identical with the Bay Espiritu Sancto and the long sand bar east of its mouth Malhado island. Northward and west of the bay in the southern part of Alabama, he groups the Miriames, and the eighteen other tribes he names. According to this hypothesis, the territory between Mobile Bay and Pearl River was the scene of his six years captivity. From this place Mr Smith traced the route northward to Muscle Shoals in the Tennessee river and thence westward to the junction of the Arkansas and the Canadian.

The translator seems subsequently to have modified this opinion and to have queried at least, whether the Bay of Espiritu Sancto in Texas was not the locality of this captivity. This hypothesis has in it many features of incredibility. The land of the Christians was so near, (the city of Vera Cruz being distant not more than five hundred miles south) that rumors of the residence or invasion of a white people must have reached the savages of the region of Matagorda bay, and thus have precluded the necessity of that immense detour of more than three thousand five hundred miles to reach the same point.

On arriving at the Arkansas however his progress is marked by indications which leave little room for uncertainty of the route he pursued. The restless energy of the Spaniards stimulated at this period many exploring expeditions to the territories of the Moquis, the Zuni, the Pimos and the Apaches.

The mysterious seven cities of these people, particularly the far famed Cibola, attracted the imaginative Spaniard with a force which he found irresistible. Cabeça's description of his finding towns with habitations, which were the first he had met having the appearance of houses, has obtained confirmation in our own day by Mr. Bartlett, and many other United States officials in New Mexico. The Indians of the tribes named erected dwellings of several stories in height, each of which is ascended by a ladder.

Here also evidences of his passage were found among the Indians in 1540, by the Spanish explorers, Melchior Diaz Nisa, Coronado, and in the relations of Castenada Nagera. Cabeça de Vaca had arrived at Petatlan, near the mouth of the Gulf of California the year before, with his companions, Andreas Dorantes, Castillo, and the negro Estivanico, the sole survivors of the exploring force which set out eight years before. Some interesting particulars which tend to fortify the narrations of Cabeça de Vaca, are given in the "*Relation du Voyage de Cibola entrepris en 1540.*"[1]

'At this epoch, three Spaniards accompanied by a negro arrived in Mexico. They were named Cabeça de Vaca, Dorantes and Castillo Maldonado. They had been shipwrecked with the fleet which Pámphilo de Narváez had conducted to Florida, and had arrived by the province of Culiacan, after having traversed the country from one sea to the other, as any one can be assured, in reading a relation which Cabeça de Vaca had dedicated to the infanta Don Philippe, now King of Spain, and my master. They recounted to Don Antonio de Mendoça that they had obtained some information in the countries they had traversed, and that they had heard spoken of, some great and powerful cities, where there were houses of four and five stories in height, and of other things very different from those which we found in reality. The Viceroy communicated these notices to the new Governor, who hastened to return to the province. He took with him the negro who had come with three Franciscan Monks. It appeared that the priests were not well content

---

[1] *Ternaux Compans*

with the negro, for he took the (Indian) women which had been given him, and thought only to enrich himself with them.

"As soon as the negro had quit the priests, he thought to procure the highest honor, in going alone to discover the cities so celebrated, and resolved to traverse the desert which separated Cibola from the habitable country where he was.

' He was very soon so far in advance of the priests, that when they had arrived at Chichicticale, which is the last village on the border of the desert, he had already reached Cibola, eighty leagues from the farther side of the desert, which commences two hundred and twenty leagues from Culiacan, distances which make in all three hundred leagues. Estevan arrived at Cibola with a great quantity of turquoises, and some handsome women which had been presented to him along the route.

"He led a great number of Indians which had been given him for guides in the places through which he had passed, and who hoped that under his protection they could traverse the entire land without having anything to fear. But as the Indians of Cibola have more wit than those whom Estevan had taken with him, they imprisoned him in a house outside the walls of their city, and there he was interrogated by the old men and caciques on the cause which had led him to their country. As the negro had said to the Indians that he preceded two white men, it seemed incredible to them that he could have come from the country of the whites when he himself was black.

"Estevan had demanded their property and their women, and it seemed hard to them to consent. They decided at last to kill him which they did without doing the least harm to those who accompanied him."

An entire year elapsed, before Cabeça de Vaca reached Spain. The interval of three years which followed before he again appears upon the stage are passed over by himself and other writers with silence. We have, regarding the extraordinary occurrences in his life which succeeded, in addition to the Commentaries of Cabeça de Vaca, the Relations of Ulrich Schmidel, a German soldier of fortune who served for nearly twenty years in the Spanish conquest of the countries of South America, and who left a record of some of the incidents of the life of Cabeça de Vaca.

The commander Ayolas, during the year 1539, had organized an expedition against the Pariembos, a fierce tribe of the grand chaco or great plains bordering the Rio de la Plata. He was decoyed by the savages into an ambuscade in which he with every one of his detachment was slain. The survivors of the colony sent the most urgent entreaties to the court of Spain for succor representing that without immediate relief they must all perish. Cabeça de Vaca who, during his three years of seclusion, had recovered from the terrible exhaustion of his wanderings, was selected as the new governor.

A contract was executed by which he undertook the rescue of his countrymen, the conquest of the territory, and the conversion of the Indians. The terms of this instrument, indicated his strong faith in his own powers, and the worthiness of the cause in which he engaged, for one of its conditions required him to expend the sum of eight thousand ducats, his entire fortune in the enterprise.

The title of Governor, Captain General and Adelantado was conferred upon him with the right to one twelfth of the produce of the countries he should conquer. At the end of September 1540 he was ready to put to sea, but the winds proving contrary he was compelled to return to Cadiz where he remained until the 2d of November. After escaping from such dangers of tempest and famine as seemed to be the peculiar fortune of Cabeça de Vaca, he arrived at St. Catherine's in Brazil with two small caravels on the 29th of March, 1541. Even the courage of this seemingly indomitable man succumbed to the perils of the ocean, and unable to overcome the horror with which it had impressed him he remained at St. Catherine's three hundred miles from those he came to succor, for more than seven months.

This period he occupied in organizing and sending exploring parties to discover a route through the unknown territories which separated him from Assomption. On the anniversary of the day of his sailing from Cadiz, he commenced his march through the forest, having dispatched his vessels with their cargoes of provisions to Buenos Ayres. His narration of the events of this terrible march, is perhaps the most interesting of his Commentaries. For nineteen days his troops toiled through dense forests, and over rugged mountains, when they reached the territories populated by tribes of Indians who looked upon them with blended terror and admiration. From these savages, who had hitherto received no evidence of the rapacity of the white strangers, the Spaniards obtained welcome supplies of food and clothing. The country abounded in fruits and farinaceous food, and the Adelantado is eloquent in eulogies of the inhabitants and their territory. Everywhere he found the evidence of unsophisticated confidence, and he was careful to leave behind him no tokens of any other feeling than sincere reciprocity of inoffensiveness and good will. It was near the 1st of January, 1542, that the first loss to his force occurred, when he was obliged to leave five of his soldiers in care of a tribe of the Guaranis. One of these had been so badly bitten by a dog that he died soon after, and only two of the others survived their maladies. Having arrived on the borders of the Yguaeu, a branch of the Parana, in latitude 25° 30′ south, Cabeça de Vaca was informed that a warlike tribe, which had some years before massacred an exploring party of Portuguese, had determined to exterminate his force in the same manner, while descending the river in canoes. His sagacious manœuvres averted such a catastrophe.

He divided his force into three companies, of which the cavalry formed two; one squad of which descended each bank of the river, while the third consisting of the foot soldiers embarked in canoes, and were carried swiftly down to the Parana. The cavalry and the infantry, as the pious Adelantado remarks, were by the favor of God, permitted to arrive at the same time. It was here that he had reason to believe that his countrymen whom he came to succor, did not look upon his coming as then governor with favor. He had sent an envoy from St Catharine's long before his departure, with an order for brigantines to meet him at this point, and although ample time had elapsed, his commands had been disregarded. It will be found that they fell upon willingly deaf ears. The lieutenant governor in command had once before rid himself of a superior, by neglecting to provide vessels to convey his worn soldiers from an inhospitable country, and he now hoped to consign Cabeça de Vaca to the miserable fate of Ayolas. Finding himself left to his own resources, the Adelantado, with characteristic energy, devised and executed other means of escape. Thirty sick soldiers, accompanied by fifty arquebusiers and arbaletriers to serve as their escort, were embarked on the native rafts called balsas, while the remainder of his force proceeded by land. In this manner he arrived at Assomption on the 11th of March, 1542.[1] More than four months had been consumed in the march and nearly a year since his arrival at St Catherine's. Schmidel says, that only three hundred men survived, of a force of more than four hundred with which he had embarked, and that one quarter of his soldiers had perished of disease and misery. He found the humor of the colonial troops unfavorable to his pretensions.

[1] Four days after the little fleet of balsas, with their freight of sick soldiers and their escort arrived at Assomption, having lost only one of their number, seized and killed by a tiger (jaguar). The report which they made of the coalition of all the river tribes of Indians to dispute their passage, was characterized by all that eloquence which is elicited by an escape from imminent peril. The river was hidden by fleets of canoes, and the canoes themselves were invisible by reason of the crowds of warriors they carried. The banks of the river were two living streams of enemies moving as rapidly as its waters, and sending constantly clouds of arrows. The cries and shouts of those on the river were momently echoed by the war whoops of their comrades on the shores, which combined with the clash of weapons, and the beating of war drums, made it seem that heaven and earth were combatting each other.

Notwithstanding all this fearful warfare, and appalling clamor, the miserable wretch who fell a prey to the jaguar was their only loss

They had waited a year to receive tidings from Ayolas then governor, after he had set out upon his fatal expedition, and it was only upon the receipt of the sad story of his massacre brought by an Indian servant, who witnessed and survived it, that they elected his successor. The crafty and unscrupulous man who received this dangerous yet coveted honor, Martin Dominick de Irala, had time to ingratiate himself with the soldiers, and thus Cabeça de Vaca found a new peril awaiting him, when he demanded their submission to his authority. He had received information while at St. Catherine's from nine fugitive Spaniards who had fled from the rigor of Irala's government, of a character not designed to inspire confidence in his representative at Assomption. Irala had been deputed by Ayolas to command the brigantines which were to meet him at a certain port on the Parana where his explorations were to terminate. The cruel and ambitious lieutenant found a pretext for abandoning his commander to his fate, and Ayolas finding his vessels gone, undertook to penetrate the terrible maze of a tropical forest and while worn down with famine sickness and fatigue perished in an assault by a warlike tribe of Indians Cabeça de Vaca was not blind to the design that the same fate was marked out for him.[1]

Thus he entered upon his government with an unfortunate prestige for himself in his long delay at St. Catherine's, and an evil foretaste of his destiny in the ill will of the man he supplanted. His first act was scarcely of a nature to inspire confidence.

Reasonably enough the old colonists required him to exhibit his authority, but his natural imperiousness or the danger and sufferings he had experienced so clouded his judgment that

---

[1] "A contest of dissimulation commenced on the first interview of the chiefs. Schmidel says he bound himself so much in friendship with Irala that they were like two brothers and in such manner as that the latter preserved all the power in the army which he formerly possessed."

he recklessly provoked the anger of those desperate men, by a haughty refusal. The only concession he would proffer, was to submit his brief of authority to two or three priests whom the council might delegate. We who are permitted to know how generous and extensive were the grants of the king, can only account for this needless mystery, by supposing that his intellect was affected by disease, or that the evil genius which had so long governed his fortunes, still led him with its fatal delusions astray. On reviewing his army he found that with his recruits he could muster eight hundred men.

As the main object of all the marvellous energy of exploration by the Spaniards, was the greed of gold and conquest Cabeça de Vaca could not long be idle. He ordered expeditions for searching the country in all directions for traces of the route to El Dorado.

Ulrich Schmidel informs us, that Cabeça de Vaca commenced his career in South America by an act of cruelty which was the precursor if not the origin, of the long train of misfortunes which ensued. The expeditions he had organized for exploring the country, and obtaining provisions for the sustenance of the colony, had found all the savage nations most amicably disposed. They were everywhere received by the natives with kindness and their requisitions cheerfully complied with.

While encamped in peaceful relations, among a nation called Achkeres, Irala who commanded this division received a letter from the Governor, directing him to execute the cacique Achkere. The Indian chief was accordingly immediately seized and hung.

Of all this Cabeça de Vaca gives us not a single word in his Commentaries, and as Schmidel was an ardent partisan of Irala, it is more than probable that he accepted the statement from Irala himself, who was quite capable of performing such a deed to bring odium on his commander.

Some months after his arrival, a similar event, of much greater atrocity, said by Schmidel to have been ordered by the captain general, was performed by the same Irala. A tribe of Indians whose name is given by Schmidel as Surucusis, and who are probably the same spoken of by the captain general himself as Guaycurus had often made war on the Guanaus allies of the Spaniards.

Cabeça de Vaca says, that to compel the warlike Guaycurus to maintain peace with his friends he was compelled to make war upon them. The story is however told by Schmidel with a coloring of ferocity that belongs more appropriately to Irala, and we are again compelled to suspect a perfidious design, animating this crafty man.

'On our report the Governor decided to advance into the country at the head of all his forces and this much against our will because the country was entirely covered with water.

'The most part of those who had been at the residence of the Orthuesens, suffered again the fatigues which this expedition induced. Besides Alvar Nuñez inspired no great confidence in the army because he had never before undertaken great charges. We rested two months among the Suracusis during which time the General was attacked with fever which obliged him to keep his bed. But we did not give ourselves much inquietude as we cared very little for him.

'I have not seen in the country of the Suracusis a single man who was more than forty or fifty years old, nor a country more unhealthy. It is situated under the tropic of Capricorn where the sun is almost vertical. The climate is more pestilential than that of St. Thomas. Our Governor Cabeça de Vaca seeing himself retarded by his sickness, sent one hundred and fifty Christians and two thousand Carios (Guaranos) Indians on board of four brigantines. He ordered them to proceed to the island of Suracusis at the distance of four miles and reduce to slavery or put to the sword the whole population and to spare no Indians under forty years of age. We have seen before in what (kind) manner the Suracusis had received us. I am going to recount how they were recompensed for it, and God knows how unjust we were on this occasion. When we arrived at their villages these Indians who had no suspicion of our design came to meet us with their bows and arrows, but with the most amicable demonstrations. Presently a quarrel broke out between them and the Guaranis, of which we profited, on the instant, by a discharge of musketry which killed a great number. We took more than two thousand Suruensis of all ages and sexes after having taken from them all which they possessed, as is the custom on similar occasions. We rejoined soon after our commandant, who was well satisfied with the success of this expedition. As we had a great number of sick, and as the army was very discontented, Alvar seeing that he could do nothing more, decided to descend the river Parabol and return to Assomption where he had left a portion of his troops. He experienced in this city an access of fever which prevented his going out for fifteen days, but I thought that he remained in his house more from pride and ill will than from necessity. He never spoke to the soldiers, and treated them with great arrogance. Our commandant had no consideration for any person, and desired that all should bend to him and to his will. The entire army united in a general assembly, decided with unanimity that he must be arrested, and sent to the emperor, to render an account to his imperial majesty of his fine qualities and of the manner in which he had treated us, and of all which had transpired.

Three of the principal officers namely the Treasurer of his majesty, Alonzo Cabrera and Garcia Vinegas, took themselves to his house at the head of two hundred soldiers, and possessed themselves of his person at the moment when he least thought it. This was in the month of April on the day of the feast of St Marc in the year 1543. We guarded him as a prisoner during more than a year, until we could prepare and furnish with provisions a caravelle, on board of which we sent him to Spain with two officers. It was necessary to choose another chief to administer the country and command the army until we could receive the orders of his majesty. Martin Dominique de Irala, who had been already governor, was proclaimed general because he was much loved by the troops. Every one was satisfied except some officers who had been friends of Alvar Nuñez but those enjoyed but little consideration.

This narration of Schmidel has its chief interest in disclosing the sentiments of Cabeça de Vaca's enemies in his government. His own relation of his arrest, is more dramatic, and minute. Of the massacre of the Surucusis, the captain general does not utter a word. If the tribe mentioned by Schmidel is identical with the Guareurus, Cabeça de Vaca has given us the provocation which originated hostilities. There is however somewhat more reason to believe that the nation of Indians called Surucusis by Schmidel is the same as the one designated Socorinos in the Commentaries. They inhabited an island a league distant from the port of Rios near which the Spaniards were encamped. The captain general narrates a long train of hostile acts performed by this tribe terminating with the murder and devouring of five Spaniards. In a single assault they subsequently slew fifty-eight Christians. On this Cabeça having duly summoned them by the process required by law and caused a formal inquest to be made declared them enemies.

Not a word more does he vouchsafe regarding the rebellious Socorinos or their punishment. At this point his narrative of his campaigns abruptly closes and he commences a relation of his own grievances.

He concedes with Schmidel in the cause of his abandonment of the campaign on account of the epidemic from which he and his troops were suffering. The general attributes his unpopularity to two measures tending to the furtherance of good morals and religion which he enforced. The first was his order for the release of one hundred Indian girls with whom his officers and men cohabited in order he says to avert the anger of God which had stricken them with the terrible fever.[1] The second

---

[1] He declared that it was the express command of His Majesty that no Indian should be reduced to slavery and that they could not hope for the favor of God if they deprived the natives of their liberty. He could not know that a greater philanthropist Bartholomew de Las Casas was at that very hour struggling for the freedom of the natives of the Northern Continent.

was his enforcement of the law against cannibalism among his savage allies. His soldiers demanded their indulgence in this loathsome diet, because the Indians threatened to abandon the Spaniards if deprived of it. Compelled by disease, and the constant attacks of the savages to return to Assomption, he had scarcely arrived there, when a conspiracy was formed to seize his person. The subtle Irala, who is believed by Herrera, Barcia, and Funes, to have been the instigator of the insurrection, does not appear once in the foreground.

The insurgents charged such designs upon the general as they thought would most readily inflame the passions of their comrades, the residents of Assomption, and Buenos Ayres.

On his arrival all his property was plundered or confiscated, consisting among other items, of ten brigantines and property amounting to one hundred thousand castellanos (about $300,000). The Governor was hurried to prison from the bed which to his malady condemned him, and heavy chains were riveted upon his feet. The guard under which he was placed were so cruelly rigid, that no person was permitted even to see him, and for a great part of the year in which he was thus immured, his friends believed him dead.

At last the vessel which had been preparing for his reception was ready, and he was taken from his cell more dead than alive. On being brought by two soldiers into the light of day, he begged them to let him fall upon his knees, that he might thank the good God who had permitted him once more to behold the sun. So feeble was his condition that he was unable to rise after this act of devotion, and the soldiers were compelled to lift him to his feet and support him while he dragged his feeble body to the ship. During all this period of suffering and imprisonment, Irala who had been elected to the supreme power, permitted no amelioration of its rigor. But the friends of the deposed Governor, although powerless in avowed hostility to the revolution, aided him in secret by securing in the most ingenious manner the transmission of his papers. Cabeza de Vaca, or rather Hernandez his secretary, narrates the circumstance as follows. "During the arming and equipment of the brigantine, in which he was to be carried away, the friends of the Governor concerted with the carpenters to cause a beam as large as one's thigh to be hollowed three palms long. In this they placed the process of general information which the Governor had prepared to submit to his Majesty, with such other papers as his friends had secured at the time of his arrest, and which were necessary to his defense. The packet enveloped in waxed linen, was then enclosed in the timber which was firmly nailed to the poop of the brigantine with six nails at the two extremities. The carpenters said that it was required in this place to strengthen the ship, and the operation was so secretly performed that no person could discover it. The master carpenter gave word to a sailor, who was one of the crew, in order that he could take these papers, when he should arrive in Spain."

During his imprisonment an incident occurred so characteristic of the temper of his enemies, the fidelity of his friends, and the ingenuity of the natives, that Cabeza de Vaca records it with great minuteness in his Commentaries. To prevent the possibility of any communication regarding the affairs of the country reaching him, only one attendant, an Indian woman, was permitted to enter his cell. Not only was she compelled to perform her service entirely naked, but her hair was closely shaved, and her person subjected to the most indecent examination whenever she returned to the prison. Notwithstanding the apparently impossible evasion of their scrutiny, the subtilty of the crafty Indian prevailed. A scroll of fine paper was enclosed in wax and concealed between the large toe and the others, and while the watchful eyes of the jailor (whose hatred the Governor had gained by his punishment of some atrocious crime) were constantly upon her, she contrived to place it within his reach. On entering his cell she announced her possession of a message by tapping the floor with her foot, and at the proper moment while appearing to be scratching it detached the message. In the same manner she supplied him with a powder, which dissolved in spittle formed an ink, by which he was able to record his instructions to his friends. The conspirators becoming aware that communications were frequently passing between the Governor and his adherents, employed every art to discover the means. Four young men were at various times selected to seduce the Indian woman, to whom they made numerous presents; but although she thought lightly of her chastity, and made no difficulty in surrendering it, no enticements could prevail upon her to become a traitress, and during the eleven months in which they made their reports they could not obtain from her a word.

As he was about to be led on board, he announced with an intrepidity almost incredible that he delegated Captain Salazar as his lieutenant in the government. Garcia de Venegas, one of his jailors, threw himself upon the Governor with his dagger, saying "If you thus prove traitor to the king I will tear your soul out of your body. If you speak again I will poniard you." In the melee which ensued, Cabeça was slightly wounded in the chest, and was both by friends and enemies hurried on board the vessel to save his life. He was loaded with chains which were secured to the deck, from which he was only released when the vessel was supposed to be foundering in a tempest. After his imprisonment the Governor affords us little more than surmises regarding the dates of the events he relates, but from comparison with other incidents we ascertain that it was near the 1st of June, 1545 when he embarked as a prisoner. So strictly was the deposed Governor guarded that even his own domestics on board were not permitted to serve him, and his food was brought him by his jailors, who were the persons that first seized him. He charges them with making three attempts to poison him with arsenic, but anticipating such an event he had taken the precaution to provide himself with some antidotes. Two monks who accompanied him down the river were not permitted to remain on the brigantine, but were sent back to Assomption as were also his servants, in doubt that they would represent the conduct of the Governor in too favorable a light. A great tempest which lasted four days, awakened such remorse in his jailors that Cabrera hastened to remove his irons, and Venegas kissed his feet, both of the pusillanimous wretches in their uncontrollable panic confessing that they had cruelly wronged him, and uttered more than two thousand lies against him. They declared that they believed God had sent this terrible tempest as an indication of his wrath against them, and in the most piteous terms supplicated his pardon. Cabeça de Vaca adds: "*As soon as they had removed the chains from the Governor the sea and winds were appeased, and the tempest which had endured for four days calmed itself.*

"We navigated the open sea during two thousand five hundred leagues without perceiving anything except the sky and sea." On his arrival at Madrid about the first of September, 1545, he found the council of the Indies in an humor that augured only ill for his cause. His friend the bishop of Cuenca, President of the council was just dead, and at the head of that important body, sat the stern bishop of Burgos the enemy of Las Casas and the advocate of the slavery of the Indians. Charlevoix says that the bishop of Cuenca had discovered the wicked design of India's emissaries, "and was preparing to punish them when death interposed." Garcias Venegas died suddenly, without having time to utter a single word, and his eyes starting out of their sockets, and pretty much about the same time Cabrera expired, after killing his wife in a fit of madness." The machinations of his enemies prevailed, and Cabeça de Vaca entered a prison to await his trial on the charges brought against him, which he did not leave for more than six years. Mr. Buckingham Smith's manuscripts contain voluminous minutes of the trial by the council of the Indies before whom he never seems to have appeared in person except to receive his sentence. The licentiate acting as prosecuting attorney recited twenty-four specifications of crimes alleged against him. The licentiate his counsel replies for him with as many rejoinders, and his legal brother makes as numerous replications.

In the mean time Cabeça de Vaca languishing in prison, petitions constantly to be released on sufficient security for his appearance, to be allowed the liberty of the court of the jail, and be indulged in other ameliorations of his imprisonment. The stern refusal of all these humble requests are clear indications of the severity of his treatment. At last, on the 18th of March, 1551, eight years after his seizure in Assomption the counsellors of the Indies delivered their judgment. He was condemned to be stripped of all the titles conferred upon him, and the privileges incident thereto, to be banished to the penal colony of Oran in Africa, and to be liable to suits for damages by any party claiming to have suffered loss, or pain during his government. Not the least severe in the details of his condemnation, was the additional sentence that he should serve His Majesty in Africa with his arms, and horse and at his own expense for five years; and that if he should seek to evade it then he should be subject to a further term of service of equal length. With this sentence terminates nearly all the recorded details of the history of this extraordinary man. An obscurity closes over his future life, and subsequent fate, which all the industry and zeal of the most indefatigable scholars have not sufficed to penetrate.

It is even uncertain if the sentence of the council was ever enforced, as Hernandez his secretary says "after eight years of arrest *at the court* he was liberated and acquitted." As his condemnation took place six years and nine months after his arrival in Spain; it is possible that after remaining in prison a year longer he was pardoned. But Hernandez certainly narrates what is untrue, when he asserts that Cabeça de Vaca was acquitted, as we have before us a transcript of the judgment.¹

¹ "In the prosecution of the Adelantado Alvar Nuñez Cabeça de Vaca, Governor of Rio de la Plata being in this court, do adjudge for the offence that has been made to appear from said action against Alvar Nuñez Cabeça de Vaca that we should and do condemn him to perpetual privation of said office of governor and Adelantado of the Provinces of said Rio de la Plata and of right of action which he claims

Charlevoix who narrates many particulars in the life of Cabeça de Vaca principally obtained from his Commentaries, and from Herrera, repeats the error, in stating that although not fully acquitted the council hesitated to send him back to Paraguay as governor, lest his presence should occasion fresh disturbances. The delay of eight years he attributed to the long absence of his Majesty from his Spanish dominions.

"At last," says Charlevoix, "the emperor granted him a pension of two thousand crowns and gave him a place in the Royal Audience of Sevilla, where he died at an advanced age."¹

Charlevoix adds, "I have indeed seen a memorial in which it is said that he was immediately gratified with a seat in the council of the Indies."²

to have of said government, and so likewise we forever suspend him from the office of governor, Adelantado or any other office of justice in all India Islands and Terra Firma belonging to his Majesty, that he may not use or exercise them under the penalties which befall and inure to those who use like offices without the license and faculty to do so, and moreover we condemn him for the time and space of five years to be computed of the first following, he serves His Majesty in Oran with his arms and horse and his expense, and he remain in such service, and for such period under penalty of having the time doubled of the five years. And we reserve their right unimpaired, to the persons injured in the charges of the accusation in the cause that for the years they sustained the injuries they may demand what shall to them appear well. And this definitive sentence we pronounce and order with costs.

Signed by six Counsellors of the Indies.

Valladolid, 18th March 1551.

Manuscript copied from the original by Mr. Buckingham Smith.

"But though his Sovereign might have amply rewarded him, he never indemnified him for all his sufferings, nor properly acknowledged the heroic manner in which he bore the many indignities that had been offered him. At this however we are not to be surprised. There are virtues which most highly monarchs can do justice to." — *Charlevoix Hist. of Paraguay.*

² Mr. Harisse says, "I do not recollect where I have seen it stated that his death occurred at Sevilla in 1564. He had perhaps seen it in

No relation of the period seems to have excited such attention as that of Cabeça de Vaca, and the cures which he modestly yet fervently records to have been vouchsafed to his prayers, drew forth the animadversion, and the advocacy of priests and scholars.

That he believed divine interposition to have been accorded in a miraculous way to his supplications is evident from a perusal of Chapters XXI, XXII and XXVI. In one place a dead man is restored to life, in many others the mortally sick are given health. The Spaniards considered those cures to be miraculous, and his reputation as a man of extraordinary piety and highly favored by God, continued during the three years succeeding his return to Spain. Cabeça de Vaca relates several incidents in his Commentaries of similar import regarding the divine favor. "The air of Santiago," he says, "is ordinarily so fatal during the spring, as that the greater part of those who land there die in a short time." During his voyage to Brazil, the leaking of his vessel compelled his entering that port, where he remained twenty-five days without losing a single man. "This so astonished the inhabitants that they regarded it as a miracle." Another instance he relates in the following words: "Having passed the equinoxial line, the commandant examined the quantity of water which the vessel carried. Of one hundred casks which had been shipped, not more than three remained to serve four hundred men and thirty horses. The Governor ordered the captain to sail towards the land which was not found three days after. The fourth night, the ships were on the point of striking on the rocks without any of the crew perceiving it, when a cricket which had been carried on board the ship by a sick soldier, who was pleased with the music of this insect, suddenly began singing. Two months and a half had passed since we had put to sea and it had been

---

Techo's *Historia Provinciae Paraguariae. Leodii,* 1673. Capitolio xiv, vol. 1, from which Ternaux Compans quotes. Mr. Buckingham Smith sought for many years to ascertain the fact, and never saw it stated by any authority he considered authentic.

silent, but the little animal now perceived the land and commenced its song. This unexpected music attracted the attention of the crew who discovered the rocks no more than a musket shot away. It is certain that if the cricket had not sung we should all have perished: the four hundred men, and thirty horses, and it was by a miracle of God in our favor that the insect was found with us."

So much attention did the assertion of his miraculous power excite that the Abbot of a Monastery in Austria named Caspar Plautus thought it necessary to disprove the possibility of the performance of miracles by a layman.[1]

A reply to the Monk's treatise, was written by Senor Don Antonio Ardoino, and published by Barcia in his *Historiadores Primitivos*. His work is entitled *Apologetic Examination of the Historical Narration of the Shipwrecks, Wanderings and Miracles of Alvar Nuñez Cabeça de Vaca, in the lands of Florida and New Mexico against the censures of the father Honorio Philopono*. The Examen occupies fifty folio pages in double columns.[2]

In addition to the number of editions of Cabeça de Vaca's works mentioned in the introduction, we may add the abridged translation, or paraphrase printed by Purchas. It is due to Mr Smith to record here, that the translation he speaks of in the same place with such reserve, was his own work.

---

[1] This monk published a treatise in 1621, entitled 'Nova Typis Transacta Navigatio Novi Orbis Indiæ Occidentalis.' He attempts an extraordinary deception in the work, prompted by his vanity. On the title page the author styles himself Philoponus, and in his preface lauds the abbot Caspar Plautus with most fulsome adulations. Hinckleman discovered that Philoponus and Caspar Plautus were the same person. On page 91 of his treatise will be found his claim for the priests, as the only persons who should be permitted to perform miracles, and his aspersions of Cabeça de Vaca.

[2] *Examen Apologetico de la Historica Narracion de los Naufragios, Peregrinaciones y Milagros de Alvar Nuñez Cabeza de Vaca en las Tierras de la Florida y del Nuevo Mexico, contra la incierta, y mal reparada censura del P. Honorio Philopono en Madrid 1736.*

The opinions of historians and writers have varied widely regarding the character of Cabeça de Vaca. By Schmidel, he is represented as a haughty tyrant who deserved his fate.

The chevalier Azara coincides with this opinion, while Herrara, considers him a victim to the machinations of the unscrupulous and cruel wretches, who formed the colony and army of Rio de La Plata. Charlevoix elevates him to the rank of a martyr, asserting that he had no other aim than the service of God and the King, which he exhibited by his fervent desire for the conversion of the Indians. Barcia also gives him the highest praise for nobility of character, and disinterestedness of motives, believing that his zeal for executing the laws that protected the natives caused the revolt. Funes, the historian of Buenos Ayres, attributes his fall to the same cause, and bestows upon him similar encomiums. He attempted the abolition of Slavery, to which the Indians had been illegally subjected, and a reform of the morals of Christians to a standard, which would entitle them to the respect of Savages, and in both he failed. He is scarcely to be decried for this, as three centuries elapsed before the first object was accomplished, and of the last, history has little to record.

MEMOIR OF THOMAS BUCKINGHAM SMITH.

The author, whose last contribution to American history is found in these pages, could never have foreseen its appearance accompanied by a sketch of his own life. But when he was cut off by an untimely fate, attended with circumstances that excited every feeling of sympathy in the hearts of his friends, cut off while the work was unfinished, and yet with the work so at heart, that even while disease at last triumphed over his last remnant of strength, he had a portion of it on his person, all will feel that a brief notice will not here be out of place.

Though born in the south and identified with a southern state, throughout his life THOMAS BUCKINGHAM SMITH was of purely New England origin and unconnected with any family in the section to which he so peculiarly belonged.

His father, Josiah Smith, a man of clear thought and extensive information, was a native of Watertown, Connecticut, and marrying his cousin Hannah Smith of the same place removed to Florida while still under the British flag, and remaining during the new Spanish rule once more found himself in the United States by the purchase of that colony.

They had two children, Thomas Buckingham Smith who was born in 1810 on Cumberland Island, Georgia, and a daughter Hannah, or as she soon grew to be called in that Spanish part Anita.

Commercial business soon carried the father to Mexico where he seems to have resided for a time, and having been appointed United States consul, resolved to remove his family to that city. His children had meanwhile been at St. Augustine, and his letters show the interest he took in their education and progress, as well as clear and intelligent views. Buckingham was for a time, when about fourteen, also in Mexico and grew up with a Spanish tone that never left him. His father was not, however, permitted to gather his family around him, having been seized with a fatal illness under which he sank in 1825.

Thus deprived of the guidance of a loving and able father, Buckingham became the ward of his maternal uncle, Robert Smith, of New Bedford, by whom he was placed in 1827, soon after his return from Mexico, at Washington, now Trinity College, Hartford, to pursue the partial or scientific portion of the course of study in that institution. Here he remained three years, and is still remembered as one full of youthful vivacity. Edward Goodman, Esq., and Professor William C. Russell, now of Cornell University were among his intimate friends and associates, and Mr. Smith then, as through life, made friends whom he never alienated or lost.

As he had resolved to devote himself to the legal profession, he was next entered at the Cambridge Law School, where he formed the acquaintance of Mr. George Gibbs, whose studies in after life were so in harmony with his own. He then studied law in Maine in the office of Judge Fessenden, the late William Pitt Fessenden being his fellow student.

Returning to his home in St. Augustine, Buckingham Smith entered on the practice of his profession, and while a business was forming with that slow growth so trying to the young aspirant for forensic honors, he, like many a lawyer similarly placed, entered the field of politics. He was soon elected to the Florida assembly, and was for a time speaker. Rigidly honest and truthful, he would have the state as honest as a man; he took a decided stand against the party of inflation, who sought to create a host of banking institutions and issue broadcast state bonds, with a facile extravagance, that ere long proved an incubus on the prosperity and progress of Florida.

Though successful in his practice at the bar, he seems not to have followed it up with zeal or energy, and a taste for historical and antiquarian studies soon developed itself, and grew with his growth. His marriage on the 20th of September, 1844, with Miss Julia G., daughter of Reuben G. and Elizabeth M. Gardner, of Maine, also seems to have tended to withdraw him from active political life, while his intimate knowledge of Spanish life and language fitted him admirably for the post of secretary of legation to Mexico, to which he was appointed on the 9th of September, 1850.

Revisiting thus the scenes familiar to his boyhood, and actually the burial place of a father whom he respected and loved, Mr. Smith at once formed a close intimacy with many gentlemen in that capital, who while holding positions of honor in the Mexican government, were devoted students of history and familiar with the rich stores of printed and unprinted material accumulated in the archives and libraries of that capital. Among these may be named especially, Don Jose F. Ramirez, and Don Lerdo de Tejada. By their aid and influence he began to collect a rich store of documents relating to the history of Florida.

His duties as secretary he discharged meanwhile, with an ability which showed his fitness for Spanish diplomacy, and when the position of minister was vacant, Mr. Smith as *chargé d'affaires* represented the United States, near the government of Mexico from Feb. 12 to Oct. 8, 1851. He then resumed his duties as secretary till his recall Feb. 2, 1852.

The first fruit of his studies was an English version of the narrative of Alvar Nuñez Cabeça de Vaca, a work of great interest as that of almost the sole survivor of the expedition of Pamphilo de Narvaez to reduce Florida. Cabeça de Vaca with a few others made their way across the continent, and although they had landed at Tampa, reached a Spanish settlement in Sinaloa. The original is at times obscure, but Mr Smith translated with care, and by his notes enabled readers to follow the course of the strange journey. This work was issued privately at Washington by Mr George W. Riggs, jr, in a beautifully printed quarto volume, with fine maps showing the course of the expedition. It was followed in 1854, by a similar volume also issued by Mr Riggs, containing Hernando de Soto's letter addressed from Florida, July 9 1539, to the Justice and Board of Magistrates in Santiago de Cuba, together with a very curious document, the *Memoir of Hernando de Escalante Fontaneda* respecting Florida, written in Spain about the year 1575. Mr Smith's notes on this curious tract were very full and satisfactory.

Under the simple title of *Espiritu Santo Bay* he added a very clear summary of the various accounts of the early portion of Soto's expedition.

He also contributed, in 1852, to the work then issuing by the United States government under the supervision of Mr Schoolcraft, a series of extracts from Mexican archives as to the Pimas and Casas Grandes, which were published in the third volume of that work (p. 296, etc.), under the title of '*History Language and Archæology of the Pimos of the River Gila, New Mexico*,' but without his name. It embraces extracts from the unpublished journals of Garces, Font, and Monge.

These works made Mr Smith known beyond the circles in which he had hitherto moved, and brought him in contact with the historical scholars of the country. The New York Historical Society, the American Ethnological Society, the American Antiquarian Society and the New England Historic-Genealogical Society at once enrolled him among their corresponding members. His eminent fitness for the diplomatic service, and the advantage to be derived by the great cause of American history from his presence at the capital of Spain led to his appointment as secretary of legation to that country on the 9th of June, 1855, the Hon. Augustus C. Dodge, of Iowa, being minister.

Here, too, Mr. Smith formed the acquaintance of congenial spirits, especially of the orientalist, Don Pascual de Gayangos, and of de Rios, the editor of Oviedo. He was enabled to explore the archives at Simancas, and at Seville, and carried out researches here and into family archives, with earnestness and zeal, and not only collected material documents, portraits, coats of arms and other objects bearing on his own projected work, a history of Florida, but also with that ready kindness which always characterized him, finding and transmitting many documents to the most distinguished of our historical students and authors.

The first fruit of these studies and researches was a volume printed under his own eye at Madrid, although bearing the imprint of a London bookseller. This was his "*Coleccion de Varios Documentos para la Historia de la Florida y Tierras adyacentes.*" The documents were of very great importance, and were printed with peculiar care and exactness, the proof being always compared with the original. This he held to be the only proper mode of printing documents, and he insisted so strongly on this, that he would not print here documents which he had copied in Spain, declaring that they must be printed where he could refer to the originals.

He was recalled Sept. 1st, 1858, and returned to the United States, his welcome home being clouded by the death of his mother, who expired at St Augustine at the advanced age of eighty-three

Mingling again with our own scholars and students, he contributed various valuable papers to the *Historical Magazine*,* and turning his attention to the study of the Indian languages, furnished for the *Bulletin* of the American Ethnological Society, a sketch of the grammar of the language of the Heve Indians of Sonora, which the writer, then issuing a series of *American Linguistics* induced him also to print in that collection. He also while in Europe printed a *fac simile* of a petition of the Apalache Indians, and one of the Timuquan tribe with a Spanish translation—documents, curious as evincing the culture of the Indians, for they are in both cases signed by the chiefs in their own hand-writing, with none of the marks or totems so common elsewhere

To the writer's series of *American Linguistics* he also contributed a "Grammar of the Pima or Nevome, a language of

---

* "A Letter of Pedro Menendez Marquez" (vol III, p 273), "Books printed in the Timuquan Language" (vol IV, p 39) "Specimen of the Apalachian Language" (vol IV, p 40), "Letter of Father Francis Palou" (vol IV, p 67), "Vespucius and his first Voyage" (vol IV, p 98) "The Siege of Pensacola in 1781" (vol IV, p 166), "The Patent to Juan de Añasco" (vol IV, p 174). "Pardo's Exploration of South Carolina, and Georgia" (vol IV, p 230), "Memoirs of Alonzo Vasquez" (vol IV, p 257) "The Will of Hernando de Soto" (vol V p 144), "Papers relating to Cartier's Voyage (vol VI, p 14). "Vocabulary of the Eudeve" (vol VI, p 18), "Memorials of the Expedition of Pamphilo de Narvaez" (vol VI, p 128) " Verrazzano as a Discoverer" (vol X 169), "Vocabularies of the Seminole and Mickasuke Tongues" (vol X, p 299). "Map of the World, containing the Discovery of Verrazzano, by Hieronimus de Verrazzano" (vol X, 308) " Discovery of the Northern Coast of North America" (vol X p 368) "Narvaez and Florida" (series II vol 1 p 24) "Instructions to the Factor" (series II, vol 1, p 109) "Relation of what befel the persons who escaped from the disaster that attended Pamphilo de Narvaez (series II, vol II, pp 141, 204, 267, 347)

Sonora" and the adjacent territory on the north, with a Doctrina Christiana y Confesionario" in the same language.

While these were going through the press he was bereaved of his wife, who had long been the partner in his varied life. She died in New York, Dec 26th, 1861.

Mr. Smith had on his return from Europe visited his home in Florida, to find the public mind intensely excited. Withdrawn for many years from local politics, not even his warm southern feelings could draw him into the vortex. His forecast enabled him to judge the relative strength, and to see the final result. On his way north, he told an old friend who shared the enthusiasm of the South over its new hopes that he could not indulge in his sanguine expectations; that on the contrary he would live to see him electioneering among his own slaves.

The war entailed no little loss to Mr Smith in the depreciation of his property and in the fact that the government set his slaves at liberty, but it is characteristic of the man that while the able-bodied then left him, he continued till death to maintain the aged and infirm negroes who had been the family slaves.

Continuing his contributions to history, he printed a curious manuscript work on Sonora, with a quaint Spanish title *Rudo Ensayo, tentativa de una prevencional Descripcion de la Provincia de Sonora* but full, accurate and showing evident marks of being the production of some missionary thoroughly acquainted with that province and its mineral resources.

The voyage of Estevan Gomez along the northern coast had been one of his subjects of study and research, and in the investigation he was led to study critically the account of Verrazano's voyage, published originally in Ramusio's large work. Convinced that that narrative was a fabrication he set forward the grounds of his opinion in his *Inquiry into the Authenticity of Documents concerning a Discovery in North America, claimed to have been made by Verrazano,* which was read before the New York Historical Society, in 1864, and printed. But as usual with him, he was not satisfied with his work, and visited Spain to seek new material for the discussion of the subject, as well as to study a very different branch, but one in which he took great interest, the culture of the orange tree, in order to select and import the best varieties, so as to preserve and extend the cultivation of the fruit in Florida.

He was successful under both points of view, and came prepared to issue in a more extended form, with ample documents, his examination into the Verrazano voyage, which, however, he never gave to the world.

Mr. Smith then for a time acted as tax commissioner in Florida, but had meanwhile undertaken, and in 1866 published, through the Bradford Club, his *Narratives of the Career of Hernando de Soto in the Conquest of Florida as told by a Knight of Elvas and in a Relation by Luys Hernandez de Biedma.*

These, with some pleasant sketches of Spanish American authors in *Duyckinck's Cyclopedia of American Literature,* embracing notices of Verrazzano, Biedma, Cancer, Pareja, Florencia, Benavides, Rochefort, Ayeta and Siguenza (*Supplement,* p. 156, etc.), formed his contributions to our literature. Critical to a nicety, he was never satisfied with his labors, but as soon as he saw them in print at once began to correct and amend. One of his most cherished projects was to issue a new edition of his first work, but as he shrank from doing anything on his own responsibility and sought no publisher, his project would have remained a mere velleity had not his old friend, Mr. Henry C. Murphy of Brooklyn, taken it in hand. The result is the present volume, which the author did not live to complete.

Disease had been insidiously impairing his constitution, and unconsciously to himself consumption had already made fatal progress. His residence at the north during the severe winter of 1870-1, hastened the crisis. Under the milder climate of Florida his valuable life might have been for a time prolonged, but he at last became alarmed, yet entertained no immediate fear. He still kept up, visiting his friends, talking over the subjects of his studies, till January 4th, when, calling on his physician, he was urged to return at once to his rooms and secure a suitable attendant, as he was more seriously ill than he imagined.

He was very much enfeebled, and before he reached his own door, after leaving the car, became bewildered. He was hurried off to a police station, and thence to an hospital, where he died the next day, before any of his many warm friends were aware of his illness.

The death of Buckingham Smith drew around his coffin the circle of literary and personal friends to whom his kindly disposition, his truthful nature, his impartiality and studies, had long endeared him. To many the life of research and investigation, solitary as it must needs be, may seem devoid of interest, and utility; but Buckingham Smith gave his early manhood to the public service, and spent in those antiquarian studies, which are so full of great lessons, the hours of relaxation given by others to pleasure, or the years of declining age, when the many seek only ease and comfort.

INDEX.

Á, prefix to native names, unaccountably taken from the Spanish, 42
Academy of History at Madrid, 18
Açamor, 205
Acaxee, agriculturists, man eaters, 78
Achkeres, Indians, 242
Achuse, bay of, 64
Acolhuan, 44
Acubadaos, Indians, 137
Adaize, Indians, 127
Adaves, Indians, 127
Adelantado, Narváez petitions to be made, 209
Adobe, residences of 78
Africa, Cabeça de Vaca sentenced to, 250
Aguar, Indian deity, 192
Aguenes Indians, 133
Ahome, river, 182
Ahome, Indians, 181
Alabama, 235
A la-Chua, instance of the double prefix, 42
Alafaya, instance of the double prefix, 42
Alaniz, Hieronymo, notary, consulted by the governor, 25, his views on the expedition, 26, gives certificate to the governor, 27
Alapaha, instance of the double prefix, 42
A la prefix to native names, unaccountably taken from the Spanish, 42
Alatamaha, instance of the double prefix, 42
A la-Tama, instance of the double prefix, 42
Alburquerque, mountains of 170
Alegre, Padre Francisco Javier, 178
Alcaraz, 189, 190, 193
Aldermen for the first town in Florida, 18
Algorrova, 143
Alhaja, Martin, begger, 234, ennobled, 234
Alligator, no mention made of the, 42
Almojarifadgo, 219

54

Alvarado, 43.
American Antiquarian Society, 259
American Ethnological Society, 259, Bulletin of the 260
American Journal of Science and Art, 170
American Linguistics, 260
Amsterdam, chart printed in, 56
Anagados, Indians, 42, 114
Anchors, stones scarce for, 48
Andalusia, 29, definitions by an authoress of, 139
Andaluz, 189
Andes, Cordillera of the, 169
Anhacan, 190
Animal magnetism, Indian juggler's knowledge of, 82
Antillas, 22, 66, destructive hurricane at, 18
Ants, eggs of food of the Yguazes, 103
Apaches, Tobosos related to, 163, extermination of, 163, account of by Oñate 163, territory of the, exploring expedition to, 235
Apalache, sought for, 31, found, 33, 41, see Apalachen
Apalache bay, 56
Apalache, Indians, fac simile of a petition of the, 260
Apalachen, town of, gold in, 21, assailed, 35, large quantities of maize found in, 35, description of houses in, 35, character of the country of, 36
Apalachian language specimen of the, 260
Apalachicola river, 235
Apalachine, 139
Apalito, Indian deity, 162
Apologetic Examination, etc, against the Censures of Father Honorio Philipono, 253
Appendix, 207-254
Aragon, 208, 234
Arbadaos, Indians, 125
Archivo de Indias, at Sevilla, 18, 207, 215, 231
Archivo General de Indias, 211
Ardomo, Antonio, Señor, 253
Areitos, amusements of Indians, 77, 141
Areyte, signification of, 79
Arkansas, river, 235, head waters of the, 234
Armor, good, of no avail against Indians' arrows, 39
Arroba, Indian measure, 138, 139
Arrows, articles of barter, 126
Arroyo de Cedros, 178, see Cedar stream
Arsenic, attempts to poison with frustrated, 248
Artichoke, Jerusalem, 178

Assomption, 239, 240, 244, 246, 248, 250
Astudillo, of Çafra, 73
Asturiano, a clergyman, 107, 116, visits Cabeça de Vaca, 84, heard from, 124
Asturian, the, stripped and shot, 101, see Asturiano
Atayos, Indians, 121, 137
Atlantic ocean, 148
Audiencia of Española, 205, letter to, ix
Auia, island of, 73
Auitzotl, 78
Austria, 253
Aute, town of, 38, 165, corpse of Avellaneda carried to, 41, houses burned, 41, expedition leaves, 45
Authorities, comparison of, 20
Autograph of Alvar Nunez Cabeça de Vaca, 200, of Pámphilo de Narváez, 210
Avavares, Indians, 116, 122, 139
Avellaneda, hidalgo, killed, 40
Ayeta, notice of, 262
Ayolas, commander, 238, 241
Azara, Chevalier, 254
Azores, 198

Bacallaos, 57
Badthing, demon, 123, 124, 127, 128
Bahía de Caballos, havea, 51, see Bahía de los Caballos
Bahía de Cavallos, number of men killed in, 50, see Bahía de Caballos
Bahía de la Cruz, 48, number of men landed at, 50
Bahía de los Caballos, appearance in 1539, 55, see Bahía de Caballos and Bahía de Cavallos
Baños, Indian, 172
Ballast, stones scarce for, 48
Bamoa, 225
Baptism of Indian children, 226, 227
Baptisms, Indian, 194
Bárcia, 20, 216, 253, 254
Bárcia Ensayo Cro, 64
Bárcia's Historiadores Primitivos de las Indias Occidentales, viii
Barrigon, sierra of, 169
Barter, articles of, 85
Bartlett, Mr, 236
Baya de Miruelo, 36
Beads presented to Indian chief, 31, 66, 67, presented, 115, 146, 150, 194

Beam hollowed to secrete papers, 247
Beans, article of traffic, 38, 41, 85, Indians' food, 159, presented, 159, 161, 166, planted three times a year, 172
Bears, 36
Beaumont, R Pe Fray Pablo, x
Béjar, 204
Benavides, 177, notice of, 262
Benitez, visits Cabeça de Vaca, 84
Bermuda, island of, storm at, 198
Bezote, derivation of, 78
Bibliothèque Impériale, map in the, 56
Biedma, 34, 64, 79, 88, notice of, 262
Biscay, 148
Bison, 163, hide of the, x
Blackberries, 77, food of the Indians, 107
Blake, W P, 170
Blankets, Indian, 107 of cowhide presented, 150, 159, 160.
Blind Indians, 145, 148
Bones, powdered, food of the Yguazes, 103
Boomerang of the Australian, 154
Bottles made from the legs of horses, 48, useless, 52
Bows, articles of barter, 126, presented, 146
Brand-burning, Indians' application of, 179
Bravo del Norte, river, 89, 162, 163
Bream, 181
Broadcloth found, 28.
Brussels, chart printed in, 56
Buenos Ayres, 246, 254, vessels dispatched to, 239
Buhío, its characteristics and signification, 22
Buhíos described, 21
Bulletin of the American Ethnological Society, 260
Buoys, floating, indication that ships were lost, 16
Burgos, bishop of, 249

Caballería, definition of, 260
Caballero, Fernan, 139
Cabbage palm, 33.
Cabeça de Vaca, Alvar Nuñez, treasurer and high sheriff, 13, 64, 73, 95, 258; summoned before the Council of Indias, x, appeared before Charles V, viii, evidences of his diligence and good conduct, x, arrival of, at Sevilla, x, left Cuba, 12, went from Verá Cruz to Spain, 12, accompanies Captain Pantoja to Trinidad, 14, remains at sea with the pilots, 14, persuaded with difficulty to go to the town, 15,

INDEX

Cabeça de Vaca, Alvar Nuñez, terrible storm while at Trinidad, 16, sends the testimony of it to the king, 16, fleet placed in his charge, 17, passed winter at Xagua, 17, in storms at sea, 20, anchored on the coast of Florida, 20, his views on penetrating the interior, 25, 26, advises the governor to secure the ships, 27, refuses lieutenancy of the ships, 27, 28, petitions governor, 30, sent to look for the sea, 30, 41, ordered to enter Apalachen, 35, explores coast, 41, reports embarrassing nature of country, 42, embarks in open boat, 49, privations, 52, wounded, 54, noticed by Charlevoix, 56, discovers a cape, consulted by the governor, 60, deserted by the governor, 62, his excessive sufferings, 62, 63, orders Lope de Ovedo to reconnoitre, 65, launches boat, 67, misfortunes, 68, beseeches Indians for shelter, 69, meets companions, 72, necessitous condition, 73, long fastings, 81, great sickness came upon him, 84, obliged to remain on the island a year, 85, resolved to flee, 85, turns merchant, 85, his merchandise, 85, his object in business, 86, hardships experienced, 86, sets off in quest of Christians, 87, supposed knowledge of extent of northern explorations, 88, remains with the Quevenes, 88, finds companions, 90, for a long time considered dead, 91, in slavery, 92, sees Indians of light color, 97, letter written by, 107, probably dated new moon from the time he first saw it, 113, in hunger and ill used, 113, his description of the country, 113, cures afflicted, 117, lost, 118, wanders with brands and sticks to make fire at night, 118, finds Christians, 119, Indians' fondness for, 121, breathes upon and blesses an Indian and performs a miraculous cure, 122, cures those sick of a stupor, 122, fame of his cures, 122, 123, went to the Malicones, 125, casts his skin like a serpent, 126, greatly tormented, 126, trades with the Arbadoes, 126, is set by the Indians to scrape skins, 127, sustained by the scraps of skins, 127, his meagre subsistence by trafficking, 127, strength after eating the dogs, 129, 130, Indians weep at his departure, 130, account of customs of Indians, 131–134, account of Indians when at war, 135, 136, opinion on the senses of the Indians, 136, enumerates nations and tongues, 137, witnesses a diabolical practice, 139, hospitably received, 140, 141, 142, 143, passed over a rapid river, 141, great inconvenience from so many followers 144, 153, time consumed in the privilege of touching, 145, mountains seen, 145, great authority over the Indians, 146, travels with Indians, 149, performed successfully a surgical operation, 151, blesses provisions, 152, his agreement with the account of Father de Moth, 154

Cabeça de Vaca, Alva Nuñez, forded a very large river, 155; fashion of being received changes, 156–160; begged by the Indians to tell the sky to rain, 160, appears to have struck the Bravo del Norte, 162, resolved to go in search of the maize, 166; handful of deer-suet his daily ration, 166, has abundance of food, 167; emerald arrow-heads presented to, 167, blesses children, 168, hears news of Christians, 173, sees traces of Christians, 175; sure signs of Christians, 183, overtakes Christians, 183; are confounded at the sight of him, 183, is ordered to be taken to their chief, 184, Alcaraz's statement to, 184; obtains certificate of date and manner of his appearance, 184, unable to convince Indians that he belongs to Christians, 187; gives glowing account of the country, 187; affirms it is the fault of the Christians if Indians do not build towns, 188; hospitably entertained by the chief alcalde, 190, detained at San Miguel, 196, entertained by Governor Nuño de Guzmán, 196, some time before he is reaccustomed to the habits of civilization, 196; arrived at Mexico, 196, distance traveled 196, leaves Mexico with Dorantes, 197, sets sail from Verá Cruz, 197; his escape from being captured, 199, instructions given to, for his observance, as treasurer to the king of Spain in the army of Narváez for the conquest of Florida, 218–223, missionary's allusion to, in the ill-starred expedition into Florida, 223, 225, petitions of, 231 232; his life, 233–254, the eminence of his family, 233, traditionary origin of the name, 233, 234, his neglect to record the direction of his journeyings, 234, terrible severity of his sufferings, 234, his route traced by Mr Smith, 235, his description of finding towns with habitations confirmed by Mr Bartlett, 236, evidences of his passage found by Spanish explorers, 236, his narrations fortified by Ternaux Compans, 236, 237, Ulrich Schmidel's records of incidents in the life of, 238, selected as governor, 238, expended his entire fortune in the enterprise of conquest, 238, his compensation, 238, put to sea, but compelled to return to Cadiz, 238, arrived at St Catharine's 238, remains at St Catharine's for more than seven months, 238, his explorations while at St Catharine's, 238, 239, eloquent in eulogies of the inhabitants and their territories, 239, his sagacious manoeuvres avert a catastrophe, 239, 240, arrives at Assomption, 240, finds colonial troops unfavorable to his pretensions, 240, Irala's enmity to, 241, colonists require him to exhibit his authority, but refuses, 241, 242, submits his brief of authority to priests, 242, reviews and musters his army, 242, orders expeditions to search the country for traces of the route to El Dorado, 242,

Cabeça de Vaca, Alvar Nuñez, directs Irala to execute Achkere, 242, makes war upon the Guaycurus, and his arrest, Schmidel's story of, 243, 244, coincides with Schmidel in the cause of his abandonment of the campaign, 245, his unpopularity, what attributed to, 245, conspiracy formed to seize his person, 246, his property confiscated, 246, hurried to prison, 246; the rigidness of his guard, 246; taken from his cell more dead than alive, 246, his thankfulness for being once more permitted to behold the sun, 246, Irala's rigor towards, 246, his friends aid him in secret, 246, 247, incident in his imprisonment, 247, delegates Captain Saluzar as his lieutenant in the government, 248, slightly wounded in a melée, 248, hurried on board the vessel to save his life, 248, chained to the deck, but released when vessel was supposed to be foundering, 248, strictly guarded, 248, attempts to poison him, 248, remorse in his jailors, 249, sea and winds were appeased when his chains were removed, 249, arrival at Madrid, 249, the machinations of his enemies prevailed, 249, awaited his trial in prison for more than six years, 249, only appeared before the council except to receive his sentence, 249, severity of his treatment in prison, 250, councillors of the Indies deliver their judgment eight years after his seizure, 250, his sentence, 250, the obscurity of his subsequent fate, 250, probably pardoned, 250, transcript of his judgment, 250, 251, Charlevoix on his acquittal, etc., 251, the attention his Relation excited as to his miraculous cures and divine interpositions, 252, 253, abridged translation of his works, 253; various opinions of historians and writers regarding the character of, 254

Cabeça de Vaca, Doña Tereça, 205

Cabrera, Alonzo, 244, death of, 249

Cabo de Santa Cruz, port, 11

Cabot, Juan, land discovered by, 57

Cabot, Sebastian, 57, mappemonde by, 56

Cacama, 42, 43

Cacine, 189

Cacique, refuses to entrust his person with Soto, 34

Cactus, 178

Cadiz, expedition returns to, by contrary winds, 238

Cahoques, Indians, 137

Calabashes, presented, 159

Caleriei, 34

California, gulf of, 236, Spanish settlements on the, Cabeça de Vaca arrived at, 12

Cambridge Law School, 256

Camoles, Indians 187.
Camones, Indians, 113
Campo, page to Antón Perez, 97
Canadian river, 235
Canaries, 205
Canarreo, shoals, 19
Cancer, notice of, 262
Cancer, tropic of, 18
Cane, joints of, in Indian's ears, 66; mats, houses of, 107
Canoes, broken up for fuel, 54
Canvas found, 28
Caoques, 139
Capricorn, tropic of, country of the Susacusis under the, 243
Captain general, Narvaez petitions for the position of, 208, salary of, 210
Cape Sant Anton, 20
Capogues, 82
Caravallo, alcalde, appointed lieutenant of the ships, 28, Lieut, 203
Carios (Guaranos) Indians, 243
Carob, mezquiquez like unto the, 140
Carolano, new voyage to, 118.
Carpenter, only one in the company, 47
Cartier's voyage, papers relating to, 260
Cases containing dead bodies, 24, 203
Castile, king of, 234.
Castilla, 97, 202, 203, 208, 210
Castillo, Captain, 41, 236; went inland to the Yguazes, 103; died, 118.
Castillo, Doctor, 204
Castro-Ferrel, 234
Catholic faith, conversion of natives to, responsibility rests on the royal conscience for, 208
Cattle, 106, 107, killed and slaughtered, 160
Cavallerias of land two, Narváez petitions for, to be given to the first conquerors, 209
Cavalleros, x
Cedars, 36
Cedar stream, 178, see Arroyo de Cedros
Cémola, Indians' food, 169
Cerra, Indians, 178, their great savagery, 170
Chacan, Indians' food, 160, its pungency, 161
Chalchi, indefinable, 171
Chalchinite, 170, see turquoises
Chalchiuhxiuatqui, signification of, 170
Chalchiuitl, definition of, 170

Charles V, king of Spain, of the Sicilies, etc., 11, 79, 98, 99, 211; Cabeça de Vaca's appearance before, x
Charlevoix, 139, 249, 251, 254, statement by, 55
Charts, ancient, 56
Chastisement of Indian infants, rat teeth used for, 158
Chata, Indians, 171
Chavavares, Indians, 137
Chaves, Indians, 17, visits Cabeça de Vaca, 84
Chiapa, bishop of, his account of Panphilo de Narváez, 99
Chiametla, town of, 177
Chicamistl, his oratory, 177
Chicasas, Indians' custom of mourning for their dead, 78, 79
Chichimecas, Indians, 206
Chief of the Heavens, Indian deity, 163
Children, Indian, nursed till twelve years old, reason of, 131
Choruco, Indians, 137
Christians, hospitable reception of, recorded by a missionary, 223
Churches, Indians commanded to build, 193, 194
Chuse, bay of, 64
Cibola, city, 165, 235, 237, invasion of, 178
Cinaloa, 78, 178, 231, 230, historian of, 179
Cinaloa, Indians, 181
Civet marten, robe of, secured, 54, fragrance of, 54
Civola, 177
Climate, condition of the, 176
Clothing, Indians' scanty, 180
Clubs, Indian, 59, astonishing precision of, 152
Coa, signification of, 229
Coayos, Indians, 121
Cohuanateo, 42, 43
Cohcán, 182
Collección de Varios Documentos Para la Historia de la Florida y Tierras adyacentes, 250
Colorado, river, 178
Comanches, symbols of the, 171
Combs, article of barter, 126
Comité d'Archéologie Américaine of France, 56
Commentarios, vii
Commissions laid before the governor, 21
Comos, Indians, 137
Compans, Ternaux, 236, 252, his edition of the Relation in French, vii
Comparison of authorities, 20
Compostela, 196

Comptroller, 113
Concessions made to Narváez by the Council of Indias, 210.
Conches used for cutting, 86; article of traffic, 85
Conchos, Indians, 162, 169
Conchos, river, 162, 165
Cones, article of traffic, 85
Constabulary of lands, Narváez petitions for, 208
Contratacion in Sevilla, 88.
Cooking, Indian mode of, 161, 162
Copper, hawkbells of, 153; traces of, seen, 176
Corals presented, 167
Corazones, 181; town of, 177; temperature of, 178; valley of, 178
Cordero, Lieut Col Antonio, 163; report of, 169
Cordillera of the Andes, 42, 169
Coronado, Spanish explorer, 153, 163, 236; march of, 178
Corral, dead body of, eaten, 74
Corrientes, cape, storm at, 20
Cortambert, M Richard, 56
Cortés, Hernando, 97, 181, his conquest of Mexico, 99, unscrupulousness of, 43; warned of an element of his ruin, 99, 100
Cotton shawls presented, 162, 166
Council of Indias, 207, 208; Cabeça de Vaca summoned before, viii
Council, order of, 232
Cow nation, Indians, 163; description of, 160
Crabs, 92, 95
Cross, sign of the, cure for Indians' diseases, 117
Cramps cured, 120
Cronica de Mechoacan, x
Cricket, music of a, prevents a ship from striking on the rocks, 252, 253
Cross, adoration of the, 226
Crosses, symbols of peace, 193
Çuaque, Indians 181
Cuba island of, 18, 71, 73, 79, 97, 98, 99, 204, 212
Cuba Cabeça de Vaca left, 12
Cuchendados 137
Cuellar, 32
Cuenca, bishop of, 249
Cuenca de Huete, 203
Cuervo, island 198
Culican, 237
Culiçan, town, 189
Culiacan, province of, 178, 236
Cutilchuc, 43

INDEX 275

Cultachulches Indians, 137
Cumanche, Indians, 163
Cumberland Island, Ga., 255
Cures, miraculous, animadversions on, and advocacy of, 252
Custom, Indian not naming the dead, 71, killing children to serve deceased ones, 71, wailing for dead, 76, disposing of their dead 76, abstaining from food 77, nether lip opened to distinguish brave, 78, of mourning among the Chacasis, 78, of marriage among the Chatis 79, weeping before speaking, 82, life taken on account of dreams, 102, daughters killed at birth, 102, 109, of taking meat 127, of salutation 130 in pregnancy, etc., 131, nursing children till twelve years old reason of 131, leaving wives when there is no conformity 131, forsaking sick in the desert, 131, in domestic disputes, 132, in night attacks, 133, in war generally 134 135, of tea drinking 138, when women are indisposed, 139, in battle mode of returning 136, of divesting Indian patient, 143, plundering 144 145 147 148, of bestowing any thing not to take it back, 156, faces turned to the wall at a reception, 160, singing and weeping at morn and eve 171, sing when going into battle 171
Cutalches Indians, 127,
Cutalchiches Indians, 139
Cuthalchuches Indians, 121, their generosity 122

Davis, W. W. H., 127
Deer hearts of presented, 172
Deaguanes Indians 88
De Alcaraz, Diego, deeds, 178 184 185
De Alvaraz, Hieronymo, 84 87
De Añasco, Juan the patent to 260, Bahia de los Caballos, visited by 55, searches for letters of adventurers, 56
De Bry's Voyages and Discoveries 78, 133
De Cebreros, Captain Lazaro 184
De Cueto, Diego alderman 18
Dedication to Charles V emperor of Germany king of Spain as Carlos I see Proem
Deer 36 dung of the food of the Yguazes 103 overtaken in the chase by Indians 104 mode of encircling them with fire 106 quantity killed 109 mode of killing 110 kinds of 172
Deer-suet handful of, a daily ration 166
De Espejo Antonio, 162, his report extant 162
De Esquivel Hernando of Badajoz 93 his son him and sh 94 96 accompanies Indian 94

De Figueroa, Vasco Porcallo, lieutenant general to Soto, 18, see Porcallo, Vasco, and Figueroa
De Gayangos, Don Pascual, the orientalist, 56, 259
De Guijón, Juan, alderman, 18
De Guzmán, Governor Nuño, 189, 194-196, Noticias Historicas, 100
De Guzmán, Padre Diego, 176, 230
De Herrera, Alonzo, alderman, 18
De Huelva, Diego, killed for diversion, 87, visits Cabeça de Vaca 84, killed in slavery, 102, 108
De Irala, Martin Dominick, 241, 242-243, 246, proclaimed governor, 244
De la Cerda, Alvara, in charge of vessel, 19, his ship to be sought for, 23
De Las Casas, Bartholomew, 245, 249, see Las Casas
Del Castillo, Alonzo, native of Salamanca, 30, 81-84, 87, 90, 91, 92 95, 112, 113-116, 125, 158-159, 173, 184, 185, 204, 205, embarks in open boat, 49, boat capsized, 72, visits Cabeça de Vaca, 84, cures Indians with the sign of the cross, 117, 120, his fame spreads, 117, a timid practitioner, 121, see Castillo
De Leon, Francisco, visits Cabeça de Vaca, 84
De los Cobas, Freo, 217
De los Covos, Francisco, 223
De Lumbreras, Miguel, alderman, 18
Del Valle, Marquis, 196
De Mayorga, Juan, alderman, 18
De Mendoca, Don Antonio, 236
De Molina, dictionary of the Mexican language, by 229
De Morfi, Father Juan Augustin, his Memoirs for the history of Texas, 154
De Naro, Don Diego Lopez, 234
De Narváez, Governor Pánphilo, 64, 113, 211, 215, 230, 234, 236, 258 attempt to trace the route of the army of, v, in command of expedition, 13, his instructions, 13, procured supplies, 14, sets out for Trinidad, 14, waits at Cabo de Santa Cruz, 41 arrives at Trinidad, 17, stays through the winter there, 17 gives the fleet into Cabeça de Vaca's charge, 17, arrived at the port of Xagua, 19, arrived at Guaniguanico, 19, anchored on the coast of Florida, 20, debarked with his people, 21, raised ensigns for the emperor, 21, acknowledged commissions, 21, finds horses and men, 22, resolves to explore the land, 23, his company, 23, consults with his officers, 25, warned not to quit the ships before securing them, 25, asks notary for a certificate, 27, begs Cabeça de Vaca to take lieutenantcy of the ships, 27, 28, victuals his men for their march, 29,

De Narváez, sends Cabeça de Vaca to look for the sea, 30, sends Valenzuela to seek a harbor, 31, presented with a painted deerskin, 31, procures Indians as guides, 32, orders Cabeça de Vaca to enter the town of Apalachen, 35, detains a cacique, 37, begs Cabeça de Vaca to look for the sea, 41, afflicted with a malady, 41, plot for abandoning, 45, seeks advice 46, embarks in open boat, 49, Indians offer hospitalities to, 53, presents cacique with trinkets, 53, struck with a stone and wounded, 54, noticed by Charlevoix, 55, 56, Indians demand hostages of, 58, his selfishness, 62, noticed by Bedma, 64, Lope Hurtado on the search after, 79, Figueroa's account of his fate, 93, 94, covered with spots, 97, portrayed by Bernal Diaz, 97, government of Florida conferred on, 97, expended and lost all his treasure, 97, place of nativity, 97, his marriage, 97, had an eye put out 97, his gentle breeding, 97, the character of his wife, 98, entreats for justice and single combat with Cortés, 98, date of his disappearance, 98, account of, by the bishop of Chiapa, 99, cautioned not to go inland, 202, greater part of his property lost 207, imprisoned and detained five years, 207, entreats the king to require him in New Spain, 207, his intention to traffic with the natives and plant the Christian faith, 207, reminds the king of his responsibility for the conversion of the natives, 208, the extent of country he wishes to be given him 208, privileges, etc. he wished the king to bestow, 208, 209, 210, his autograph 210, memorandum of orders made in Council of Indies on the back of enclosure of petition, 210–211, petitions of, to the king of Spain with notes of concessions made to him by the Council of Indies for the conquest of Florida, 207–211, memorials of the expedition of 260, relation of what befel the persons that attended him, 260

De Niça, Marcos, friar of the order of St Francis 177
De Oñate, Juan, 163
De Oviedo Lope, 84, 86, 90, with the Indians, 65
De Rios, the editor of Oviedo 259
De Palos, Juan, lay brother, 99 100, accompanies expedition 29
De Paz, Augustin, printer of books 205
De Salazar, Juan Velazquez, first commission for mayor in Florida, 18
De Silvera, Diego, 199
De Solis, Alonzo, distributor and assessor, 13, 66, accompanies the governor to explore the land, 23, consulted by the governor, 25, assails the town of Apalachen, 35, embarks in open boat, 49, drowned 68

De Soto, Hernando, 55, 64, expedition of, 34, 42, 66, his letter from Florida, 258, the will of, 260, misunderstanding with De Figueroa, 18, narratives of the career of, 262, relation of the march of, 42

De Tapia, Padre Gonzalo, struck down by a sorcerer, 154

De Tejada, Don Lerdo, 257

De Urdaide, Diego Martinez, 224

De Valencia, prelate, 99

De Valenzuela, Maria, 97, compared to Penelope, 98

De Varnhagen, F. A., 58

De Venegas, Garcia, 248, death of, 249

De Vera, Francisco, 205

De Vera, Pedro, conqueror of the Canaries, 205

Devoropa, missionary station, 154

Diabolical practice, 139

Diaz, Bernal, his portraiture of Pánfilo de Narváez, 97

Diaz, Melchior, alcalde, 188, 191

Disease and hunger, number of men died of, 50

Doctrina Christiana y Confesionario, in the Pima language, 261

Documents, accompanying President's message, 127, proper mode of printing, 259

Dodge, Hon. Augustus C., minister to Spain, 259

Dog, fatal bite by a, 239

Dogs bought for food, 125

Doguenes, Indians, 137, 139

Don Carlos, emperor, 57, 215

Don Pedro, a lord of Tescuco, killed, 38

Don Philippe, infant of Spain, 236

Don Theodoro, Greek, 48, killed, 64

Dorantes, Andrés, 23, 41, 81, 84, 87, 90, 92, 95, 107, 109, 112, 113, 115, 121, 123, 125, 150, 184, 185, 197, 204, 236, alderman, 18, embarks in open boat, 49, in ambuscade, 54, his boat capsized, 72, visits Cabeça de Vaca, 84, escaped from slavery, 102, 103, shown articles of Esquivel, 102, presented with open hearts of deer, 172, sailed for Spain, 206, put back, 206, invited by Mendoça to the capital, 206, joyfully receives appointment to retrace on discoveries in company with some religious fathers, 206

Dorantes, Diego, 95, visits Cabeça de Vaca, 84, killed for diversion, 87, killed in slavery, 102, 108

Dorantes, Pablo, 204

Dorantes, Pedro, 231

Dreams, Indians' superstition of, 180, life taken by the Indians in obedience to, 102

Drunkards, Indians, 104
Dry scratching, punishment for Indian boys, 165
Ducks, 36
Duero, 97
Dulchanchellin, Indian chief, 32
Dumont, 139
Duran, Padre, his account of a ball in Mexico, 78
Duty, free, on horses, arms, etc., Narvaez petitions for, 209
Duyckinck's Cyclopedia of American Literature, 262
Dwarf fan-palm, 33
Dwellings, Indian, several stories in height, 236
Dyeing hair of deer for tassels, 85

Eagles, 58
Earth, food of the Yguazes, 103, a constituent in food, 140 houses of, 167
El Dorado, expedition ordered to search for, 242
Electioneering among slaves, prediction, 261
Eliu, ó la España Trienta Años ha, 139
Emasculated Indians, 139
Emeralda basta, 170
Emerald arrow heads presented 167 lost 186
Emeralds, x
Encomienda, Indians to be excluded from the tribute of, 228
English version of the Relation in, the only, viii
Enriquez, Alonzo, comptroller 13, 44 89, 95, 109, landed on an island in Florida, 21, barters with Indians, 24 consulted by the governor, 25, petitions governor, 30 embarks in open boat, 49 his boat found 92, Figueroa's account of his end, 93 his commission recalled, 93
Ensayo Cro, 20
Española, 20, 66 212, 213, 219, storm at, 18, wretchedness in, 18
Español, audience of, 205 letter to, ix
Espiritu Sancto bay, 57, 87, 89, 234 identical with Mobile bay, 235
Espiritu, Sancto river, 96
Espiritu Santo Bay, work by Buckingham Smith, 258
Esquivel, 89, 93, 113 slain by the Mariames, in consequence of a dream, 87, 102, 107, relation received from, 101
Estevanico, a black 91, 112, 121, 122, 158, 159 205, 236, visits Cabeza de Vaca, 84 went inland to the Yguazes, 103 parted with to the Viceroy, 206, killed, 237
Estrada, visits Cabeza de Vaca, 84
Estuary entered, 55
Eudeve language, 178 dialect of the Pima 88 vocabulary of, 260

Europeans, slow introduction of American fruits and vegetables among, 165
Exchequer, provisions for the security of the, 212, 213, 214, 215, 220, 221, 222

Falcons, 37, 58
Factor of Florida, no appointment to the office of, seems ever to have been made, 211; instructions to the, 260
Farinaceous food, abundance of, 239
Feathers, bunches of, found 24; presented, 191, 194
Feather work presented, 162
Feet cut with oysters in wading, 30
Females marry, etc., again, when their husbands went inland 203; Indian, destroyed at birth, 180
Fernandez, Alvaro, Portuguese carpenter, 73
Fernandez, Bartolomé, consulted by the governor 25
Fernandez, Pero xii
Fernandina, island of, 208, 212
Fessenden, Judge 256
Fessenden, William Pitt, of Maine, vi, 256
Festival, Indian, hearts of brutes prepared for, 177
Fidalgo of Elvas, 34
Figueroa, 73, 92, 94, 95, 96, 107, 116; received relation from Esquivel, 101; escaped, 101; heard from, 124
Fires, Indian, 179
First-land-seen 57
Fish, Indian mode of taking, 181; in great plenty, 204
Florencia, notice of, 262
Florida 42, 100, 139, 181, 202, 207, 208, 235, 236, 255, 261; Cabeça de Vaca summoned before the Council of Indias to declare, x; Cabeça de Vaca landed in, 12; cape of, boundary of conquest, 13; first mayor and aldermen for, 18; coast of, expedition arrived on the, 20; coast of, explorations on the, 23; cape of, 20, 71, 83, 210, 215; description of Indians in, 39; peninsula of, 58; government of conferred on Pánphilo de Narváez, 97; cattle in, 107; Romans's history of, 139; instructions to the factor of, 211; memoirs on the prosperity of, 257; documents relating to the history of, 257; history of, Buckingham Smith's earnestness in collecting materials for the, 259; mild climate of, 262
Flints, valuable, presented, 121
Fly-catchers, 37
Font, unpublished journals of, 258
Fontaneda, Hernando de Escalante, 83; memoir of, 258
Force, Peter, library of x

Forests, vast, 33
Fortifications, custody of lands for, Narváez petitions for, 209.
Fortresses to be made at Narváez's cost, 210
Fragrance of the civet marten skin, 54
Franciscan monks, 154, 239
Franco, Bartholomé Hernández, alderman, 18
French, single edition of the Relation in, viii
Friars accompany expedition, 13
Fruit, abundance of, 239
Fuel, thirty canoes broken up for, 54
Funes, 254.

GAILNA, pulverized, presented, 150
Galisteo, valley of the, 170
Galvano, Antonio, 73
Garay, 20, 88.
Garces, unpublished journals of, 258
García, Bartholomé, friar 153
Garcilasso de la Vega, 18, 34, 55
Gardner, Elizabeth M., 257
Gardner, Julia G. 257
Gardner, Reuben G., 257
Gartish teeth, scratching with, punishment for Indian boys, 164 165
Geese, 36
Gelves, 86
Genealogía de la noble y antigua de Cabeça de Vaca, 233
General Historia de las Yndias, por Don Fray Bartolomé de las Casas, 99
Geografía de las Lenguas y Carta Etnografía de Mexico, 163
Georgia, state of, 66
Gerfalcons 37
Germany, 208
Giants, natives likened to, 39
Gibbs, George 256
Gibraleon 204
Glass broken, scratching with, punishment for Indian boys, 164
Glyph of Don Pedro Tetlahuehuetzquititzin, 11
Gold, traces of 24 176, tinklets of, found, 21, appearance of 153 from barter and from mines, the tenth, Narváez petitions for, 209
Gomara, Monarchia Indiana, 100
Gomez, Estevan voyage of, 261
Goodman, Edward, 256

Gourds, bored, sacred instruments of the Indians, 142, presented, 149, 191
Governor and chief justice for life, Narváez petitions for, 208, salary of, 210
Grand del Norte, river, 89
Grass, houses of, 162, seed of, Indians' food, 169, 179
Guadalquiver, river, 143, 162
Guadalupe, delta of the, 89
Guanignanico, storm at, 19
Guañin, definition of, 219
Guaranis, Indians, 239, 244
Guasives, 230
Guaycones, Indians, 137
Guaycurus, warlike Indians, 242, 245
Guatimo, emperor, 13
Guaymas, 178
Gulf of Mexico, 20
Gum, sweet, 42
Gutierrez, visits Cabeça de Vaca, 84
Guzmán, 184

HADAILS, Indians, 127
Hakluyt's Voyages and Discoveries, 128, 164
Han Indians, 82, 137
Hand, pictures of the, Indian symbols, 171
Hare-hunting, 152
Hares, 36
Hariot, M. Tho., 163
Harrisse, Mr., 251
Harvest, Indian festivals at, 177
Havana, Cuba, 20, 23, 204, vessel left on the shore of, 19, harbor of, 198.
Haven of Bahía de Caballos, 51
Hawk-bell of copper, presented, 150
Hawkbells given to Indians, 66, 67, given to Indian chief, 31
Hawkins, 83
Hearts, town of, description of, by Benavides, 177
Hernandez, Cabeça de Vaca's secretary, 246, 250
Herrara, 34, 73, 184, 246, 251, 254, quotation, 18
Heve, language, 178, dialect of the Pima, 188, Indians of Sonora, grammar of the language of, 260, see Eudeve
Hiaquis, Indians, 230
Histoire de la Floride la Port d'Aute, 55
Historia Apologetica de las Yndias Occidentales, 147
Historia General y Natural de las Indias, 22

INDEX.

Historia de la Compañia de Jesus en Nueva España, 178
Historia de las Indias de Nueva España y Islas de Tierra Firme, 78, 206; relation given in the, ix
Historia de los Chichimecas, 43
Historia Verdadera de la Conquista de Nueva España, 97
Historiadores Primitivos de las Indias Occidentales of Barcia, viii, 253
Historical Collection of Ramusio, viii
Historical Magazine, 260
Historical Society of New York, 154
History, Language, and Archæology, of the Piaros of the River Gila, New Mexico, 258
History of Paraguay, 251
Horcasitas, captain general of Cuba, 71
Hornachos, a Moorish woman of, 203
Horses, bottles made from the legs of, 48; all consumed, 49; number of, killed for subsistence, 50
House of Contractacion of the Indies, 212, 218
Houses, Indian, how constructed, 104
Huchotzinco, 44
Huehue, old man, 44
Huexotzinco, convent of, 100
Huitzilaputzli, 44
Hurricane at Trinidad, account of, 16; visited the Antillas, 18
Hurtado, Lope, 79; killed, 181

Ibulkas, mission of, 43
Idolatry called in question, 24, 28
Ilex vomitiva, 139
Imprint, first of the Relation, vi
Indians, small pox among the, 18; first appearance of, 21; captured, 24; their evidence of a vessel lost, 28; insult expedition, 29; seen wearing many plumes, 31; hostility of, 32; serve as guides, 32; clothing of, 35; attack from behind trees, 38; contest the passage of a lake, 39; their archers, 39; personal appearance, 39; fell upon the rear guard, 40; assault by, 41; contentions with, 48; attack expedition, 48, 53, 54; powerful archers of, 48; abandon canoes, 51; fishermen, 52; well formed, 53; demand hostages, 59; huts of the tenantless, 65; pledge of friendship, 66; bring food, 67; are besought for shelter, 69; hospitality of, 70; their duty to mourn with friends in bereavement, 70; custom of not naming the dead, 70; destitution among, 74; great commotion among for Christians eating their dead, 74; visited by a disease of the bowels, 74; their nipples and lips bored, 75

Indians, their women accustomed to excessive hard labor, 75, 79; precarious mode of subsistence, 75, their love of offspring, 75, matrimony among, 76; customs, 75, 76, 77, nether lip opened, the sign of a brave, 78, live on oysters three months of the year, 79, their idea of increasing their wives' line and not their own, 79, their physicians, 80, their use of cauteries, 81, kind treatment by the, 81 go naked, 82, their mode of healing early observed, 82, generosity of the, 82, incapable of exertion in the winter, 86, cruelty of, 87, locality of walnut eating, 88, subsist on walnuts one sixth of the year, 90, blind, 92, Christians slaves to, 101, abused Christians, 101, their habit of running, 104, cured by having made over them the sign of the cross, 117, ignorant of time, 124, bestow all their time in obtaining food, 126, food scarce among, 129, custom of leaving sick to perish, 131, mode of settling quarrels, 132, their strategy against their enemies, 132, 133, women sometimes the cause of war, 133, gross barbarity of, 134, vigilance of, in war, 135, 136, method of fighting, 135, their effectual manœuvering, 135, advice to those who would fight them, 136, keener senses than any other in the world, 136, produce stupefaction with smoke, 138, 139, their tea, 138, 139, emasculated and impotent, 139, bored gourds sacred instruments of the, 142, clouded of an eye, and blind, 145, great liars, 148, their astonishing precision with clubs, 152, their great fear, 155, 157, sicken from privation and labor, 156, 157, great sympathy of relations when suffering, and no feeling displayed when dead, 157, their mode of cooking, 161, fear and superstition of, instance of by Hariot, 163, their arcanum against all diseases, 165, their punishment to boys, 165, rapid introduction of vegetables among, 165, instruction to, 169, originally worshipers of the sun, 171, flee to the mountains from the Christians, 174, 175, to become Christianized must be won by kindness, 175, carried away by Christians in chains, 175, regard silver and gold with indifference, 177, festivals with hearts of brutes, 179, Ceri, tribe of, in a state of great savagery, 179, their protection against the weather, 179, Cabeça de Vaca's remarks on, 179, 180, Christianized, 195

Indians to be made slaves, Narvaez petitions for, 209

Indias, Council of, Cabeça de Vaca summoned before, x

Indisposition, custom in Indian woman's, 139

Infants, Indian, rat teeth used for chastising, 158

Instruction, given to Cabeça de Vaca for his observance as treasurer to the king of Spain in the army of Narvaez for the conquest of Florida, 218-223 to the factor of Florida, 211-215

INDEX.

Iron found, 28, manufactured, 47; scoria of, 170, traces of, seen, 176; nails of, Indian ornaments, 181.
Italian, translation of the Relation published in, viii
Itenerario del Nuevo Mundo por Mendoca, 162
Ito, termination, generally misspelled etto, 33
Jumanos, Indians, 163, description of, 162
Ixtlilxochitl, 43, 44.

Jamaica, island of, 212
Jaramillo, Captain, 163, 181
Jerusalem artichoke, 178
Jesuit mission of Sonora, 82
Jesuits, 71
Joana, Doña, queen, mother of Spain, 18
Jomard, ancient charts published by, 56
Jornada, length of a, 18
Joust of reeds, with bulls, 196
Juego de herradura, 64
Juego de la barra, 64

Kayo, Jesuits, visit to the, 71
Kelly's Universal Cambist, 49
Keith, Prof., U. S. N., tabular statement of old and new styles, 114
Keys, three different, to be used to obviate fraud, 214, 222
Kin, Indian, 180
Kingsborough, 44

Ladder, dwellings ascended by, 236
Lakes in the country of Apalachea, 36, troublesome of fording, 36
Land, twenty leagues square of, Narváez petitions for, 209
Landonnière, 83
Lancerados, Indians, 112
Language of signs, 168, 171
Languages, Indian, differences in, 168
Larramendi, 188
Las Casas, Friar Bartolome de, 177, his General Historia de las Yndias, 99
Laudonnière René, his second voyage, 127
Laurel trees, 36
Lawson, John, surveyor general of North Carolina, 148
Lead, traces of, seen, 176
League distance of a, in the narrative, 18
Le Moyne, 83, 139
Le premier voyage de Amerigo Vespucci, 59

Letter, from a missionary to the Provincial of New Spain, respecting the arrival of Indians in Cinaloa from the Pimeria Baja in quest of friends, who, eighty years before had followed Alvar Nuñez and his comrades, 223-231; of the survivors under Narváez, ix
Liars, Indians 104
Library of Peter Force, v
Libro de la Florida de Capitulaciones, Asientos, 218
Linnets, 58
Linen cloth discovered, 24
Lions, [Cougar], 36; skin used, 59
Lip bored, Indian fashion, 75
Lipstones, fashion of the, 78
Liquid amber trees, 36
Lisbon, port of, 200
Lizards, Indians' food, 79; food of the Yguazes, 103
Locusts, Indians' food, 179
Lonja manuscript in the, v
Lopez, Diego, dead body of, eaten, 74
Lopez, Geronimo, alderman, 18
Los Cerillos, turquoises obtained among, 170
Louisiane, memoires Historiques sur la, 139

Macana, club, 154
Madrid, 249, 259; Academy of History at, 18
Magdalena, river of the, 41
Magnetism, animal, Indian jugglers' knowledge of, 82
Magrum, desert of, 163
Maine, 256, 257
Maize, brought from Aute, 47; fields in the country of Apalachen, 36, 37; flour of, 247; found, 24, 29, 35; not planted for want of rain, 160; planted three times a year, 172
Maldonado, Castillo, 236
Maldonado, Doña Aldonça, 204
Maliconcs, Indians, 121, 125, 127
Malhado, island of, 73, 75, 92, 104, 113, 116, 131, 137, 180; discovery of, 89
Mallards, 36
Manual para administrar los Santos Sacramentos, 154
Mappemonde by Sebastian Cabot, 56
Maps and notes, attempt to trace the route of the army of Narváez with, v
Mares to be taken from the Islands, Narváez petitions for, 209
Mariame, Indians, 101, 102, 116, 137, 179, 180, 235

Mariams, Indians, 92
Mariames, Indians, 93
Marriage state, among Yguazes 102, its duration 103
Marten skins, cloak of, given for passage, 84
Marquesate presented, 150
Marquez, Pedro Menendez, a letter of, 260
Matachin dances of the ancient Mexicans, 44
Matagorda, bay of, 89, 235
Mats, articles of barter, 126, tribute paid in, 193
Maury, M. F., letter from, 113, 114
Mavila, town of, 64
Mayor for the first town in Florida, 18
Meat, raw, better for digestion than roasted, 127
Medina del Campo, 205
Megre, Father, 178
Melon, early introduction of, among the Indians, 165
Memoir of Hernando de Escalante Fontaneda, 258
Menaces from the natives, 22
Men old, held by the Yguazes in little esteem, 104
Mendez, 73, 93, killed in consequence of a dream, 87
Mendica, Indians, 137
Mendoça his project 206, letter of to the king, 206, his Itenerario del Nuevo Mundo 162, requires of the survivors, a map of the territories over which they traveled, ix
Merlins, 37
Mexicans, Matachin dances of the ancient, 44
Mexico, ix, 100, 196, 197, 205, 224, 225, 231, 236, 255, 256, coast of, 165, description of a ball in 78, gulf of, 20, 88, retreat from, 43, Mr Smith appointed secretary of legation to, 257
Mezquiquez, wholesome food when eaten with earth, 140, method of preparing, 140, see Mezquite
Mezquite its classification, 143
Mimosæ, 143
Miracles, 252, 253
Miruelo, bay 58
Miruelo, Diego 20
Miruelo pilot, his knowledge of the position of the river Palmas, 19, puts vessels among the shoals, 19, his ignorance of locality, 23
Mississippi, river, 64, 143
Mitote mystic singing and dancing 79
Mobile bay and Pensacola, territory between, probably the scene of Cabeça de Vaca's six years captivity, 235, identified with the Bay Espiritu Sancto, 235

Moctezuma, 42, 43, 193
Moles, seed eaters, 160
Monarchia Indyana 3a P Gomara, 100
Mongé, unpublished journals of, 258.
Moors, Christian army advances against the, 234
Moquis, territory of the exploring expedition to the, 235
Mortars, for cracking maize, 35
Morton, Jackson, senator from Florida, vi.
Mosquitos, plentiful supply of, 77 mode of protection against, 105, 106, their tormenting qualities, 106
Motonia, Padre, 206
Mountains, none seen, nor information of any whatsoever, 49, seen, 145
Mulatos, stream, 178
Mulberries, 92
Mullet, 181 dried, found, 51.
Muñoz's Collection, 18
Murphy, Hon. Henry C., of Brooklyn, iv, 262
Muscle shoals, 235
Musetti, Juan Pedro, book merchant of Medina del Campo, 205
Muskokes, Indians, 164

Nacabeba, 154
Nagadoch, Indians, 42, 114
Nachitoches, river, 127.
Nagera, Castenada, Relations of, 236.
Narváez and Florida, 260
Navajos, Indians, 170
Navarra, yeomen of, exercise of juego de la barra among, 64
Navarre, King of, 234
Navarrete Viages Menores, 20
Navas, battle of, 233
Navigation, want of knowledge of, 49
Needle, scratching with, punishment for Indian child, 167
Negroes, aged and infirm, Buckingham Smith's humanity to, 261
Nets, articles of barter, 126
Netzahualcoyotl, 43
Netzaxualpilli, 42, 43
Nevomes, Indians, 178, 230, evidence of their early attachment to the Spaniards, 224, their settlements, 224, information of, the earliest and most accurate, 223, character of, 223, 224, their modesty and honesty, 224, ask holy baptism and residence among Christians, 224, 225
New England Historic-Genealogical Society, 259

New Galicia, 182; province of, 184
New Mexico, 236
New Spain, 66, 69, 97, 202, 204, 205
New York Historical Society, 259, 262
Nieremberg, Juan Eusebio, 230
Night herons, 37
Nipples bored, Indian fashion, 75
Nisa, Melchior Diaz, Spanish explorer, 236
Novi Typis Transacta Navigatio Novi Orbis Indiae Occidentalis, 253.
North America, discovery of the northern coast of, 260
North sea, 145, 148, 162
Noticias Historicas de Nuño de Guzmán, 100
Nuevo Mexico, 163

Oaks, evergreen, 36.
Oars, made from savins, 48
Obligation, admissions of, to patrons, vi
Ocean sea, 208
Ochete, 42
Ochile, Indian chief, 34
Ochre presented, 115
Ohque, 163, see San Juan
Oma Slakkeuche, river, 34
Ojuelos, 184
Olid, 43
Opata, language 188
Oran Africa, penal colony, 250, 251
Orange tree, culture of the, 262
Orden Real, 154, 223
Orozco y Berra 163, his map of Mexico 169
Orthuesens, Indians, 243
Osachile, Indian chief, 34
Oviedo, 17, 18, 22, 23, 34, 64, 66, 98, 107, 116 text of tangled, 97
    translator's strictures on ix
Oviedo Lope, returns with the Deaguanes 88
Oysters, 81, abundant, 41; feet cut with, 90 Indians food for quarter of the year, 77, 79

Pacific Ocean, 148
Paluche, 42
Palachen, differently spelled, 28 gold in, 24
Palacios dead body of eaten, 74
Palmas river 51, 218 boundary of conquest, 13 pilot Miruelo's knowledge of the position of 19

Palmitos, 29, 36 used for tow, 47, 48
Palou, Father Francis, letter of, 260
Panamá, 148
Pantoja, Captain, 61, 93 ordered to go for stores, 11, lieutenant governor, 94, his severity, 94, killed, 94
Panuco, 20, 26, 73, 89, 93, 94, 95, 96, 203
Panzacola, 64
Parabol, river, 244
Paraconsi, Floridian, 127
Pariguay, 251
Parana, river, 239
Pardo's exploration of South Carolina and Georgia, 260
Pareja notice of, 262
Paricmbos, fierce tribe of Indians, 238
Parrots, feathers of, article of barter, 167
Partidos of the island of Santo Domingo, 14
Partridges, 37, 58.
Passaguates, Indians, 162
Patarabueyes, Indians, 162, see Jumanos, 162
Patronato of the Lonja, Sevilla, 162
Pearls, 195
Pearl river and Mobile bay, territory between, probably the scene of Cabeça de Vaca's six years' captivity, 235
Pensacola bay, 116.
Pensacola, the siege of, in 1781, 260
Peñaloza, Captain, 62, 113, in ambuscade, 54
People of the Figs, Indians, 116, 124, 137.
People of-the-Flat Roof Houses, Indians, 163, see Querechos
Pequeño, signification of, 66
Perez, Anton, pilot, 97
Perez, Father Martin, 154, 230, visitant, 223
Perrillo pequeño, signification of, 66
Perro mudo, 66
Persian turquoise, 170
Petaan, 193
Petachan, river, 191
Petatlán, river, 178, 181, 184, 193, 206, fort erected on the banks of, for safety, 224
Petition of Cabeça de Vaca, governor of La Plata, to the Council of the Indies, 231
Petlatltlan, meaning of, 193
Petlatl, meaning of, 193
Petatan, river, 176
Philipon is, Father Honorio, 273

Physicians without diplomas, 89
Pilu, 64
Picardo, Juan, printer of books, 205
Pike, 57
Pima nation, 178, 230; or Névome, language, 188, 199; grammar of the, 200
Pimentel, fifth Count of Benevente, 206
Pecos, territory of the, exploring expedition to the 235
Pin, scratching with, a punishment for Indian child, 165
Pine, seed of, for food, 150; how prepared, 150; trees, 56
Pineda, 20; first voyage of 88
Pinole, Indians' food, 169
Pipkins, Indians' ignorance of the use of, 161
Pitahaya, prickly pear, 179
Pitchers, clay, 73
Pitchlynn, Peter P., chief of the Chatas, 70, 79, 171
Placer ridges, 170
Plantations destroyed at Española, and Portorico, 18
Plautus, Caspar, abbot, 253
Plot to abandon the governor and the sick, 45
Poison for Indian arrows, 172; effect on deer 173; used to catch fish 181
Poisoning, Indian method of curing, 83
Porcallo, Vasco, of Cuba, 91; gift of provisions, 11
Port, the best in the world, 204
Portorico, letter to the emperor from, 18; storm at, 18
Portuguese, discoverers, 57; explorers massacred, 239; navigators usage of in measuring, 18
Practice a diabolical, 139
Pregnancy, custom in, 131
Presidio del Norte, 165, 169
Prickly pears, 116, 117, 118, 119, 120, 122, 125, 126, 147, 150, 153, 179; description of, 91; food for Indians quarter of the year, 92, 109, 111; several kinds of, 112; season of, the happiest time for the Indians, 104, 110; mode of preparing, 105; leaves of the, for food, 129, 130
Priests, brief of authority submitted to, 212
Primahaitu, 187
Proclamation to, and requirement to be made of, the Inhabitants of the countries and provinces that there are from Rio de Palmas to the Cape of Florida, 215–218
Procyon lotor, 66
Proem, 11
Property, depreciation of, through the Southern war, 264

Ptolomeus, 57
Pueblo de los Corazones, 172, founded, 178
Pumpkins, 38, 41, Indians' food, 159, presented, 159, 161, 166, early introduction of, among the Indians, 165
Purchas, 253

Quarrá, valley of, 163
Quarrels, Indian, how settled, 182
Quetzalitztli, derivation of, 171
Quevenes, Indians, 88, 93, 97, 133, 137, 163
Quitoks, Indians, 137
Quivara, 153

Rabbits, 36
Raccoon, 66
Rain prayed for, 160
Rain water, beverage of Indians, 112
Ramirez Jose Fernando, 78, 100, 257
Ramusio, 261, his Historical Collection, viii
Ranjel, 34
Rat, sharp teeth of, Indian instrument of chastisement for infants, 158
Rats, Indians' food, 79
Recopilacion Mejico, 205
Red oaks, 36
Reeds, joust of, with bulls, 196
Relaçam Verdadeira, 42, by the Knight of Elvas, 42
Relation, first imprint of the, vi, its title page and colophon, vi vii, next edition, in black letter, connected with a work in another hand, vi, its title page, vi, difference in the two editions vii, title of the third and last issue in Spanish, vii translation of published in Italian, viii single edition of, in French, viii only literal version in English, viii
Relation du Voyage de Cibola entrepris en 1540, 236
Repartimientos, Indians to be set free from, 228
Report of the U S Coast surveyor 1859 89
Reptiles, Indians' food, 179
Republic, the freest among the Indians, 181
Residents, duty free for ten years Narvaez petitions for, 209
Resin, 48
Review of force to date, 50
Ribas, Padre, 143 230 missionary in Cinaloa, 78, account of Indian, physicians 83
Riggs, George W, Jr, v, 258
Rio Bravo del Norte, 143, 170

INDEX

Rio de las Palmas, 208, 211, 213, 218, 219 latitude of 17
Rio de la Plata, 238, 254, province of 231, 250
Rio Grande, river, 165
Rios, port of, 245
Rochefort, notice of, 262
Rockweed 92, 95
Roes, dried, found, 51
Romans 78, 164 History of Florida, 189
Romen, Don Garcia 234
Ropes made of horse hair, 48
Royal Audience of Sevilla 251
Royal ducks, 37
Royal rents, Narváez petitions for the tenth of 209
Rudo Ensayo, tentativa de una prevencional Descripcion de la Provincia de Sonora, 261
Ruiz, Gonçalo, dead body of, eaten, 74
Rush, powder of Indians' food 172
Russell Prof. William C., 256

Sails made from shirts 48
St. Andrews, 116
St. Augustine, Fla., 255, 256, 260 harbor of 128
St. Catharine's, Brazil 238, 240, 241
St. Francis, order of, 177
Saint Iago, vespers of, 196
Saint John's day, 33
Saint Lawrence 200
St. Thomas, 243
Sabine, river, 127
Salamanders, food of Yguazes 103
Salmon 37
Salt duty free for ten years Narvaez petitions for 209 from the lakes 162
Salt water, men crazed with drinking, 52
Salazar, captain, delegated lieutenant in the government 248
San Antonio mission of, 134
San Antonio, bay of, 89
San Bartolomé valley of, 162
Sand mounds 89
San Juan, island of 18, 212 213, town 163
San Lucar de Barrameda fleet sailed from 13
San Marcos de Apalache 55
San Miguel, town 184, 194, 196
San Saba mountains 148

Santa Barbara, mines of, 162.
Santa Fé, 170, river 128.
Santa Fee, Historia de los Triumphos de nuestra, 143
Santander, 232
Sant Joan, island 57
Sant Miguel, strait, 51
Santo Domingo, 99, number of men left fleet at, 50, island of fleet arrived at, 12, 13, ship bought at 14
Santiago de Cuba, 79, 212, 252, 258, municipality of, 34, port of Cuba, supplies obtained at, 14
Satourioua, 127
Savin trees, 36
Sawane river, 34
Saya, root, 178
Scarcity, year of, 225
Schmidel, Ulrich, 240, 241, 242, 243, 245, 254, relation of, 237
Schoolcraft, Mr, 258, Indian tribes, 165
Sea birds, article of traffic, 86
Sea snail, pieces of, articles of traffic, 85
Seed time, Indian festivals at, 177
Seminole, 34
Seminole and Mickasuke tongues, vocabularies of the, 260
Señora, valley of, 177
Senses, Indians, keener than any other in the world, 136
Sevilla, 143, 162, 218, 222, Archivo de Indias at, 207, 215, 218, arrival of Alvar Nuñez at, x, city of, 211, 212, 213, 214
Seville, 251, archives explored at, 259, Archivo general de Indias at, 211
Sexual intercourse, Indian, not permitted in his own nation, 180
Shawls presented, 174, 193
Shea, John Gilmary, iv
Shoals, dangerous, 19
Shoes, pieces of, found, 28
Ships lost on the breakers, 202
Shirts, Indian, 167
Sibola, herds of, 163
Sierra, dead body of, eaten, 74
Sierra Madre, 42
Signs, language of, 168, 171
Siguenza, notice of 262
Silver, bags of [small pearls] presented, 145
Simancas, archives explored at, 259
Sinaloa, 178, 230, 258, province of, 223
Sins, weight of, a prevention to heal, 121

Skins cast like serpents, 125
Slavery amongst the Indians, 101, 102; Indians in Narvaez expedition, 209; abolition of, 254
slings, Indian, 79
Small pox finished the Indians in Española, 18
Smith, Thomas Buckingham, 251-252, admissions of obligation to patrons, vi; fills an official position in Mexico, vi; finds a field for historical investigation, vi; holds a position near the court of Madrid, vi; strictures on Oviedo, ix; letter from M. F. Maury, 114; memoir of 255-264; of New England origin, 255; his parentage, 255; in Mexico in his youth, 256; becomes the ward of his uncle at the death of his father, 256; placed in Trinity College, Hartford, 256; his friendships, 256; entered the Cambridge Law School, 256; studied law in Maine, 256; returned to St. Augustine and practiced his profession, 256; entered the field of politics, 256; elected to the Florida assembly, 256; took a decided stand against the party of inflation, 257; taste for historical studies developed itself, 257; his marriage, 257; withdrew from active political life, 257; appointed to the post of secretary of legation to Mexico, 257; by aid of friends began to collect documents relating to the history of Florida, 257; his fitness for Spanish diplomacy, 257; represented the United States as chargé d'affaires, 257; resumed duties as secretary, 257; recalled, 257; his English version of the narrative of Alvar Nuñez Cabeça de Vaca, 258; translated with care, 258; his notes on the memoir of Hernando de Escalante Fontaneda, 258; his summary of Soto's expedition, 258; contributed a series of Mexican extracts for Mr. Schoolcraft's work, 258; enrolled as corresponding member in various learned societies, 259; appointed secretary of legation to Spain, 259; his zeal in exploring archives, etc., for his history of Florida, 259; always compared his proof with the original document, 259; recalled, 259; death of his mother, 260; his contributions to history, 260, 261, 262; bereaved of his wife, 261; did not share in the enthusiasm of the South in the late war, 261; his property depreciated through the war, 261; maintained aged family slaves after emancipation, 261; visits Spain and was successful in seeking new material for historical discussion, and imported the best varieties of the orange tree, 262; acted as tax commissioner in Florida, 262; never satisfied with his labors, 262; shrunk from responsibility, 262; consumption had made fatal progress, 263; urged by his physician to return at once to his rooms, 263; became bewildered, hurried to a hospital and died, 263; eulogy on, 263

Smith, Hannah [Anita], 255
Smith, Josiah, 255.
Smith, Robert, 256
Smoke, used by Indians to produce stupefaction, 138, 139
Snakes, food of the Yguazes, 103, Indians' food, 79
Socorro, 163
Socorinos, Indians, 244
Sole, 57
Song of spring, extract from the, 43
Sonora, 177, 178, 179, Jesuit mission of the, 82, Indians of, 143, province of the valley of, 177
Soto Mayor, camp-master, kills Pantoja, 94, died, 94, eaten by Esquivel, 94
South America, Spanish conquests in, 238
South, enthusiasm of the, 261
South sea, 148, 152 176, 177, 182, 195
Southern states, 139
Spaniards, discoveries, 67, the Nevomes always kept good faith with the, 223
Spanish, the third and last issue of the Relation in, vii, settlements on the gulf of California, Cabeça de Vaca arrived at, 12, goods, price of, raised through war with France, 18, cases containing dead bodies, 24, 203, navigators, usage of, in measuring, 18, conquest of New Mexico, 127, diplomacy, Smith's fitness for, 257
Spain, 36, fleet from, 12, number of men sailed from, 50, exercise of juego de la barra in, 64, court of, urgent entreaties sent to the, for succor, 238, Buckingham Smith appointed secretary of legation to, 259
Sparrow-hawks, 37
Spelling of Indian names, difference in, vii
Spiders, food of the Yguazes, 103, Indians' food, 79, presented to be blessed, 153
Statue, covered with blood, 177
Stick, curved, of the bird hunter of the Nile, 154
Stone and lime, houses of, 162
Stone, scarce for ballast, 48
Stone, Gen Carlos P, his map, 168
Stony mountains, 170, 171
Straw, armful of, tied at the top, Indians' only protection from the weather, 179, powder of, Indians' food, 167, 172
Strait Sant Miguel, 51
Stupefaction produced by smoke, 138, 139
Styles, old and new, tabular statement by Prof Keith, 111

Sugar works destroyed at Española, 18
Sun, children of the, cognomen, 123, Indians originally worshipers of the, 171 salutation to the, 171
Surucusis, Island of, 243, Indians, 242, 243, 244, 245
Susolas, Indians, 121, 137
Swan, Major Caleb, 164
Sweet gum, 42

TABLE-TIPPING, Indian jugglers' knowledge of the force of, 82
Tabula Prima, referred to in chart, 56
Tabula Secunda, referred to in chart, 56
Tampa bay, 34, 78, 258 expedition represented to have landed at, 235
Tangier, Arab boys darting sticks in, 154
Tarahumar, 169
Tavera, died, 73
Tudela on the Duero, 97
Tea, Indian 138, 139, Charlevoix's account of preparing 139
Techo's Historia Provinciæ Paraguariæ Leodii, 252
Tegucca, Indians, 181
Teguaican, town of, 205
Tehora, town of 178
Tellez, Captain, 62, 113 in ambuscade 54
Temistitan (Temachtitian) 230 signification of, 225
Tempest, calmed miraculously, 249
Temochula, river, 181, 182
Teneriffe, 163
Tenessee river, 235
Tepeguages, 143, see mezquiquez and mezquite
Tercera, island, 200
Ternaux, M., 233
Tesento, 38
Tetlahuchuezquizitl, prince (Don Pedro), 43, his elph 44
Tetzcoco, city of 42, 43
Texan lagoons, 181
Texas, 89, 179, 235
Texas, memoria for the history of 154 warring savages in 153
Tezuco, 42
Tezcucano, 44
Thatch used for covering houses, 35
Thebes tombs of, representations on 154
Theodoro 116 Dorotheo, Greek accompanies Indians, 55
Theology Indians instructed in, 192, 193, their ideas of, 192
Thieves Indians, 104

Thirst, seven men died of, 188.
Thread, mantelets of, 35
Tierre firma, 66
Tiger [jaguar], one of the expedition killed by a, 240.
Tiguex, province of, 153
Tillandsia usneoides, covering for Indians, 83
Timuquan tribe, 42, 139, fac simile of a petition of the, 260, book printed in the, 260
Tinklet of gold, found, 21
Tlacotell, definition of, 170
Tlaltelalco, convent of, gallery of paintings, 100
Tlascála, Indians of, 230
Tlatolli, signification of, 229
Tobosos, Indians, 162, 163
Tocobaga, bay, 58
Toledo, 98, council in, 208
Topia, mountains of, 78, 181
Torquemada, 99, 100, 229
Torre del Oro, 143
Tostado, visits Cabeça de Vaca, 84
Totontzin (Lion arm), 43
Tow, palmitos used for, 47
Town of Hearts, 177
Towns burned by the Christians, 174, with habitations, 236
Translados de la Florida, Capitulaciones, Asientos, 215
Translation, first, of the Relation, v
Treasurer of Rio de las Palmas, the duties of his office, 218-223.
Trees, astonishingly high, 33, river from top to bottom, 33
Trima, 113
Tribute, assessed anew on the Indians, 206
Trinidad, port of, 14, terrible storm at, 16, arrival and stay of De Narváez at, 17, number of men lost in the ships at, 50
Triumphos, 230
Tropic of Cancer, 18
Truffles, Indians' food, 79
Turkey, no mention made of the, 42
Turquoises, x, 237, account of, 170, presented 167, 191
Tzinaloa, 184

Ugachile, Indian chief, 34
United States, Buckingham Smith represented the, near the government of Mexico, 257
Urdaide, captain, 231
Uric in at Española, and Portorico, 18

INDEX. 299

Utina, Oliti Ouae, 128
Uzachil, Indian chief, 34

VAQUEROS, Indians, 163
Valdivieso, Pedro, 95, visits Cabeça de Vaca, 84, killed for diversion 87, 102, 108
Valenquela, captain, sent to seek m harbor, 30, returned, unsuccessful, 31
Valladolid, 97, 223, 251, 232; Cabeça de Vaca appeared before Charles V, ix, x
Vandersipi, Father, 230
Vasconçalos, 187
Viscuence, 189
Vinegas, Garcia, 244
Vasquez, Alonzo, Memoirs of, 260
Veachile, Indian chief, 34
Velasquez, Juan, native of Cuellar, 94, drowned, 32, dictionary of, 209
Vera Cruz, 15, 165, 197, 205, 235, Cabeça de Vaca's departure from, 12
Verrazano, inquiry into the authenticity of documents concerning a discovery in North America claimed to have been made by, 262, his map of the world, 260, as a discoverer, 260, his voyage, 261, notice of, 262
Verrazano voyage, examination into the, 262
Vespucius and his first voyage, 260
Vidas Exemplares, 230
Vipers food of the Yguazes, 103
Virginia, 163
Voyages and Discoveries, Hakluyts, 164
Voyages Relations et Memoires de l'Amerique, 233

WALNUT trees, 86
Walnuts, how prepared for food, 90
War, Indians waging continual, 180
War with France raised the price of Spanish goods, in Española, 18
Washington (D. C.), 113
Washington (now Trinity) College, Hartford, 256
Water, lack of, 126
Watertown, Conn, 255
Waxed linen used to conceal papers, 247
Wears, skillfully made, 78, of one Indian mode of fishing, 74, 75
Wheat, cracked, Indians food, 169
Wind, north east, prevalent, 204
Wiroans Wingina, Indians, 164

Withlacoochie, river, 34
Wives, Indian, obtained from the enemy, 180
Women, Indian, movement of, pernicious effect of, 138, custom in indisposition of, 139, held by the Yguazes in little esteem, 104, sometimes the cause of war 133; mat carriers, 152; handsome, presented to Estevan, 237.
Wood, food of the Yguazes, 103
Woolen cloth discovered, 24
Worms, food of the Yguazes, 103; presented, to be sanctified, 153.

XAGUA, port of, fleet passes winter at, 17, number of men sailed from, 50
Xamo, island, 73
Xerex de la Frontera, 205
Xiuhtic, meaning of, 171
Xantl, meaning of, 171
Xuarez, Juan, commissary, 13, 38, 73, 95, 99, 100 accompanies the governor in his explorations, 23, burns cases with dead bodies, 24, consulted by the governor, 25, his views on embarking, 26, accompanies expedition, 29, petitions governor, 30, embarks in open boat, 40

YAKEMI, river, 182
Yastasitasitan-ne, Indian deity, 163
Yecori, town of, 178
Yeguaz, Indians, 180
Yerba, poison used on arrows, 181
Yguacu, river, 229
Yguazes, Indians, 92, 102, 137, good archers, 103
Ynca, statement by the, 55
Yupon, Indian tea, 139
Yxtlilxochitl, 42, 44

ZAMORA, city of, 205
Zandia, mountains of, 170
Zarate, x
Zeburos, alcalde, 188
Zuaque, 178, see Cinaloa
Zuaque, Indians, 181
Zuni, territory of the, exploring expedition to the, 235

CPSIA information can be obtained
at www.ICGtesting.com
Printed in the USA
LVOW01s0236100417
530211LV00005B/457/P

9 781275 799967